graphic 08

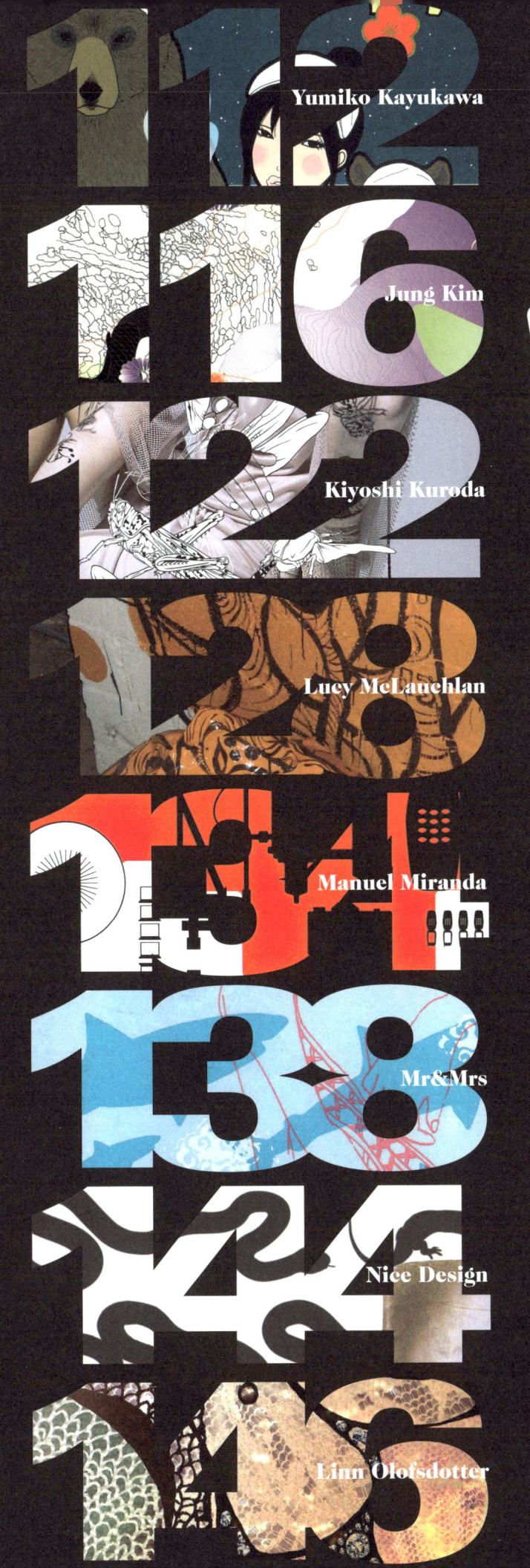

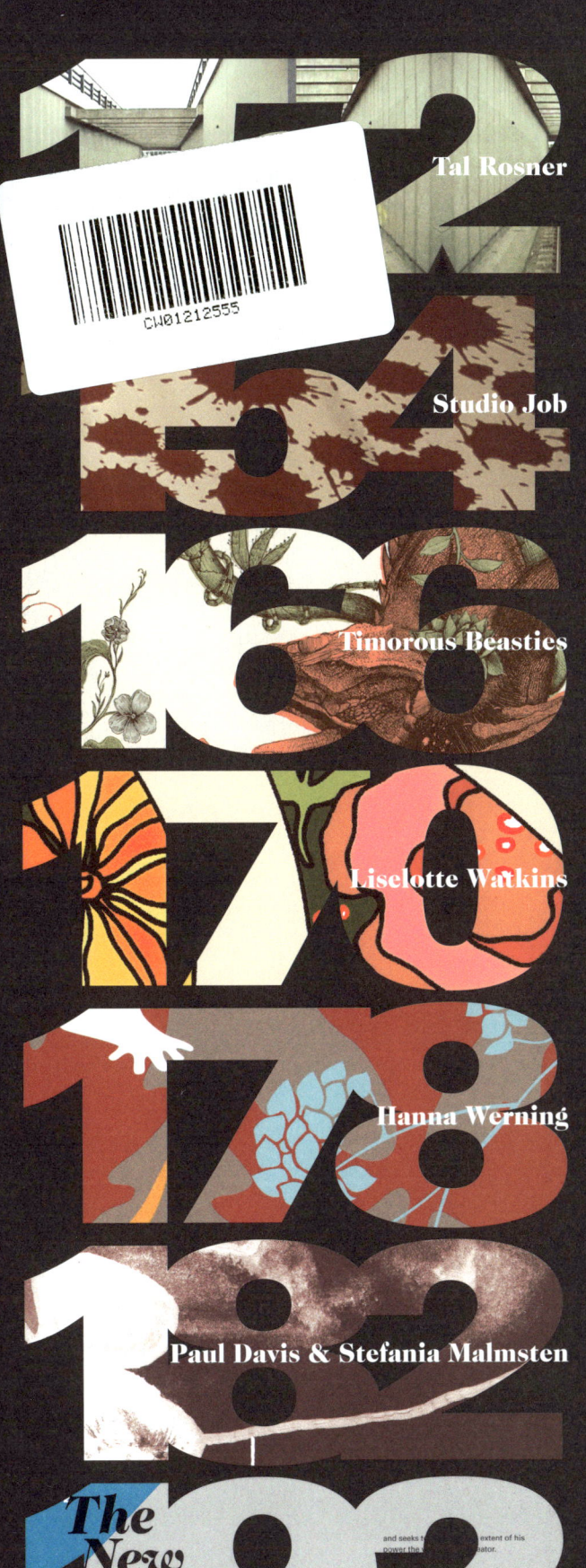

- 112 Yumiko Kayukawa
- 116 Jung Kim
- 122 Kiyoshi Kuroda
- 128 Lucy McLauchlan
- 134 Manuel Miranda
- 138 Mr&Mrs
- 144 Nice Design
- 146 Linn Olofsdotter
- 152 Tal Rosner
- 154 Studio Job
- 166 Timorous Beasties
- 170 Liselotte Watkins
- 178 Hanna Werning
- 182 Paul Davis & Stefania Malmsten
- 192 Adrian Shaughnessy — The New Graphic Ornate

Graphic is distributed by:

Australia
Tower Books
Unit 2, 17 Rodborough Road
Frenchs Forest, NSW 2086
T +62 2 9975 5566
F +62 2 9975 5599
E towerbks@zipworld.com.au
www.foliograph.com.au

Belgium
Bookstores
Exhibitions International
Kol. Begaultlaan 17
B-3012 Leuven
T +32 16 296 900
F +32 16 284 540
E orders@exhibitionsinternational.be
www.exhibitionsinternational.be

Other
Imapress
Brugstraat 51
B-2300 Turnhout

China & Hong Kong
Foreign Press Distributors Ltd
Room 6, Ground Floor, Block B
Proficient Industrial Center
6 Wang Kwun Road
T +852 2756 8193
F +852 2799 8840

France
Critique Livre Distribution SAS
BP 93-94 rue Malmaison
93172 Bagnolet Cedex
T +33 1 4360 3910
F +33 1 4897 3706
E critique.livres@wanadoo.fr

Germany
Bookstores
Sales representative South Germany:
Stefan Schempp
Wiener Platz 7
D-81667 München
T +49 89-230 77 737
F +49 89-230 77 738
E verlagsvertretung.schempp@t-online.de

Sales representative North Germany:
Kurt Salchli
Immanuelkirchstraße 12
D-10405 Berlin
T +49 30 4171 7530
F +49 30 4171 7531
E salchli@t-online.de

Germany, Austria & Switzerland
Distribution / Auslieferung
GVA Gemeinsame Verlagsauslieferung Göttingen
Anna-Vandenhoeck-Ring 36
37081 Göttingen
Germany
T +49 551 487 177
F +49 051 413 92
E krause@gva-verlage.de

Other
ISS Pressevertrieb GmbH
Carl-Zeiss-Straße 5
D-53340 Meckenheim
T +49 22 258801 122
F +49 22 258801 199
E publishing@ips-pressevertrieb.de
www.ips-pressevertrieb.de

Indonesia
Aksara
Jalan Kemang Raya 8b
Jakarta 12730
T +62 21 7199 288
F +62 21 7199 282
E info@aksara.com
www.aksara.com

Italy
Idea srl
Via Lago Trasimeno, 23/2 (ZI)
36015 Schio (VI)
T +39 455 576 574
F +39 445 577 764
E info@ideabooks.it
www.ideabooks.it

Red Edizioni Sas
Viale Prampolini 110
41100 Modena
T +39 59 212 792
F +39 59 4392 133
E info@redonline.it

Librimport Sas
Via Biondelli 9
20141 Milano
T +39 2 8950 1422
F +39 2 8950 2811
E librimport@libero.it

Japan
Shimada Yosho
T.Place, 5-5-25, Minami-Aoyama, Minato-ku
Tokyo, 107-0062
T +81 3 3407 3937
F +81 3 3407 0989
E sales@shimada.attnet.ne.jp

Korea
Beatboy Inc.
Kangnam-Ku Shinsa-Dong 666-11
Baegang Building 135-897
Seoul
T +82 2 3444 8367
F +82 2 541 8358
E yourbeatboy@hanmail.net

Malaysia
How & Why Sdn Bhd
101A, Jalan SS2/24
47300 Petaling Jaya
Selangor
T +60 3 7877 4800
F +60 3 7877 4600
E info@howwwhy.com
www.howwhy.com

Mexico
LHR Distribuidor de Libros
Calle 11 No. 69-1
Col. V. Gomez Farias Mexico
D.F. 15010 Mexico
T +52 55 5785 8996
F +52 55 5785 7816
E lhrlibro@prodigy.net.mx
www.lhrlibros.com

The Netherlands
Bookstores
Betapress BV
Burg. Krollaan 14
5126 PT Gilze
T +31 161 457 800
F +31 161 457 224

Other
BIS Publishers
Herengracht 370–372
1016 CH Amsterdam
T +31 20 524 7560
F +31 20 524 7557
E bis@bispublishers.nl
www.bispublishers.nl

Russia
Design Books
3 Maly Kislovsky Lane office 315
Moscow 103009
T +7 095 203 65 94
F +7 095 203 65 94

Scandinavia
(Denmark, Finland, Norway, Sweden)
Sales Representative
Bo Rudin
Box 5058
SE-165 11 Hasselby
T +46 8 894 080
F +46 8 388 320
E rudins@swipnet.se

Singapore
Basheer Graphic Books
Block 231, Bain Street
#04–19 Bras Basah Complex
180231 Singapore
T +65 336 0810
F +65 334 1950

Page One Pte Ltd
20 Kaki Bukit View
Kaki Bukit Techpark II
415956 Singapore
T +65 744 2088
F +65 744 2088
E pageone@singnet.com.sg

Spain
ACTAR
Roca i Batlle 2 i 4
08023 Barcelona
T +34 93 418 77 59
F +34 93 418 67 07
E info@actar-mail.com
www.actar.es

Taiwan
Long Sea International Book Co., Ltd.
1/F No. 204 Si Wei Rd
Taipei 106 Taiwan ROC
T +886 2 2702 6838
F +886 2 2706 6109
E thfang@ms16.hinet.net
www.longsea.co.tw

Turkey
Evrensel Grafikir Yayincilik
Gulbahar Mahl
Gayret SK No:11
80300-01 Mecidiyekoy / Istanbul
T +90 212 356 7276
F +90 212 356 7278
E evrensely@superonline.com

United Kingdom
Bookstores
Airlift Book Company
8 The Arena
Mollison Avenue
Enfield, Middlesex EN3 7NL
T +44 20 8804 0400
F +44 20 8804 0044
E info@airlift.co.uk
www.airlift.co.uk

Other
Comag Specialist
Tavistock Works
Tavistock Road
West Drayton, Middlesex UB7 7QX
T +44 1895 433 800
F +44 1895 433 801

USA / Canada
Lords News International
133 Jefferson Avenue
Jersey City, NJ 07306
T +1 201 798 2555
F +1 201 798 5335
E lordnewsinc@hotmail.com
www.lordusa.com

USA / West Coast
Trucatriche
3800 Main Street Suite 8
Chula Vista, CA 91911
California
T +1 619 426 2690
F +1 619 426 2695
E info@trucatriche.com

Subscriptions to Graphic
(all prices include airmail)
1 year (2 issues)
Europe EUR40
USA / Canada EUR45
Other countries EUR50
2 years (4 issues)
○ Europe EUR80
○ USA / Canada EUR90
○ Other countries EUR100

Students subscription (valid only with a copy of your student registration form):
1 year (2 issues)
○ Europe EUR33
○ USA / Canada EUR38
○ Other Countries EUR40

Fax this form to:
+31 20 524 75 57
or send to:
Graphic
Herengracht 370–372
1016 CH Amsterdam
the Netherlands

code GR/BZ/08

Payment (for prompt delivery please pay by credit card)
○ Please charge my: ○ Visa ○ AmEx ○ Euro / MasterCard
○ Please invoice me / my company (first issue will be sent on receipt of payment)

Mr/Ms/Mrs   Name   Surname

Card number   CVC-2 Code*

Expiry date   Signature

Company

Address**

City   Postcode/Zip

Country   Telephone

Email   Fax

* Please add your CVC-2 code (the last 3 digits of the number printed on the signature strip on the back of your card) if paying by MasterCard.

** Please also attach details of card billing address if different from delivery address.

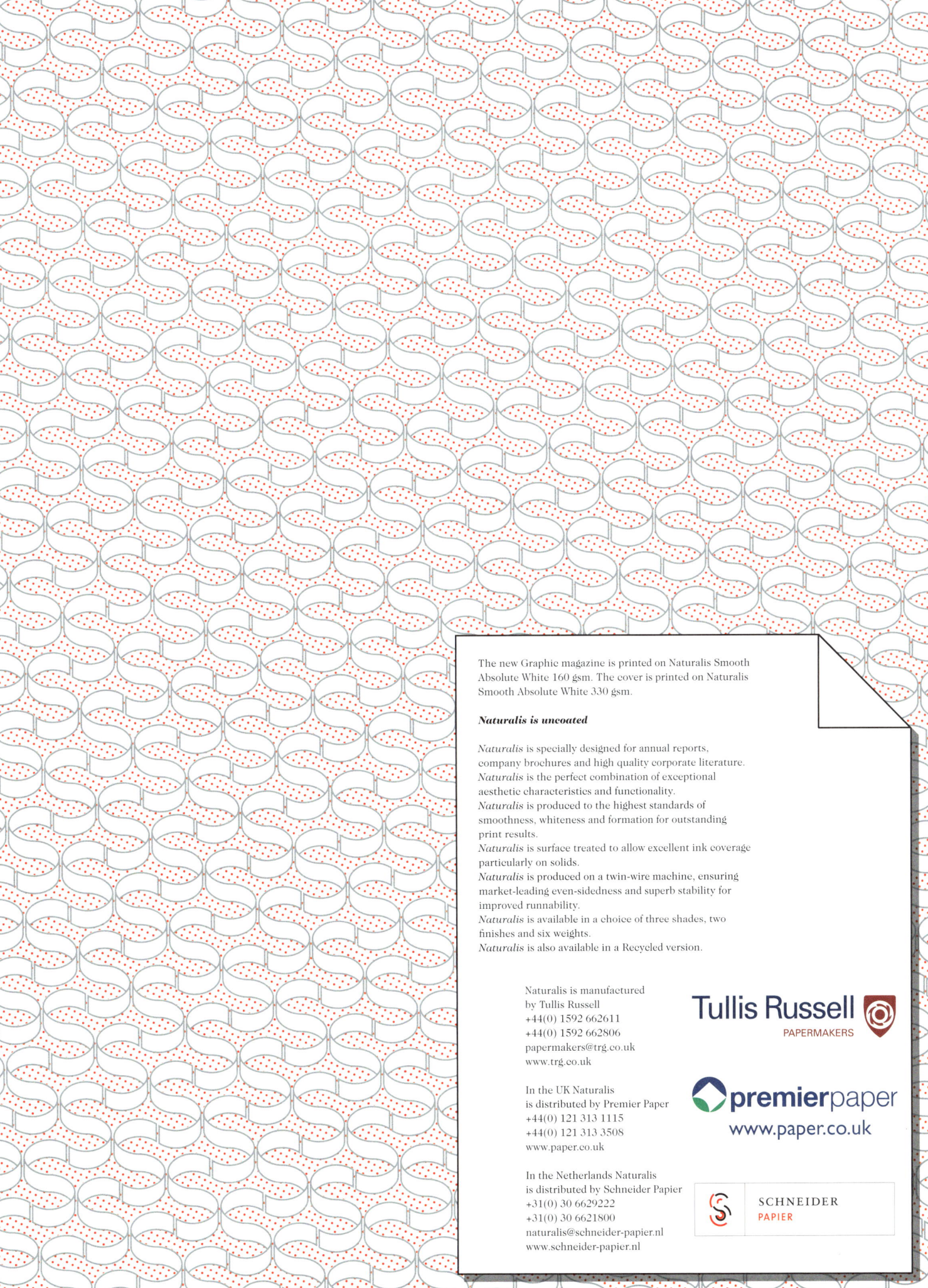

Akroe

Pattern emerging: Paris-based painter, graffiti artist and graphic designer Akroe talks to Simon Armstrong about his very personal approach to art and graphics.

'Being attentive to objects, and collecting, is an education in detail. And Akroe's world is alive with details, tiny figures and things picked up and gathered together'
  Jean-René Étienne

Slowly and surely, in the streets and boutiques of France and beyond, Etienne Bardelli, better known as Akroe, has built up an admirable parallel reputation as both graffiti artist and graphic designer. Each profession subverts the other. He makes walls look like screengrabs and designer products look like alleyway interventions. An obsession with patterns, clean lines and the cool minimalism of designers such as Peter Saville, Akroe's talent stands out in both occupations. Evolution and development, old codes into new chaos, Akroe is a unique talent. Being thoroughly immersed in two creative fields ensures he is perpetually at once remove from both, a position on the peripheries that has resulted in some impressive artistic delights. After admiring his work for some time, I finally seized on an opportunity to find out more. The only problem with answers is they inevitably lead to more questions, like what is Jurasian cheese? Never mind that though, here's how it started…

Where does the name Akroe come from? Cocoreako. I'm a coco-boy. **Can you tell us a bit about your background?** I grew up in a small town in the east of France, a county named Jura. Nice house, a big garden, cats, stupid friends at school, very appreciable TV programmes, rainy Wednesday afternoons, sunny holidays, cycling through snowy fields, holes in my trousers… The good, simple life. All of which totally collapsed when I discovered skateboards,

And what about your art and design training? When I was seventeen or eighteen, I was already decorating shops, bars and nightclubs with my spray-cans. It was usually awful but I could get some money that way, instead of working in a factory during summer like everyone else. I always managed to keep leftover spray-cans for my own use. I never considered this work to be graffiti; making popular paintings on shop windows and sandwich billboards doesn't really give you many meaningful sensations! I even felt guilty about it, a little ashamed of selling something so non-personal.

It often felt like a waste of time. However, I always knew what was the pure, real graffiti – when it's risky, stressful, fast and strong. Making big paintings in hard and strange conditions always procures great satisfactions. Now I prefer to make graffiti only in this state of mind, and as a personal game.

Was there a defining moment when you decided to become a visual artist? When i saw this advertising for shampoo, I remember Cindy Crawford shaking her head and showing white cardboards in a white futuristic advertising agency. It was a wonderful revelation to me. **Is there a separation between your design work and your graffiti? What is the difference for you?** Graphic design, as a job, is a discipline where it's difficult to express yourself. You operate as a visual translator. Somebody gives you a message, and you have to make it visible and comprehensible. To translate this message you usually adopt and adapt recurrent things from your own personal universe, constructions and shapes, through those choices you can still express yourself within the brief. Today my graffiti is seen more as personal work. It is a mix of graffiti and graphic design. I use illustration, typography, photography, and especially intentions. At the end it looks like graphic design. The visible barrier between my professional works and personal works is not so clear. Basically, the separation is that while the message or impression you give may differ, you use same tools to obtain it. On my website, I named the graffiti part 'l'atelier – the workshop' because it is an experimentation space for my ideas rather than just graffiti work.

When are you most aware of design? When I'm not designing.

I often notice that graphic designers that come from a graffiti background have strong feelings regarding commercial design projects. There often seems to be a lot of animosity towards those who succeed – what are your thoughts on this? I think this feeling does exist, and is linked to the loss of a reference mark. Graffiti has always been associated with rebellion, an opposition to society. It's shocking to see how graffiti or the work of a graffiti artist is used to sell products for mass consumption. That totally breaks graffiti's codes and values. Also, because the community spirit is so very strong in the graffiti movement, people can feel betrayed if their peers successfully move into other fields of creativity. As graffiti has been so savagely rebellious, spray-can artists could be afraid their clients come to them only because of what they represent, more than a real interest in their work. Often the client would like to buy some rebel credibility, or 'cool' attitude.

As far as I'm concerned, I don't feel involved in the graffiti scene as such, maybe more post-graffiti. When a client comes to me, I respond as a graphic designer. I'm not taking advantage of the

'I always knew what was the pure, real graffiti – when it's risky, stressful, fast and strong'

Green bubblegum
2003
Part of the eight-piece Bubblegum Project, exhibition at Shutzmarket, Anvers, Belgium

Right
Wallstickers
Each side of the pattern connects with other three

Below
Motif for Les Galeries Lafayette

Below right
The Echelle Pattern
Corsica, 2005
'Corsicamouflage' – Part of a series of 'camouflages contre nature' paintings. *Contre,* meaning 'against', has two meanings here: The camouflage opposes its environment by being an unnatural application, yet the design also complements its surroundings as if the two are now interdependent and leaning against each other.

Far right
Pink Bubblegum
2003
Part of the eight-piece Bubblegum Project, exhibition at Shutzmarket, Anvers, Belgium

6

graffiti essence on a professional level, but saying that I've never felt concerned by animosity anyway.

Can you tell me about your 2003 'Bubblegum Project'? Bubblegum was a show I did with my friend KRSN in a place named Shutzmarket in Anvers, Belgium. It's a shop / gallery that focuses on graphic and urban culture. It's a nice place. We felt it was a place for futilities, where every object has a short but sweet lifespan because of evolving trends. The things there seemed born to disappear very quickly after they arrived. A lot like bubbles. So, KRSN and I did a mural painting together, and also presented individual works. I did a photographic series about futility, using big graffiti bubbles. The aim was to paint on surfaces that would be separated soon after – this separation was the bubblegum explosion. The surface could be a car and the floor, or the door and the wall around it. According to the point of view, it could also be surfaces separated by several metres. The photography was important because it gives the only evidence of the short life of the painting and makes you understand things will not stay in this state for long. There was also an interesting parallel in this project between photography and graffiti; spray-can artists always carry their cameras when they go painting. It's an absolute priority because every piece is cleaned up so quickly now, or sometimes covered by another artist, your painting often only exists in a photograph rather than on a wall. My bubblegums were made to exist only in photographs.

What was the old cheese factory like? What happened there? It's a secret now. Everything's disappeared.

Which design projects have you been most satisfied with and why? The second album artworks for TTC (the French hip-hop group). I did these with the photographer Manuel Lagos Cid. It was enjoyable because I was entirely free to produce what I wanted and very conscious of the group's motivation and goals. Our states of mind were in perfect accordance, made easier because we are friends too. This freedom allowed me to make strong graphic choices, and the project turned out to be like a mirror for me, I learned a lot about my way of working. I probably prefer this type work to a lot of my paintings. The music is also really better than yours. Check www.batards-sensibles.com.

How did you find working with Hixsept clothing? They are stupid.

Do you have any exciting plans or projects the coming year? At the moment I'm working for Galeries Lafayettes in Paris, designing shop windows and interior decorations. A big event, and quite cool. I will also enjoy doing sleeve design for Institubes crew, for my friend Tacteel, mixtapes for DJ Orgasmic and a smelly dirty tape for Pimp Cuiz too, also some non-lucrative ideas with Sixpack, and some beautiful secrets with KRSN…

What is happening right now in the Akroe mansion? Everybody's dancing with cocogirls, come in! We got Jurasian cheese!

www.akroe.net

The book *Akroe – design & designer*, published by Pyramyd Editions, is available at £11.99.

'The aim was to paint on surfaces that would be separated soon after – this separation was the bubblegum explosion'

Basso & Brooke

Bruno Basso and Christopher Brooke emerged from the London Fashion Fringe 2004 with their heady fusion of fashion and graphic design. Their distinctive style employs densely illustrated fabric prints and colourful themes to produce fantastic and irreverent collections. From their studio in Brixton, Bruno Basso discusses the use of symbols and imagery, digital prints and the crossover into high quality bespoke products for the home.

By Lachlan Blackley

Far right
Poodle Portrait

Right
The Cost of Beauty
Spring / Summer 2006
At Sao Paulo Fashion Week
Photography: Fernanda Calfat

Where did you both study? Chris did a BA at Kingston and a Masters in Fashion at Central St Martins (womenswear). I studied journalism in Brazil and studied advertising but didn't finish my course. I started very early in the industry when I was 15 years old as an artist's assistant in an advertising company. I did advertising focused on Graphic design then I started to work as a consultant. *How did you meet and begin working together?* At a party – I had just come to London from Brazil and a good friend of mine is a friend of Chris. We met and I saw his work and I just loved what he was doing at the time. He was styling pop stars like Robbie and Kylie, Jamelia, loads of people. When I first came to London I expected to do something much more related to graphics and nothing stimulated me. I was thirsty to see new things and when I arrived nothing surprised me. I met Chris and got really excited with what he's doing. When you work for shows and you do stage clothes, the clothes need to be seen and you need to make a distinctive look – and he's outstanding. I was really interested in working with the digital process and it started basically like that. When we started digital printing, it was so expensive we couldn't afford to make a proper garment. I told Chris we should have a portfolio, we worked for three or four months and we got around a hundred designs done. And this really attracted people. Our first collection was really sexual, very blunt. I was really interested in misplacing things. The designs looked like Art Nouveau and Liberty prints but once you look closer it's spurting cocks etc., and really strong imagery. But it attracted so many people. We sold for people like Coco de Mer and special commissions for Chris' clients. Everything was bespoke based. It was really magical the first moment. We were extremely excited about the digital process and how incredible a digitally printed garment can be – because you can do whatever you want.

You were discovered at the London Fashion Fringe competition in 2004. Can you talk about this? Chris saw an advertisement in a newspaper somewhere and thought 'this is a good opportunity to get the investment we need'. Because basically fashion is money and more than any other creative field, to build a capsule collection, you need a backer. And I think as well, fashion marketing is really decisive. I mean, if you show something that attracts you can keep on going. If you show something that people don't give you creditability for or value, you are dead in the market. The fashion world is too small to give you second chances. *You have to wow them immediately.* Exactly. And this was our intention with the first collection. First we were selected from 300 people and then we got a grant to produce the collection. We produced it in 2 months, then we had the show and we won the prize.

What did this enable you to do? That gave us £100,000 – but not in cash. It gave us business support, consultants, lawyers and all the administration side of the business. We created a company. It gave us loads of press and interest from people all around the world basically. And all the consultancy work, working with the best people in their areas – like hats from Stephen Jones who are one of the best hat-makers in the world. We do our shoes and bags with Pollini – one of the best Italian manufacturers. It opened the possibility for everything. It's a long walk I can imagine for a fashion designer and we got this position

immediately. We had Colin McDowell, one of the most respected fashion journalists promoting us and it was fantastic. From this we got the contract with the Italian company Aeffe (they produce Gaultier, Alberta Ferretti, and Moschino). It was not related to Fashion Fringe but they saw our work. We have, inside this big group, the possibility to produce anything that we want in terms of garments. Of course we're designers not artists, and the thing that distinguishes a designer from an artist is that you have a compromised industry. We will not do cardboard blouses; we'll be doing proper wearable pieces. We need to think economy and we need to think what suits the market. We'll seek consultancy about what neck is the neck at the time or whatever… but of course we have creative freedom to interpret this in the way that we like. **And the only condition is that you have to show in London for five years?** Yes (four years now because we've shown for one). And it's fantastic. I think London is good to show now because we have the share of the cake and it's good when you're in this position.

Your style has been likened to designers such as Galliano, Westwood, McQueen, Versace… Have they been an influence? I think it has been compared because our work is highly recognisable. I don't think it's compared in any other sense. We've got our own cut, we've got our own style. It's difficult; you're being pragmatic so someone can recognise your work at the first glance. I'm always interested in the first second. The digital print and how we apply this, is one design consistency in everything that we do. Even if the teams are different, the drawings are different, the time is different… that is the thing that echoes in every single piece. And this is why we're compared with them – because Galliano is highly recognisable, Westwood as well, McQueen… they've got a really strong mark. **Do you think it's also because in a sense there's a high theatricality to the work?** Yes… To tell you the truth, minimalism and this kind of 90s thing really bores me. I just think that it's too clinical and it's dated, it's 90s. I think 'theatrical' is ever, because when you go to a show you want to see a 'show' and I think that what we do is just supply people with expectation. But I think it's important that if you take apart everything from the show and see it in hand, these are beautifully made clothes and not just created for the burst of the show. As separate pieces they work as well. A show just as a show doesn't make sense for me. I think it should work in both ways.

Can you talk a little about inspiration and the use of image? There are some basic ideas that follow all my work. I'm interested in social relations and follow some personal anthropological studies I've made. How different classes understand each other – the interaction between social classes. Another thing that interests me is Dandyism… frivolity, the frivolous aspects of life, all the things that you don't need to do but you just do for the sake of it. I'm really interested in symbolism. I've been studying symbols for a while now. How symbols can be digested by certain groups and what you can get from the symbols working with them in a proper way. Our work is music based as well – I can describe sound with images. And I've been really interested in synaesthetics – how we can cross over sensations and give image to the sound or give smell to the image. I'm interested in aspects of sense behaviour. And I'm interested in 'What is power?' What makes people think that they are powerful? I've always been interested in illusion and how your mind understands image. How the psyche works and how people understand things. How an image can provoke action and reaction, what an image can do. How I can approach certain parts of the brain with colour and with shapes and how I can bring out feelings from you as a comfort or a disturbance etc. I think I know how to manipulate, to provoke a feeling that I'm looking for. **Is this something you learnt from advertising?** Maybe yeah… I've been studying people like Goebbels as well and how you can convince people with image. I was always interested in the social aspect of image. How you can identify at the first glance social

'I've always been interested in illusion and how your mind understands image. How I can approach certain parts of the brain with colour and with shapes and how I can bring out feelings from you'

Opposite page
Fashion Fringe
2004
Photography: Chris Moore

'I love to misplace information. I think it's fun to create a new cover for things'

positions. What distinguishes the first moment? What this means for you. And we applied this to our garments. I'm interested in the mass. Our clothes are not selling for the masses but I'm interested in the mass consciousness. You feel something about our clothes. Whether you like it or you don't like it, you're going to have an attention to it. **There's a sense of irreverence as well.** Yeah, the first season 'The Garden of Earthly Delights' was about sex, the second 'Succubus' was hierarchy and the third show 'The Cost of Beauty' in Sao Paulo was about vanity. Now we're still working on vanity and what makes people think that they are happy. And we play a lot with bourgeois 'good taste' (we've got icons like Ivana Trump). Chris likes working with the idea of bad taste, transforming it in a sense that you don't actually perceive it as bad taste… but it's so intense and so obvious, that it's fun. I love misplacing things. I love it when you have something so repugnant but you present it in a way that is so delicious or so eye-catching. I love to misplace information. I think its fun to create a new cover for things – make things that are really cheap become expensive and make expensive things become really cheap.

What ideas are you working with for the London Fashion Week Spring / Summer '06 Collection? This season we're going to work with Pop and with product ideas… it's quite Jeff

Succubus And Other Tales
Autumn / Winter 2005
At London Fashion Week
Photography: Chris Moore

'It's possible to create a bespoke product with the same equality as an industrial product created for the masses'

Below
Lady Garden

Below right
The King's Fart

Far right
Wheel of Fortune

Koons inspired. We've started to develop a 'Musical Garden'. We're going to have references from all of the styles like Mick Jagger and The Stones, Prince etc. It's a magical theme garden and it's a collection of 15 flowers printed on fabric.

Your designs are heavily print-based. Can you tell us more about the digital process? Well I think that in the creative industry now, we have a new 'good time'. It's the perfect time for new development. I think that we're going to have an 'after war' time. In 2005 it's possible to create a bespoke product with the same equality as an industrial product created for the masses. And with the digital process it's fantastic because you can control everything. You can just produce one. I can just print 30cm of fabric if I want, which was impossible 5 years ago because it was a highly expensive process. The printing is really high resolution. We're printing in the Netherlands and we print with the same quality as the musicological process. Nobody wants to wear the same thing that somebody else is wearing and I think people are looking much more to being individual again. And I think the digital process helps a lot for this because you can do whatever you want. **What fabrics are you printing?** Silks, Lycra, leather, denim, chiffon, organza… we have developed taffeta and we print on wool. The Lycra we print stretched. We glue it to the paper and we stretch the artwork as well so you don't have the white mark on the fabric when you stretch it. Leather is difficult to print on because it's an organic shape. But there is one process now where they vulcanise it – they transfer an image on to leather and then a sand shower is shot onto it and perforates, creating a new layer on top. **What's the process roughly from design to production?** How we work is a very interesting process. Everyone depends on each other and our time is very short. I work on the art direction, colouring and style etc. and put the print together. Chris is the fashion director and the tailor. We always talk about how we're going to approach the season. We always start with music and we ask what sensation we want. Because we need to go deep, I have my dictionary of symbols and we first make an overall research about certain highly recognisable symbols. We develop a series and we

think how many drawings to draw for each series and the consistency of the line etc. and we decide what we want. We have a group of illustrators – the head of our illustration is Alexis Panayiotou. We do a couple of drawings and make some tests and see if it can be applied or not. If it is, we go to the second step which is Chris doing the patterns. After that we measure everything and map it on the computer. And we work as if it was on paper, we work at real size and just place things on the actual pattern. Depending on the type of material, it goes off to the Netherlands or Italy or Portugal to be printed and then it goes to Italy to be constructed as a garment. And then it comes to London to show. It's an intricate process. It requires loads of attention and a very well established network because we work in a really tight time. We use really good people to develop our things like Dupont for Lycra and very good people in the Netherlands that produce our fabric with A-certificate colours, and so on.

What are your thoughts on ornamentation, decoration and the repeated image in your work? Ornament and decoration are storytellers.

This page
The Cost of Beauty
Spring / Summer 2006
At Sao Paulo Fashion Week
Photography: Fernanda Calfat

Opposite page, top
Born Beauty

Opposite page, bottom
Vice Brain

It can be contemplative, it can carry time and history, evoke mood, and alter perception. It can add new emotional and social value to almost anything. I think ornament is fantastic. I love the Chinese and Japanese and I love the Middle Eastern. We just came from Russia and the ornament of the Byzantine is fabulous. It's good that you talk about repeats. A repetition of something is a pathological system of something. Once you repeat, it means that something is not right. Our work seems to be a repetition of things but really our criteria is not to repeat things. It looks the same but it's not the same. It can be a multiple of the same but not a repetition. I've been really interested in Leonardo da Vinci's concept of the 'golden mean' and I apply this as much as I can to the print design. The visual centre point is never the proper centre point. Everything should be slightly moved out or off centre. You can't tell it's not in the centre and this makes it more like natural mistakes. It makes it more human, more accessible and you kind of digest it better – it's not clinical. It's comfortable. **Finally, can you tell us a little about the homeware products you're**

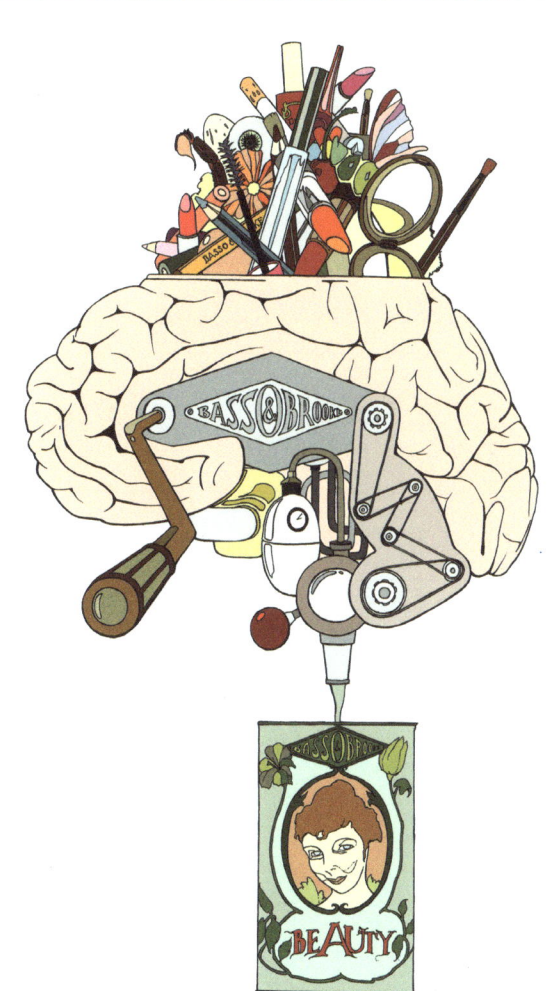

'I will always see myself as a graphic designer, because I don't know how to sew or to cut clothes, but I understand fashion in the wider sense'

Opposite page
Symphony

This page
Interior range for Harrods

doing and your thoughts on the crossover with graphics and fashion? Our work is really collaborative. We're developing printed ceramics, hand-woven silk carpets, wallpaper, laminated surfaces, china crockery, crystal glassware and ceramic tiles (for use everywhere from the kitchen to the pool). We're also doing an interior range for Harrods for next year – wallpapers, dinner plates, chairs, and creating one-off pieces of furniture (both antique and modern) upholstered in our fabric designs. And we're collaborating with the best and oldest manufacturers, British companies mostly. I was watching Peter Greenaway's film *The Cook, The Thief, His Wife And Her Lover* recently, and that is a perfect example of how fashion can work with cinema for example. It's absolutely stunning. Jean Paul Gaultier. The scenes where she goes to the bathroom and the clothes and everything change colour. At the time this was new. This inspires me – when two industries can talk. I think we're here to cross over between graphic and fashion. I will always see myself as a graphic designer, because I don't know how to sew or to cut clothes, but I understand fashion in the wider sense. I think fashion is something you don't know yet that you'll be attracted to – but you will be, because there's an industry working for it. And I think the way to progress is to crossover. I think people should provoke and go further and to get experience from others.

www.bassoandbrooke.com

Aya Kato

Aya Kato is a self-taught illustrator from Aichi, Japan, who creates from a dark and passionate fantasy world. Her rich, heavily styled images draw from the traditional Japanese and stories of the fairytale. At just 23, her first collaboration with music video director Laurent Briet brings her romantic characters to life in the Tori Amos video *Sleeps with Butterflies*.

By Lachlan Blackley

Where did you train? Can you tell us a little about your studies and how this has shaped your work? I studied art education and graphic design at the Aichi College of Education and I started working as a freelance illustrator in 2005. I learnt illustration by complete self-study because practice is hardly taught at my university. I kept drawing at home every day and I researched fairytales of the world. I was enchanted by the words of a creative, fantastic world. I wanted to unite my dream world with the world of the fairytale. ***What or who is your biggest influence in terms of style? What attracted you to this?*** I think that Japanese traditional art is the foundation of my expression. I sincerely love line in Japan. For me, the beauty of Japanese art is in its two dimensions – its deepness and the beauty of the outlines. The picture is a place of meeting for me. I draw inspiration from my Japanese roots and traditions and became interested in the print process having studied the work of Hokusai and the world of Ukiyo-e. ***Tell us more about the dark worlds you create?*** My dark worlds are the influences of the fairytale. I am comparing the fairytale to the black well. I think that black is the noblest colour – strong and beautiful. I like devilish black beauty. And, I yearn to black strength. It is thought that black is the colour that shows woman the most beautiful. I want to draw the world where black power was drawn out to its maximum. And I want to draw a person's eyes that seem to be sad. But, they are eyes that are turned to the future. I am attaching importance to the eyes most. I am drawing the person as an inspiring soul. Sad eyes are drawn because I want you to be opposite to the person in the picture. And, I want you to read the person's mind. ***Your illustrations also have a very strong Art Nouveau feel. Has this been an influence?*** My foundation is Japanese

Above
Fuuzinraizin

Far left
Red Moon

Left
Samurai Girl

Following spread, left
12 Dancing Princesses

Following spread, right
Little Tiny / Thumbelina

'It is a girl's world. The world of bare feet – the world of a girl who dreams. It is a world like the fairy tale, it is pure and romantic and with a little poison'

Below
Ali Baba

Below right
Aladdin

Opposite page
Sleeps With Butterflies

Following spread, left
Otohime

Following spread, right
Batoukannon

traditional art. Art Nouveau is an influence from there. However, it is not only that. I capture and want to draw the world quite freely. I think that this desire became an expression like Art Nouveau. I think that it is one shape of my passion. If I draw with my intuition, it becomes such an expression.

What stimulates your creative ideas? It is from love. I think that I can draw the picture because I am falling in love. Love gives me power most. And it is from music. There is occasionally music that sounds directly to the mind. I am always helped by music in which a lot of messages are put. It is from a world of telling. I often find inspiration from books or poetic language and my pieces extend from there. I may read a book and discover a new world. It is also influenced by my passion. I am always noting the one that boils up from inside me. It is fantasy and the passionate world. A girl's world – the world where dreams are had. I am playing in my world as the child plays with the doll. I do not want ever to lose the child's mind. I believe that my child's mind draws such a world. For me, the inspiration is all. I often think while the car is driving and float. **Which artists do you respect most for their work?** Katsushika Hokusai and the illustrators Arthur Rackham and Errol Le Cain. I am interested in popular art. I respect the artist who is widely known and accepted. **Can you tell us about the process of creating your illustration?** First of all, the idea is written by words and sentences. The image of the world is a written picture. The line is drawn quite freely. It is very much sense work. The inspiration that floats at that time is valued most. I am drawing the picture by using a PC. However, I am drawing the point and the line in the analogue. I am using the PC to colour as paint. In a sense that puts a digital colour to my picture. It is half analogue and half digital.

The recording artist Tori Amos features your illustrations in her music video 'Sleeps with Butterflies'. Can you tell us how this happened and about your collaboration with director Laurent Briet? It began when Laurent Briet saw my website (*Cheval Noir*). He found a common feature between me and the world of Tori and connected us. He and I reported many times through email. The compatibility of working with each other was confirmed after that. I think it is work that can be done by such a compromise with each other. It shortened the distance with each other. This was my first collaboration. This was the moment that determined holding out as an artist. **What was the brief for the video? The central ideas?** It is a girl's world. The world of bare feet – the world of a girl who dreams. It is a world like the fairy tale, it is pure and romantic

and with a little poison. I drew one new picture for this video. It is a picture of the butterfly of water and the lotus. I drew a deep, beautiful, pure world imaging it. **How was it for you to have your 2D work transformed into 3D moving image?** Laurent Briet proposed the method. Because I had no experience, I relied on his power. I completely trusted him and I left it to him. This was the first job for me. I seemed to be crushed by pressure at first because I had not expected that such big work was able to be done the first time working. The uneasiness disappeared gradually, and this changed into feelings of pleasure when it became a very wonderful experience. Tori is a great person. Her world and my world felt connected somewhere; therefore, I sincerely wanted to offer a wonderful picture for her. And, I was able to draw a perfect picture thanks to Laurent and John Winter (the producer) who had invited me. They were really supportive and I was helped many times. I think that I have done wonderful work because there was a trust in them and empathy with Tori. It was reborn from my world to Laurent's world, and transformed to a deeper, more beautiful world by the singing voice of Tori Amos. When I saw the video I was very proud to be one of those who expressed it. This experience is a treasure for me. **Have you been approached to do other commercial projects as a result?** I did work for a TV commercial for Microsoft Windows XP, *Trekker* (USA) – though whether it was a result of this video I'm not sure. And work for many magazines as well (Nylon, Rojo, Etapes, Beautiful Decay). There were a lot of people who sent personal mail, too. They helped me. I am really glad a lot of people are seeing my work.

What projects are you planning for the future? What would you most like to do?
I want to challenge a lot of things now. I want to work with people from many countries and in various fields – fashion, music, and the image etc... What I want to do most is send one book off into this world. It is a book that scatters love and the dream. I want to make the picture book that ties the person to the person, like a letter that the lover dedicates for the lover. And I plan to do a one-woman show soon in Japan. Then, I plan to sell the work for the first time.

www.geocities.jp/b_ba_a0530/cheval_noir_files/top00.html
b_ba_a0530@ybb.ne.jp

Opposite page
Rapun

Above
Kaguyahime

Florence Manlik

Orgiastic visions from a lost Symbolist unfold on 'parcels of nothingness'. In her abstract fantasy worlds, Parisian illustrator Florence Manlik explores the obsessive nature of the *volute*, and the idea of *la justesse*. Her beautiful, hand-drawn work has since found its way to a broad range of products which include book and CD covers, snowboards, clothing and windows for Cacharel.

By Lachlan Blackley

When did you first realise your desire to create as an artist, and how did this develop? I was always drawing anorexic figures to play with my sister. Stabilo felt-tip pen on paper cut out with scissors. They got names, and were admirable flat puppets. This didn't develop, since the figures I draw today still look anorexic. Some things never change. ***How did your studies shape your work?*** I adored learning to draw. I had more than 40 hours studies per week, and 75% of them were drawing lessons. We had lessons with naked models, portrait, sculpture drawing, drawing from memory, plant drawing, lettering… and then an optional four hours drawing on Saturday morning, which I never missed: I was quite addicted. But then it became so fantastically automatic, after these school years I had to put paper and pen away for more than four years to recover a personal line, a style which was me. Learning, and then un-learning – both were essential. In the meantime I became a performance artist, and I produced small epoxy resin or latex objects; strange shapes, impossible to name, so they were called 'soft object, or hard object'. My first notable exhibition was in the museum for contemporary art, in Marseille, where I lived in 1994.

What's your biggest influence in terms of style? You can't really talk about influences with me. It's all reversed. I do something, and then a kind of family emerges. It is not new, it has always been reversed. It sounds bizarre I know, but it's true. This can't be influence, influence usually

happens before someone's own stuff. But right now I would say I'm the last, a late, or a lost Symbolist. Because the drawings look like a 'reaction against literal representation of objects and subjects, where instead there is an attempt to create more suggestive, metaphorical and evocative work' – as with Symbolism. **Which artists or people do you admire most?** Science-fiction writer Roger Zelazny. Jean Painlevé – fabulous for his poetic underwater creatures documentaries. Hieronymous Bosch, Aubrey Beardsley, Marcel Dzama – for their cruel and elegant drawings. Multi-talented living artist, Momus. Some Japanese *kawaii* designers. Unconventional people or works. People / works with fantasy. The people who built all those buildings we live in, the engines we use, picked all these fruits we eat, had all these great and sometimes horrible ideas. But over all, people who appreciate where they are, what they are and possess (whatever their condition is) may be the most admirable thing to me.

What do you like to explore with your work? Are there recurring themes or ideas? The 'simple' process of life itself, the essence of things, their disappearance. Passing things forward without any mental restriction. The ability to face any situation with elegance and style. Paradoxical things, contradictions, absurdity, nonsense, synthesis, spirit. A non-pompous way to express some recurrent abstract concepts. **Can you talk about the element of fantasy?** All is fantasy here; it seems I have an organ called fantasy instead of a brain. It's not genetic. Something occurred at some time, I don't know. Anyway, everything ends up on the same level, abstraction, representation of things, control, absurdity, organisation and chaos, to build up something which sounds right. I'm obsessed with *la justesse,* in French. Soundness. It has to be *juste*. Balanced, whatever it is made of. It has to stand, even if bended. A *juste* fantasy. In the end it's all quite serious, it only looks like fantasy. Or the contrary.

Above left
Cage san dreams
2005
'Pattern featuring my bird, John Cage'
Original drawing 41cm × 31cm

Below left
Shark pattern
'Work for French fashion designer Robert Normand's summer collection 2006. He came up with these amusing ideas of flying sharks in stormy water'

Following spread, left
52 Designers' shoes
Spring / Summer 2005 collection
Gouache

Following spread, right
36 Chihuahuas
2005
Gouache

29

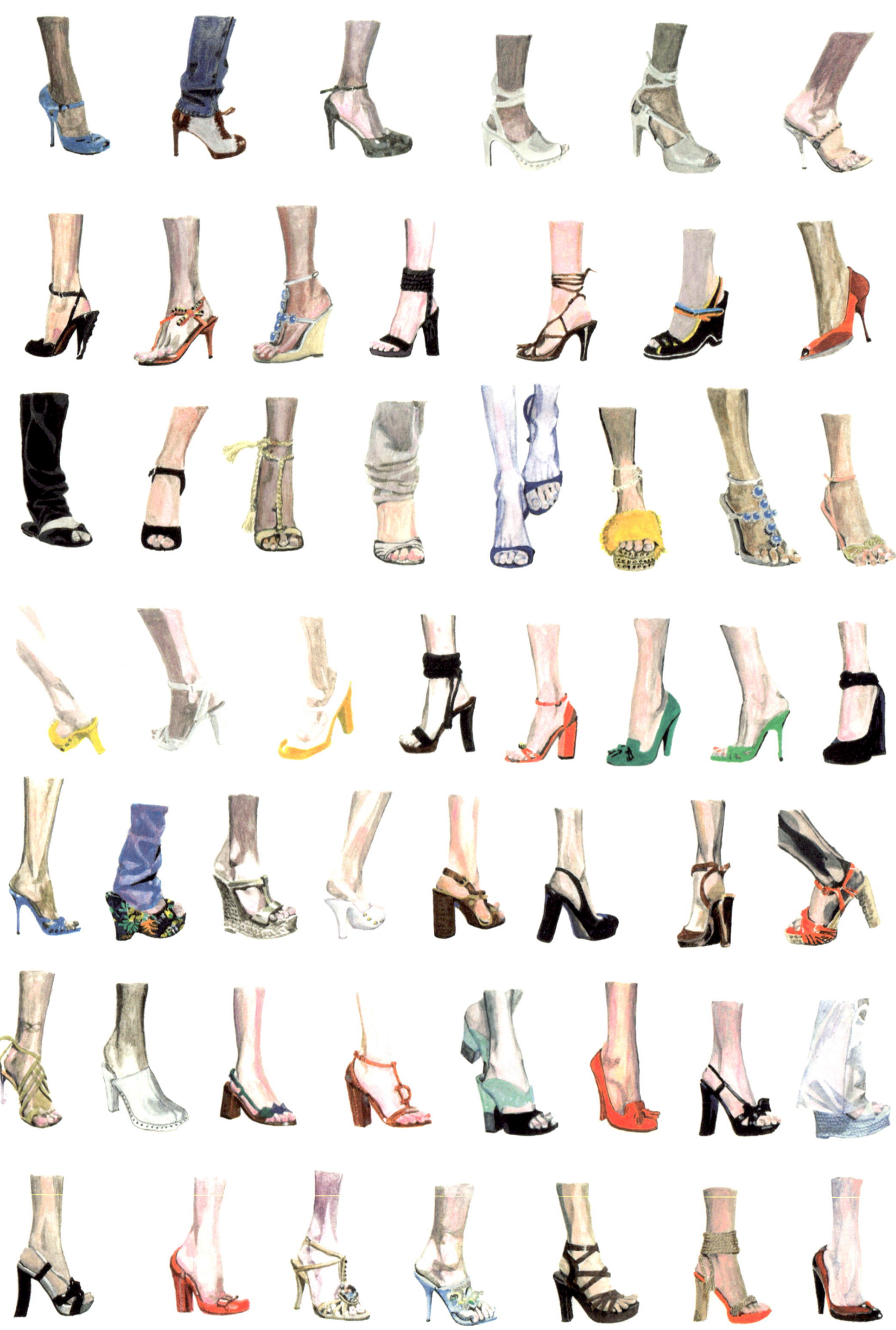

Airlute
2005
61cm × 41cm

'The volute is something full and empty at the same time. It's somewhere between attractive and uncanny. It's abstract rock & roll. The huge volutes are orgiastic visions, a debauchery of shapes, an indigestion'

Your 'volutes' are very organic and abstract. You mention that 'the beauty of a volute is that it represents nothing special'. Can you explain? A volute seems to be an evocation of something beginning or passing, light but invasive, enveloping, tortuous, twisted, plain or stuffed with fantastic creatures, mushrooms, micro skulls, fountains, bats… the volute is something full and empty at the same time. It's somewhere between attractive and uncanny. It's abstract rock & roll. The huge volutes are orgiastic visions, a debauchery of shapes, an indigestion. The full shapes are quite repulsive, but the double lecture phenomenon saves them from being rejected. It needs an effort. I quite like this idea – not 'ready to be consumed'. It is a risk, but it's gratifying and… *juste*. **Tell us a little about the process of creating a volute?** Volutes are a movie without scenario. Each drawing is lead by its own rules. Each line / element is an impulsion to the next one. It feels almost automatic, but I can't deny there is control all along the way. No idea, only execution. Once a drawing is started, it is almost impossible to make me do anything else, to have lunch, to meet friends or so on. Time doesn't matter anymore. This is out of all known dimensions. This is metaphysical.

Can you explain further the nature of this abstract form in your work? When I used to do exhibitions, a gallery or the place which was offered to me in a museum appeared to me like a parcel of nothingness. I could place something – or myself for a performance – in the space, and there was nothing else. It was like placing something in an abstraction. A sheet of paper is like an empty space. It is already a parcel of nothingness, already fully abstract, almost immaterial. My drawing gets abstract before it's even started. It seems natural to me. I'm fascinated by things like margins, borders of the sheet of paper, by the missing part, by the format itself. What was before, what's coming after, above, below. **You work mostly with pen and pencil. What is it you like about this medium?** Yes, mostly 0.05 ink micron pen on very smooth paper. It fits my character, to the idea of making an effort before eating it, and to my strong assertions disgust. It is a handicap for some kinds of reproduction. Like everything in this world, it has its limits. It's

Red (detail)
2004
Drawing, 86cm × 70cm

unfair to my eyes. I'll have to change this bad habit sometime. Hand drawn technique is nice. Computer work is nice. I'm not a militant for hand drawn, but it is my favourite and most comfortable technique. It is a question of rhythm. I like the morning trembling lines, the visible hesitation, doubt, sometimes fear, it is a very honest technique in this sense. Accidents and clumsiness are welcome; turning the disaster into some tragic beauty is an excellent exercise – a succession of chances and mistakes as a rule. I look for the best imbalance. The drawing must appear as having always been there, engraved in the depth, somehow.

Where is Bisland? The Bisland project is a series of ink pencil highly hypnotic drawings of architectures. A kind of Science-fiction landscape, with structures such as the 'Catharsis building'… Bisland is like haunted nothingness. Bisland is in my heart, it is a collection of abstract notions which are the cement of my work. **And what's the story with the 36 Chihuahuas gouache?** Chihuahuas were found on the internet because so many Japanese girls wanted to get rid of them – not fashionable anymore (peach caniche replaced them). There is also the *52 Designer Shoes* gouache. The shoes on Vogue's website are samples of what I'm frustrated not being able to wear since I would be two metres tall. The chihuahuas and the shoes on these gouaches are about 2–4 cm high: tiny. It is the same kind of work as the other things I do (detail and intricacy), with colour in addition. The brush I use must be the brother of the 0.05 pen. It is the accumulation which makes it interesting.

There is such detail and intricacy to your style. What are your thoughts on ornament and decoration in your design? How does it contribute to what you do? Sure, it is very ornamental. I'm lucky, because this saves me from being a bit too personal, which I'm aware I can be. It helps to open up my own limits, offers me the possibility of work, to collaborate with people interested in things other than my own mystical investigations! No one ever asks about the content (but I'm glad you did!). Because it is ornamental we had the chance to be printed on CD sleeves, clothes, windows, book jackets… and this is fantastic, it helps to go further.

Blue (detail)
2004
Drawing, 86 × 70cm

'I contact the people I wish to work with myself. I have no agency. I put on my beautiful Balenciaga trousers, and let's go'

Yours is a very personal style. How does it fit with doing commercial work? How do you find these contracts and is there work that you won't do? This is reality. Yes. This is my micro fight. But I'm still alive, I'm still drawing. I contact the people I wish to work with myself. I have no agency. I put on my beautiful Balenciaga trousers, and let's go. Or then some adorable people offer me publication in their magazines, this helps too. And recently, the creation of my blog, is a good thing. The question about work I wouldn't do hasn't come up yet. If there is one advantage in producing a very specific work – it prevents this kind of disagreement! **Can you talk about the range of projects you've done?** Around 2000 I decided to work differently. Drawing became my priority. The idea was to experience other possibilities of exhibitions, through collaborations with existing structures such as the music industry, fashion, advertising... To be printed on things, for a larger public's eyes. It took quite a while to get started, but it all becomes real, little by little; I'm getting more and more samples of my work printed on several kinds of supports, in magazines, CD and LP sleeves (Colleen – *Leaf*, 2003). I also did Cacharel's last Christmas window. Having a drawing printed in their windows was a nice exhibition all around the world. I've even engraved on wood! Pyrogravure for Stéphane Parmentier's kitchen planks, Paris.

Work coming out soon? A book jacket and CD sleeve for *La Volte* (a novel and its original soundtrack) which is out in September 2005. Work for French fashion designer Robert Normand's summer collection 2006. He came up with these amusing ideas of flying sharks in stormy water, and bunches of flowers made out of hair, which I adored drawing. Drawings for K2 snowboards 'Luna' line (USA) – worldwide next winter. And T-shirt designs for 'Trees are so special' (Tokyo), and for ex-Pélagique's new label Tricolore (Paris). **Do you have plans for a book of your own?** Ooh, not yet, but I would love to! **What would you most like to do next?** In the future I wish to be able to use a 0.1 pen! I wish to work with fashion designers, to design patterns, to create wallpaper designs, such as *Cagesansdreams*. I would love to give my project *Bisland* a true visibility, sometime.

manlik.florence@neuf.fr
manlik.blogspot.com

Robert Ryan

London-based illustrator Rob Ryan has found a medium that not many designers would covet. With paper, scalpel and a sketch book of words Rob creates detailed paper-cut stories by hand that evoke another time and place – when women wore big skirts and men always wore a hat. From album covers to pub signs, his commercial work extends to fashion with illustrations for Paul Smith, Project Alabama, Sazaby and the Christmas windows for Liberty's.

By Lachlan Blackley

Right
Rob Ryan

Far right
John Harding book cover
08.2005
Client: Transworld Publishing

When did you start drawing and telling stories? I always loved drawing. I remember when my dad bought a new shirt he used to take the piece of paper out, the card – it was kind of white on one side and grey on the other and it was really smooth and a nice piece of card to draw on. When I went to secondary school I had a good art teacher. I remember me and this other boy used to draw cartoons and stuff together. One day we were standing around admiring an older boy's drawing that was like super realism, and we were just going 'that's incredible, it's fantastic…' And this teacher overheard us and came up and said, 'That's rubbish, it isn't. You're much better than that. He's just copying a photo – you actually think of funny things and you come up with your own stories', and stuff like that. And I think when somebody says that to you, you kind of actually believe you're ok.

Then you went to art school? I did a foundation course in Birmingham for one year. Then I went to Trent Polytechnic in Nottingham and did Fine Art, which was good. The course was left over from the 70s, so you could really explore. I got into print making and got into screen printing quite a bit. And from there I went the Royal College of Art and did Printmaking. **When did the paper-cut illustrations begin?** I started doing that about three or four years ago. I was mainly painting. I wasn't really doing a lot of printmaking because I didn't have a printmaking studio. And I was doing a lot of writing. I've always been into the idea of sketch books, and sketch books are mainly words for me. I wanted to do something new and I was doing a lot of these pictures where I was folding the paper and they were totally symmetrical, they were very regular, very balanced. I always like the quite formal positioning. So I started doing these paper cuts, not really knowing what I was doing, and of course I started cutting the words out as well.

What is the fascination with words for you – the phrases and telling stories? I don't know, I suppose maybe it comes from it being a starting point. In some pictures the title will almost tie the whole picture together. Sometimes the phrase is the starting point of the picture and I think sometimes I tend to put that in and then build around it with other words. And you can use words like building blocks, like you have certain imagery that turns up again a few pictures later. **What feeds your imagination for stories?** If you're really, really happy it's quite difficult to do a picture about misery or sadness, because you've got it quite good. Sometimes you have to amplify those emotions. If you split up with your girlfriend or boyfriend, that source of material is so rich and so intense that you'd have enough material for five years possibly from just a month. But working day to day I think you have to dig a bit deeper than that. You have to imagine what other people are feeling a bit more and look at people. I'm happily married, I've got two kids and I've been with my wife for 25 years. It's quite difficult for me to complain! I almost have to empathise with people more. Because if you're going to write about experiences and stuff, and your own existence is fairly kind of… It's like being a writer, you have to make up stories, almost put yourself in people's shoes and imagine.

JOHN HARDING
ONE BIG DAMN PUZZLER

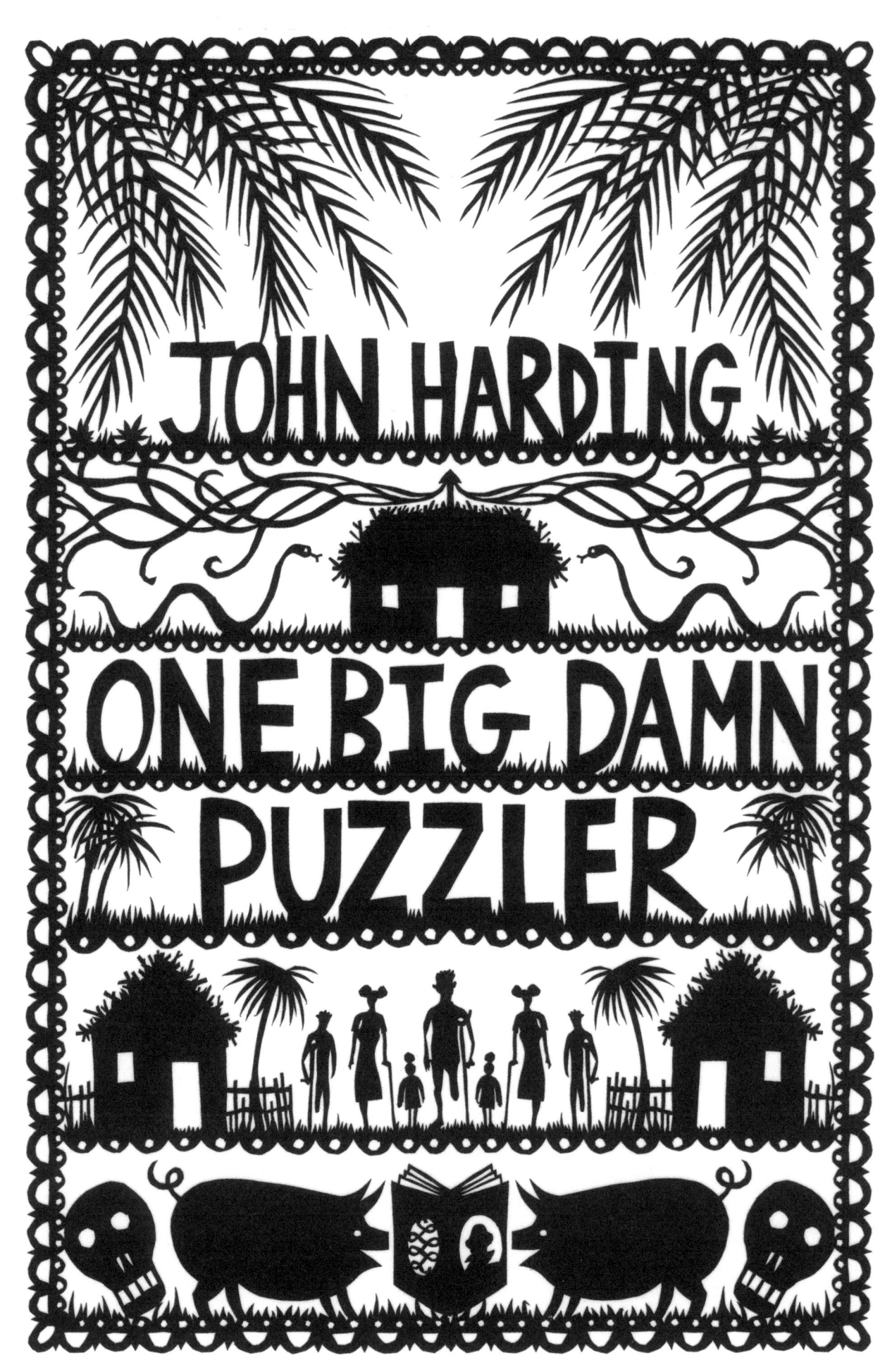

Above
Kissing Gate
2003

Above right
Museum of Us
11.2004
Papercut
From one man exhibition at the Horse Hospital, London WC2

Right
Nightbird cover
Original artwork
Client: Mute Records
Photography: Des Willie

Has there been an influence on your style with the paper cuts? It's difficult… when I started no-one was really doing it. Kara Walker was doing them at the same time, a bit before I started doing them. But her pictures are so different – they're such huge grand things, so I couldn't really say that. You know, it sounds weird, but in a way I think of Gilbert & George. I can see their pictures like paper cuts; in fact they are like paper cuts because all their work is stencilled on in that really time consuming way. And I'm a big fan of theirs – they use words and they're very symmetrical… and funny.

There is a kind of traditional folk feeling to your subject. Where does this come from? You know what – I couldn't draw someone and put an iPod and headphones on them. I can hardly draw a car, or a plane! All my people look like they're from the 40s or the 50s. The women all have big skirts and the men have trousers and a hat… I don't think I'm going for some sort of timeless quality! There will be picket fences and an ornamental path – and I don't know what that's about. What's that about? I don't know. I do have an aversion to making anything look too contemporary. So I think that might be the kind of reason it ends up looking like that, because it's quite a generalised view. If I do a picture of a man or a woman it's not really a specific person and the silhouette adds to that – it's just 'man' or 'woman'. This is what it represents. And the words link them and make the story without necessarily showing any emotion in the face, because in a silhouette you can't do that. You have to make the story with the words. ***And the folk element?*** When people see my pictures they might say 'oh, that reminds me of something I saw in Siam' or someone will go 'that's like a Philadelphia quilt', or someone will say Norway or Switzerland or Spain or Mexico. It's weird; it will be a worldwide response. From ten people it will be split all over the place. ***It reminds me of old story books from the 30s and 40s I had as a kid.*** Yeah people have these memories of Grimm's fairytales and things like that. And a funny thing that's happened is that people think the work is quite dark and I never think it is. My wife always laughs when I say I'm quite an optimistic person, but I think I am. When people say my work's got quite a dark, almost Tim Burton kind of feel, I think somehow they confuse their own memories of what the work reminds them of. And I think when they see the work they see themselves as children again and possibly being scared… A silhouette's a scary thing isn't it? Because you can't see anything, it's almost like somebody hiding. You kind of imagine a fairytale character hidden behind a tree, and I think they kind of take that with them. ***You use a lot of nature elements – birds and trees and flowers etc. Do they have a symbolic meaning for you?*** They do in a way… the birds I suppose have a symbolism that goes back to St Francis of Assisi with his famous prayer about the birds being the messengers of God – they don't have to do anything but fly from place to place and inspire people just because they're beautiful. I think there's a sense of that. Birds spring up quite a lot, almost like they're silent observers of us. They're kind of perfect, birds, aren't they? And we're flawed. And flora and fauna… to tell the truth, it's very interconnecting. I mean, if you look at a tree all it does is split up into different parts. It's very good for holding bits of paper together! I have lots of pictures where people are in trees and climbing trees. And borders feature quite a lot as well. You know, if I looked at a picture, the picture that I would like is the one where there are four things in each corner or something in the middle and something around it. There's something about symmetry that appeals to me. And for me the border can be the end point or the starting point of a picture to sort of get that in place. I love American quilts where there's just layers within layers. I like the organisation of that.

What attracts you to paper and the hands-on approach to cutting out? I don't want to think about things too much, I don't want to change them or rub them out. I want to kind of have the idea and let's do it! And I mean paper – cutting paper – is the ultimate extension of that really, because you can plan the picture to a certain extent. And I don't plan them totally. I kind of have an idea of how it's going to work and I draw it and cut it as I go along. It has to interconnect to hold together because they're always one sheet of paper. It's quite important that it's from one sheet – there's nothing added to it. It's one simple thing. A beginning and an end. It's quite a nice thing to do, you know, it's sort of satisfying. ***Do you get lost in it?*** Oh yeah. It's like doing a jigsaw, you can sit there and you only realise you've been doing it for a long time because your back hurts. And of course the big question is how long did that take to do? You can spend ten hours a day and it's absorbing. ***On average how long do you spend on a piece?*** I wouldn't want to spend longer than four days. There's only so much paper that you can cut in four days. You get quite fast at it, and I do have people who help me. ***How many?*** Never more than one at a time. I'll draw and they'll

'I couldn't draw someone and put an iPod and headphones on them. I can hardly draw a car, or a plane! All my people look like they're from the 40s or the 50s. The women all have big skirts and the men have trousers and a hat… I don't think I'm going for some sort of timeless quality'

'If I looked at a picture, the picture that I would like is the one where there are four things in each corner or something in the middle and something around it. There's something about symmetry that appeals to me'

Right
Paul Smith fabric
2006
Client: Paul Smith for *PS Pink*, Spring / Summer

Below
Transfer images
Screen printed iron-on transfers

sit next to me and assist me. I mean at the end of the day it's following a line. But it's demanding on your eyes especially. It's very, very tiring. **Do you have a specific or favourite paper that you use?** I had a great paper and I can't get it any more. It was a really big leaf-end paper. **What did you like about it?** It had a really smooth surface and it was 70gsm. You start cutting anything over 100gsm and you really feel it. It was available in very big sizes as well like A0, so it was quite nice. It was the end of a line they got from some warehouse and I haven't found anything as good. **So, many scalpel injuries?** Yeah I used to cut myself quite a lot. I used to cut my fingers a fair bit, but not really doing it – changing the blades! And I used to cut myself in the leg. I'd kind of be talking to people and I'd walk into the table with the scalpel sticking out… it's a dangerous world!

You're with the creative agency This Is Real Art. How does it work with getting projects? Well they obviously try and marry me up with people and they're good for showing my book around. And I very rarely say no to something. But the interesting thing about the work that This Is Real Art has hooked me up with is, it's work that I wouldn't have gone out and sought. I did a big thing for Erasure last year. I did quite a lot of work with them and I wouldn't have thought I'd show my work to record companies. **Why is that?** I don't know, I just think that there'd be too many doors for me to knock on before I found somebody sympathetic. I just cannot sell at all! You know, I'd rather starve than sell myself. I just find it can be excruciating.

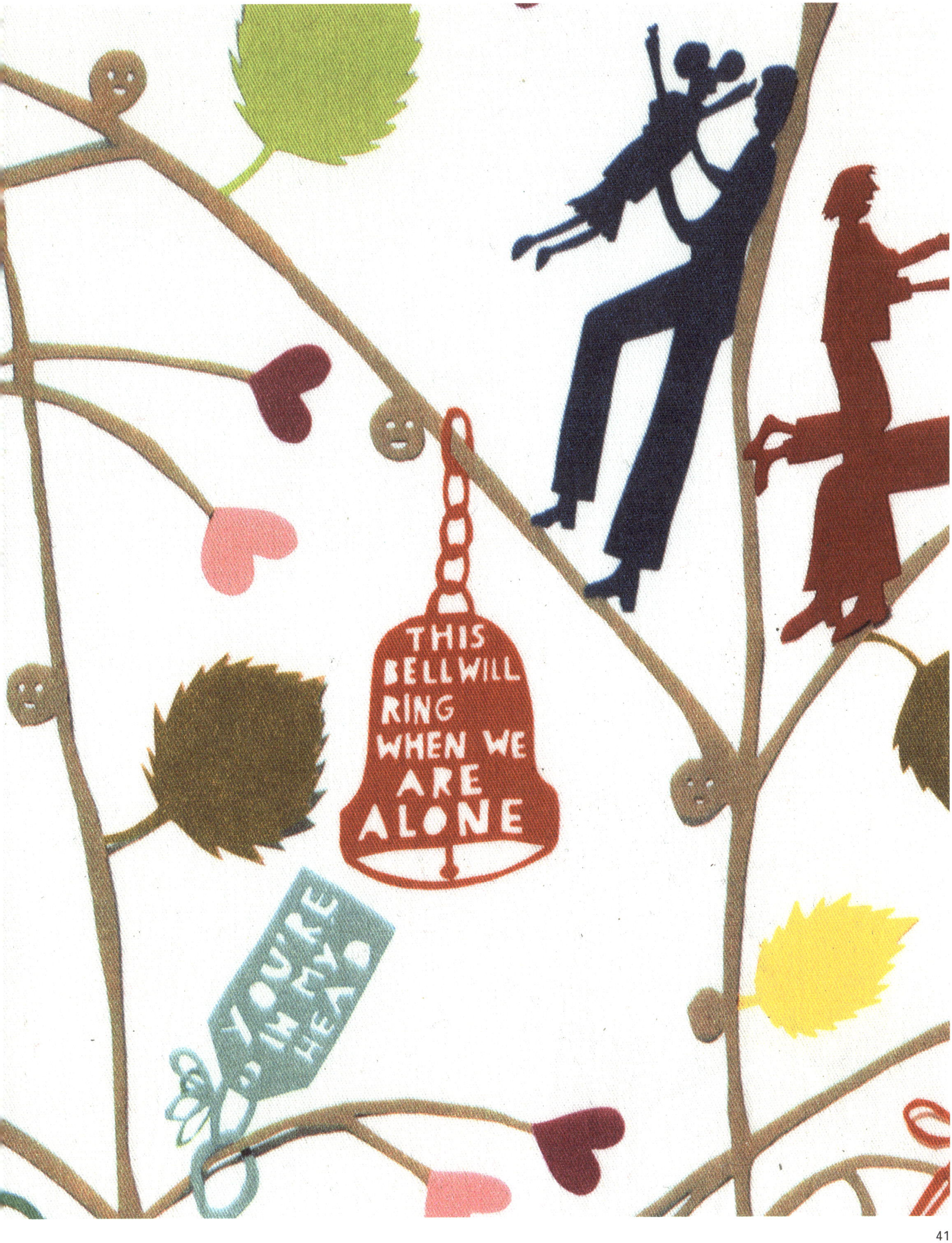
THIS BELLWILL RING WHEN WE ARE ALONE
YOU'RE IN MY HEAD

WE HAD NOTHING
WE HAD NOT MUCH
WE
HAD EVERYT
PLEASE GOD DONT LET ME HAVE TOO MUCH

Do you have creative freedom with most of the work you do? I do. I think I've been really lucky. I pretty much get my own way quite a lot of the time. And I must admit I come from a fine art background, so I've never been told by anybody: listen, if you want to work, you've got to compromise. But I think I'm open to suggestions and I will take things on and try and come up with my take on it.

You mentioned the Nightbird cover for Erasure. Can you talk about this project? Well the original idea for that was… I wanted to do the whole thing in camera. I wanted to build a set where you would look through the lens and everything that you saw, we built. I had the idea of making up this dreamy night bird out of all these light bulbs. So we had a photo studio and we had this brilliant photographer who was dealing with a depth of field that was 30 feet. We had this paper cut in the foreground. And in the background we hung these lights in this hot room for 3 days! All different lengths. The idea was for it to be almost like a still of a theatre piece. And I would have liked it to have stayed, but the record company had their own idea. Basically, they took elements of it and just kind of Photoshopped them really. It's still the same idea, just a more Photoshopped version. **And the cover for issue 2 of Amelia's Magazine?** That was a good job. She approached me about it and she'd researched the people that laser cut it. And to tell the truth, I did the art work but their laser cutting is fantastic! It's really impressive, what they can do with this machine. There's only one of them in the country that can do that kind of level for production. I think it was a good brief. She said, 'this is what I want to do. I want to have a laser cut image but also, for twenty pages deep I want to have a hole that this piece of jewellery will fit into. And then we'll have the paper-cut going over the top and then it will be shrink-wrapped…' So within that framework we thought, well ok we've got the jewellery, let's put that in a kind of egg shape, let's put the egg in a nest and stick a few birds on and

'I must admit that I come from a fine art background, so I've never been told by anybody: listen, if you want to work you've got to compromise'

Left
We had everything
11.2004
Papercut
From one man exhibition at the Horse Hospital, London WC2

43

'There can be something that you can work with, where originally you see the pattern and the colours, and then within that there's a second story to be discovered'

kind of built the picture up around that physical brief. And it worked out pretty good I think. **You use the colour red quite a lot.** With the paper cuts it's really just going to be one colour or black. Red draws you immediately and it's almost like a second colour to black, isn't it? It's the colour version of black for me. A lot of those Amish quilts were red and white and they're quite similar to my work. I always really liked those. When you see those old Pennsylvanian quilts they're like red and white. And they're almost sort of shocking, like a Jasper Johns picture.

What are your thoughts about ornament and decoration in your work? I think it can be very seductive. You can almost get drawn into it so much that it can be like a bit of a crutch. I think it works when it has a story woven into it. You used to find this in a lot of illustration, especially children's illustrations from the 40s, 50s, early 60s possibly, where decorative motifs and borders were used. But also a story was woven into them that related to the text or maybe a central illustration in the middle. I think for its own sake it can be limited, but then it has its place. I did an illustration for Vogue that was pretty much purely decorative. There is quite a repetitive quality in it. You do have to look into the picture to see what's going on. And sometimes that required looking into something… When you say decorative I almost immediately imagine repeated motifs, almost quite natural forms. There can be something that you can work with, where originally you see the pattern and the colours, and then within that there's the second story to be discovered. Decorative art almost used to be a kind of dirty word, especially in fine art circles. I think people these days do what they want to do a lot more and I don't think it's taking the easy way out at all. I think it's just finding your own path. **Tell us about your work for the Liberty's Christmas window?** I'm working on that now for October and it's quite difficult in the heat of the studio trying to get into the Christmas-y atmosphere. It's a big job, it's going to be blown up by somebody else, laser cut out of steel and it's a lot of windows all the way around the shop. 42 pieces of glass within like 20 windows or whatever… so you know, it's a lot of work and it has to tie in and it all has to fit together. The thing is, you want to tell a story and unfortunately a story has a beginning and an end. But people don't walk past a shop window in one direction so somehow you have to try and get this story across in multi-directions which is a sort of challenge in a way. Liberty's goes around a corner, there's a road in between and the windows are all different shapes… so you're kind of trying to have a whole story going on and to break it up into digestible pieces.

Right
Listen to the world
05.2005
Screenprint on foil card
Exhibited at Galerie Frank, London W1

Plans for the future? I keep exploring new things. People always keep asking me to do stuff that's quite different. In the last few months I've been working with this interior designer who's refitting pubs, so I've been doing pub signs. I'm working on a book jacket for Bloomsbury at the moment. And I've just finished doing some work for Paul Smith for their 2006 womenswear [available from Paul Smith Pink Spring / Summer 2006]. Basically that will be work of mine turned into textile prints and then turned into a range. ***Is this your first venture into fashion?*** No, I did something that will be launched in September for an American company called Project Alabama (www.projectalabama.com). They do a lot of hand-sewn appliqué and embroidery and their concept is almost like haute couture. Some of their garments sell for $4,000, because it's all labour-intensive cotton. And they really went to town on my work, cutting out all these shapes and sewing them on and different layers. I also did a range for a Japanese company called Sazaby last year – printed stuff for bags and purses and all that sort of thing. ***What would you most like to do?*** The hardest thing for me to do is to sit down and write something. You know, so many people tell me 'Rob, you should write children's stories'. And for me that's a hard thing to do. It takes a certain amount of time and in between doing all this other stuff, you find that you don't have a spare minute. So whether I stop at some point, take some time out and sit down and write, that's really what I want to do. But you know, I'm not really that bothered. I always keep saying to myself, if I don't enjoy it, I'm going to stop doing it. You know what I mean? Just like any other job really. And as long as it keeps moving and I still have a laugh while I'm doing it, then that's enough for me really.

www.thisisrealart.com

Robert Ryan will be exhibiting in February 2006 at Jaguar Shoes Gallery, 17 Kingsland Road, London E2 8AA
+44 (0) 20 7729 7606
For further details go to:
www.jaguarshoes.com/robertryan

Above and left
Amelia's cover
Autumn / Winter 2004
Commissioned laser-cut cover for *Amelia's Magazine*

Sweden Graphics

Sweden Graphics, or Sweden Interiors? Graphic goes fact finding

When we put an early cover for this issue on the web we had people emailing us asking whether it had been designed by Sweden Graphics. We let them know that it hadn't, though we were planning to feature their work inside the book. What this reaction highlighted, however, was just how present the work of Sweden Graphics is in today's graphic design scene. If one were to look for the most influential graphic styles of the past few years, their work would have to be placed alongside that of M/M Paris and GTF and Geoff McFetridge. They have lead a generation of visual artists and shaped our current graphic taste.

Two 'tiles' projects with Tham Videgård Hansson Architects – ceiling tiles are designed for the kitchen ceiling of a private residence in Stockholm and floor tiles are designed for a nationwide chain of fast food stores – gave us a good excuse to ask them a few questions.

Sweden Graphics is Nille Svensson and Magnus Åström. They have been around in different forms since 1997 and work with design, illustration, animation etc. They are also part owner of the publishing house Pocky.

In the past few years you have made several projects involving patterns: several wallpaper designs [see issue 1 of Graphic Magazine], ceiling tiles, and now a set of floor tiles. Where does this interest in patterns come from? It is hard to be interested in graphic design without being interested in patterns. Patterns seem to please the brain. One particularly satisfying thing when working with pattern design is the step when the designed element is duplicated and repeated to form the pattern. It is almost impossible to foresee the effects that this change in complexity and scale creates. Often you have to go back and forth a lot before you have a pattern element that works well repeated as a pattern. Its part design, part puzzle game.

In a note accompanying the wallpaper designs published in the first issue of Graphic you spoke of 'narrative decoration'. Could you tell us a bit more about that? The wallpapers came out of an idea of making illustrations in a new way. We often do illustrations in a fairly simple and straightforward way. By repeating illustrations in a pattern the content or meaning of the illustration is somehow shrouded. From a distance you see a pattern, a decorative element. Then if you look closer you realise there is a content, something to be read and understood. So the 'narrative decoration' is a way of still using illustration to speak quite clearly but at the same time make the work a bit more ambiguous and intriguing to the viewer.

Can you think of other people interested in making this kind of work? I don't think this is something new at all. Patterns and decorative elements have always had some kind of inherent meaning. With time, however, a more widely spread understanding and use of symbols have got lost and the ornaments become mere decoration, while they were probably saturated with symbolic value when they were originally created. We just thought we could use pattern elements and a form that could be easily interpreted and still appreciated for its decorative quality.

Do you feel that after the (sometimes) misunderstood minimalism and anti-form of the late 90s there is now room for designers to take on richer and more ornate forms?
Form follows fashion and fashion is always moving towards its own opposite. There is definitely a growing output of a certain kind of 'ordered' design, patterns and what you may call classic typography in search for better words, which follows the anti-design that followed minimalism. A lot of time is wasted on establishing what is not trendy any longer – something we thought was good but turned out not to be. The 'untrendy' is treated as something that has been revealed or exposed as pretending to be something it wasn't, while the 'new' promises everything the 'old' failed to live up to. To me this is a fallacy, but maybe that is what you mean when you describe minimalism as misunderstood. Minimalism has but one problem and that is that it is not fashionable anymore, if that's even a problem. But what has followed it is not any less elitist or uninhibited in any relevant

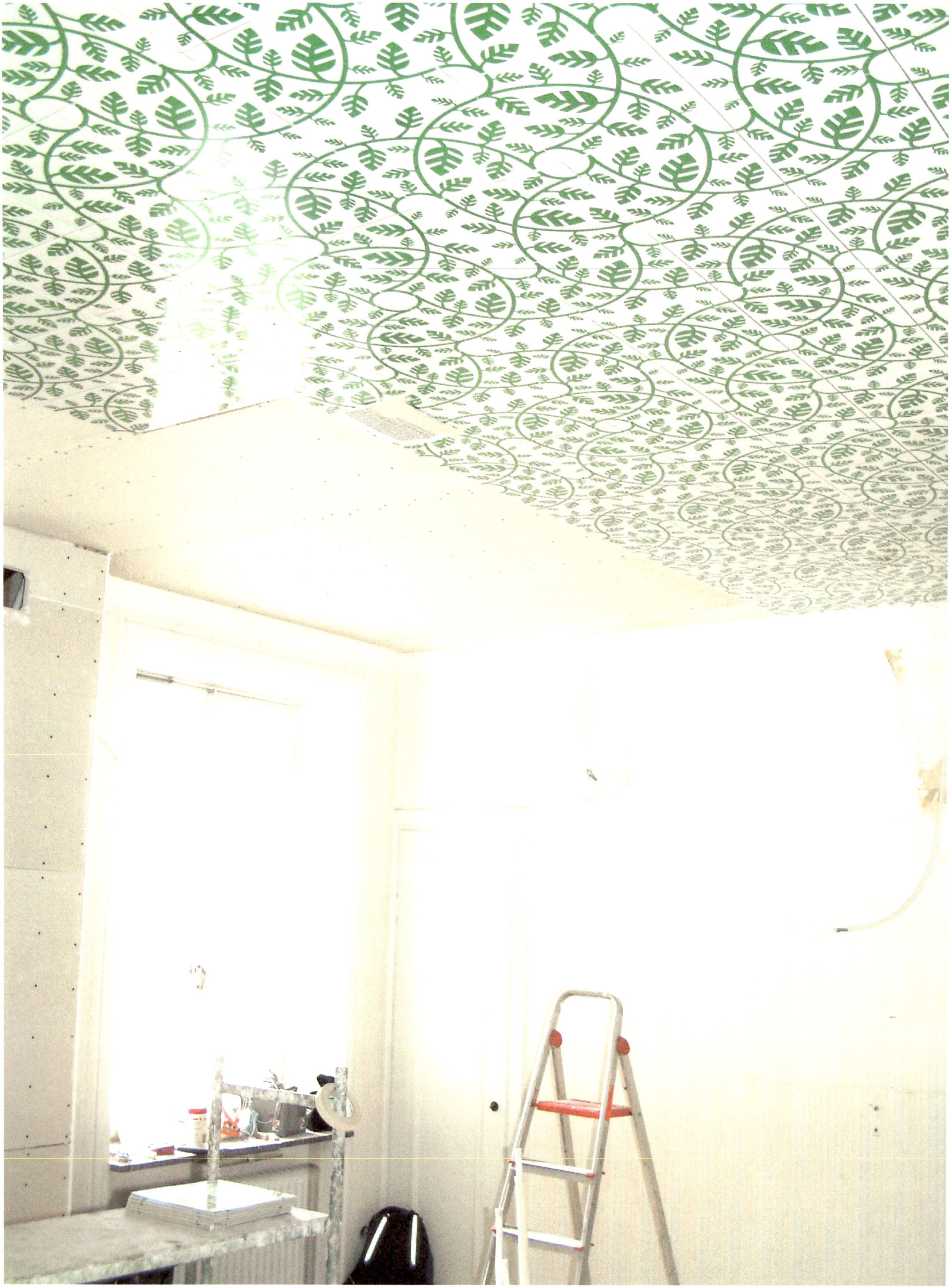

50

way. The trend towards ornament and decoration conforms as much as anything that has preceded it. It is a trend and therefore limiting and uniform by definition. So, in order to answer your question, it is as much a room of opportunity as a dictate.

How did the tile designs come about? The ceiling project was initiated by Tham Videgård Hansson Architects who made the interior design of the apartment. They asked us for a concept to decorate the kitchen ceiling and suggested a tile design solution. ***Are the two projects related?*** The two tile projects are definitely related. Though also quite different. While the ceiling pattern is constructed with one tile design only, the floor is built up by eight different tiles (nine if you count the blanks). Strictly speaking it is not even a pattern but more a large illustration or puzzle, laid out using this set of eight designed elements. The plan is that we will make a new floor layout for every new store that opens.

What were the ideas behind the ceiling tiles? The form of the ceiling tiles were much governed by the fact that the budget limited us to one tile design only. At the same time we wanted a large-scale pattern since the surface was so big and the tile would always be placed at some distance from the viewer. So we made a pattern element that could be rotated and thus be combined with itself. In that way the scale automatically became much bigger as the pattern was not repeated with every tile. The pattern is conceived as being constructed by quite large curved elements but the repeated element is just as big as a tile. ***How did they change when it came to designing the floor tiles?*** The floor tiles were designed in collaboration with Wilhelmson Arkitekter as part of an interior design system for a chain of fast food restaurants. So while the ceiling was part of a private residence the floor was a semi public space. Here we had the opportunity to design many different tiles and through that we saw the possibility of making an irregular decoration instead of a repeating pattern. ***Did the project run the way you expected it?*** It was hard to find a good way of producing the tiles.

Does form always follow function? 'No, almost never. And if it does try it hardly ever catches up'

Even harder for the floor ones since they would take a lot more wear and tear than ceiling ones. This fact did limit us to some extent but as it turned out we found an acceptable compromise.

Are the tiles going to be mass produced? We are still looking for methods and partners that could make it possible to manufacture tiles like this on a larger scale. **Did you feel the tile sets were a natural progression from the wallpaper designs?** Not really. The projects are quite different in the way that the wallpapers were an experiment in finding new ways of making and using illustrations. The result was more of a hybrid form. The tiles are perhaps more conventional as a concept in the way that there is nothing surprising with a decorated tile. But through our design we have tried to push it and still make something somewhat 'out of the ordinary'. **How does all this work with patterns fit in with the rest of your output?** As a designer, everything you are interested in should be thrown in there, regardless of the project's prerequisites. You often get the most interesting results if you don't kill your babies, but put them to work. While working on the patterns we were asked to make a fake tattoo design. Pressed for time we took bits and leftovers from the pattern designs and made a little set of quadratic fake tattoos that can be cut out and puzzled together on your skin much like the floor tiles.

What's special about decorative forms? It can effectively sum up or capture the essence of a style or aesthetic approach. **Is ornament not a crime anymore?** Certainly not, it's a superficial indulgence at worst. **Does form always follow function?** No, almost never. And if it does try it hardly ever catches up. **On a scale of 1 to 10 – where 1 is fanatical minimalism and 10 is gilded rococo – where would you place your work? Why?** Cut up the scale in little pieces and put them in a bag and every time you do a project you draw a number. That is how it feels. **What is your definition of ornament?** I guess the answer is something along the lines of 'form that is applied for extra functional purposes', but it's not a very satisfactory one. The idea of the functional is so diffuse in consumer society and it is hard to define what functionality really is. **What styles do you most identify with?** Fun, intelligent, friendly work. **Computers, more or less?** One per capita is enough. **Wallpaper or paint?** Wallpapers are definitely more fun to design.

Is this kind of work something you intend to continue making in the future? Hopefully we will do more work in connection with architecture and interior design. The collaboration has been really inspiring on these projects. **Anything you're already working on?** It looks like we are going to do a whole kitchen, ceiling, floors, walls and cabinets for a private residence later this year.

www.swedengraphics.com
hello@swedengraphics.com

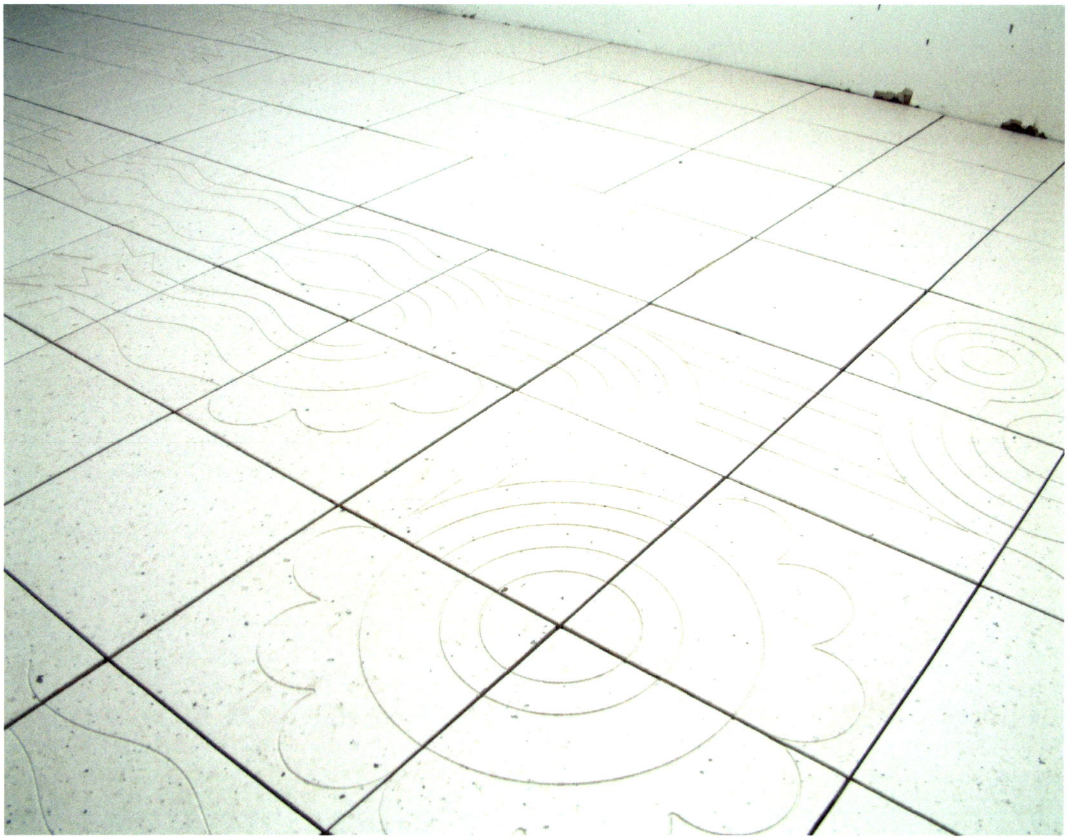

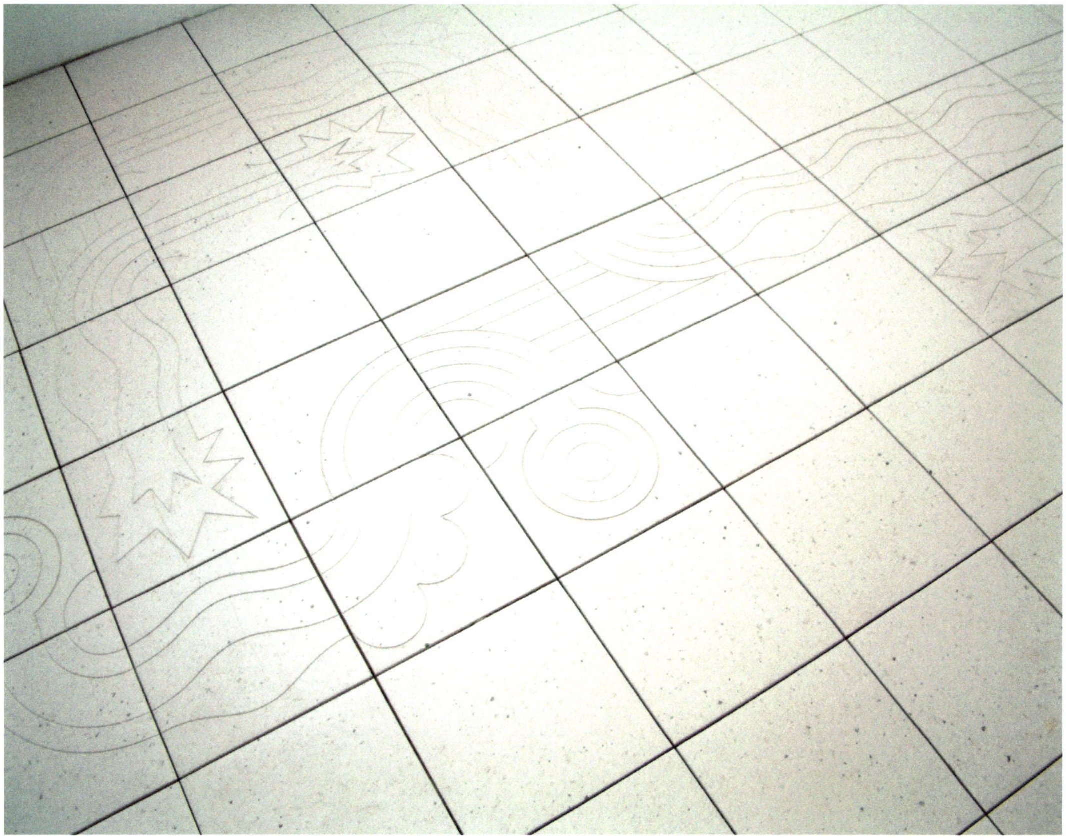

Kam Tang

Graphic designer and illustrator Kam Tang engages a diverse variety of medium and styles. Best known for his work with *Wallpaper** magazine and the new identity for London's Design Museum, Kam's designs have also appeared in large-scale advertising campaigns for Adidas, Nike and Sony. New personal explorations materialise with his exhibitions in Japan and the Big Active book *Head Heart & Hips*.

By Lachlan Blackley

Opposite page
Navigator: Amsterdam
For *Wallpaper** magazine

When did you first realise your desire to create as a designer? I grew up in Brighton, on a voracious diet of Marvel comics, Tex Avery and Disney. I was never sure whether this was simply something I enjoyed (as kids do) or whether it was something more 'career defining' as such. It wasn't until later, during college, when I started applying myself seriously to study that I realized doing something creative and visual was what I wanted to pursue.

You studied graphic design at Brighton University and a Masters at the Royal College of Art. Can you tell us briefly about your studies and how this has shaped your work? I was lucky enough to be under the tutelage of George Hardie to whom I'm much indebted (he is the designer of the Pink Floyd and Led Zeppelin album covers). His approach to ideas and problem solving, and his draughtsmanship, were second to none. The whole notion and process of taking a problem, analyzing and interpreting the 'answer' is really gratifying (assuming the pieces fall into place). It's like a game, using your imagination, drawing and having fun (again, as kids do). Back then, we didn't have to use a computer, instead we had to manage drawing a perfect circle by hand with a pen, and this skill really meant a lot in my illustration work. When I was studying design, everyone had to find a way to execute their graphic solution – some chose typography, but I pursued drawing instead. Design is a more disciplined and functional practice, whereas illustration is more personal and expressive. Therefore, I tend to use my illustration in more of a design way. I chose to continue my studies at the Royal College of Art for more in-depth exploration. Then when I graduated I started my first freelance illustration job with GTF [Graphic Thought Facility].

Your style is quite varied. What or who would you say is your biggest influence? It's hard to single out individuals and movements, as influences have varying impacts upon me at different times and circumstances. I find the greatest inspiration in the natural world, but I'm open to a lot of things. I think you have to be pretty broad minded, as everything you encounter adds to your artillery of knowledge – to draw upon when needed. At the moment I love Mozart's operas and the world of freemasonry, but how this will affect my work is anybody's guess. Now when I look back at my work, I find that they often have common themes – the lines and shapes are quite familiar. ***Which artists or people do you admire most for their work?*** More recently the epic works of sculptor Michael Heizer has excited me a lot. And the Stubbs show at the National Gallery was great. I find people who have pioneered and mastered their field of expertise the most admirable – Mozart, Fischer, all seem to possess and be possessed by a dogged persistence and call to take things to the fore... unfortunately they are also the ones who tragically burn out. ***What feeds you for inspiration, ideas?*** I'm reading a lot more literature for inspiration these days. Art and design exhibitions don't seem to stimulate me as they used to. I am always interested in the everyday things, such as the pattern, structure, colours – usually they are just little things which I will write notes and make simple drawings with. Most of the sketches look like industrial drawings and I often look back to these sketches for inspiration and reference afterwards. I enjoy the process of looking and seeing things, where I can observe and collect the visual images.

Could you explain how you work and the process of coming up with an idea to its execution? Everything begins with sitting down and thinking, digesting the task at hand. I like to start jobs just drawing stuff to ease my way in. When things are down on paper I get a clearer picture of the possibilities and potentials. These are then given further thought until it starts standing up for itself when you ask questions of it. The execution is usually decided upon as the idea develops – although in a commercial world it can be dictated by time, money and the art director's requirements. I usually get up early in the morning and then work until noon. Later I will go out for a walk (seeing things etc). I have to keep up with my schedule, and manage my time month by month according to my workload.

You're now with the creative management agency Big Active. How has this changed things for you? It's been great. I've worked freelance since leaving the RCA, without an agent. Now with Big Active, I can focus more on the creative side, without the burdens of 'running a business' – job hunting, money haggling and avoid getting humped. ***Tell us a little about your commercial work?*** A lot of what I do is governed by the job at hand. Every client wants something specific, the 'clothes' may look different but they are all created and laboriously stitched by the same hand. Thanks to the aid of internet technology, I can manage to work with Japanese clients and other international partners. ***Is there a difference between the commercial work you do and***

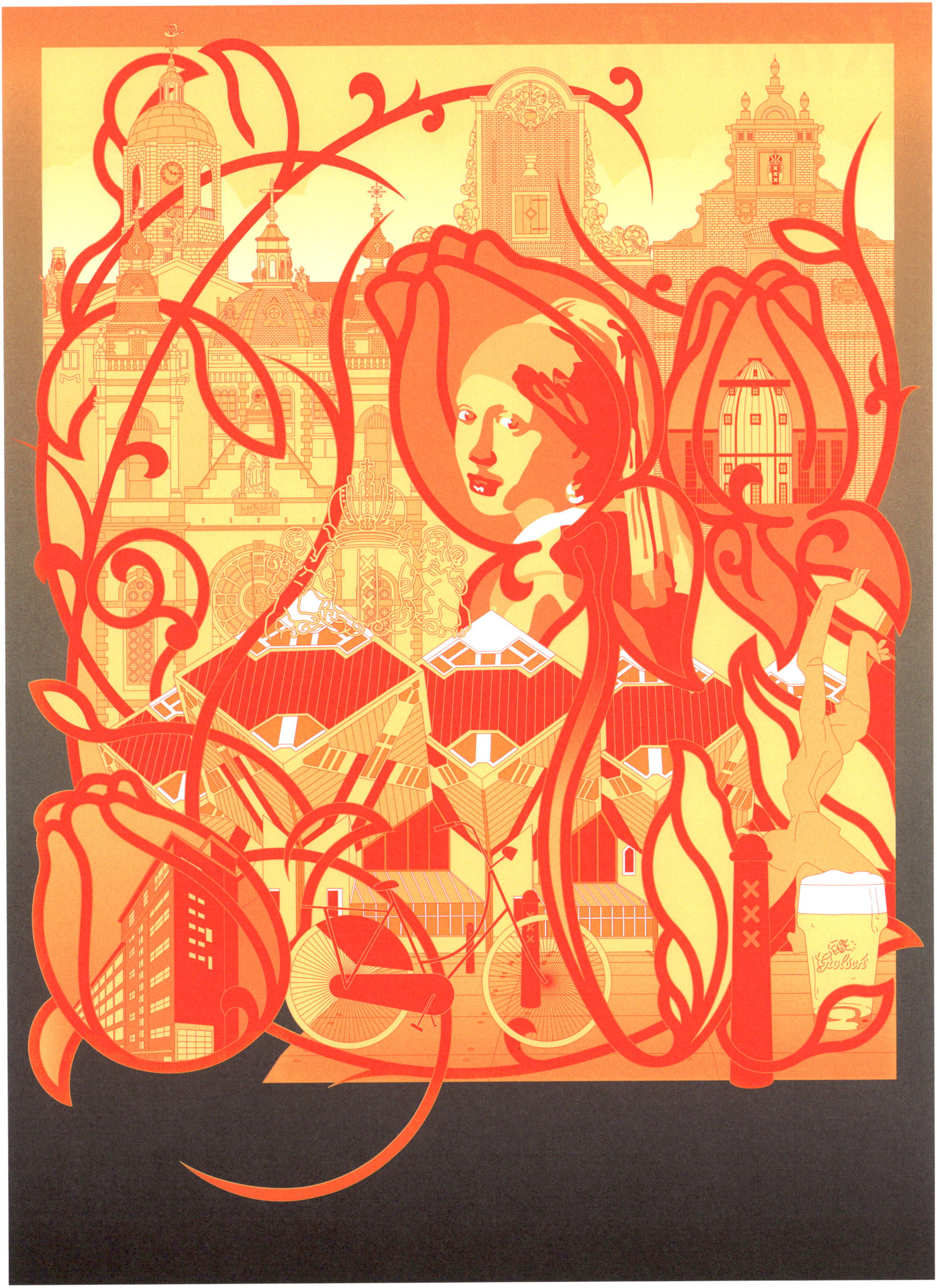
Grolsch

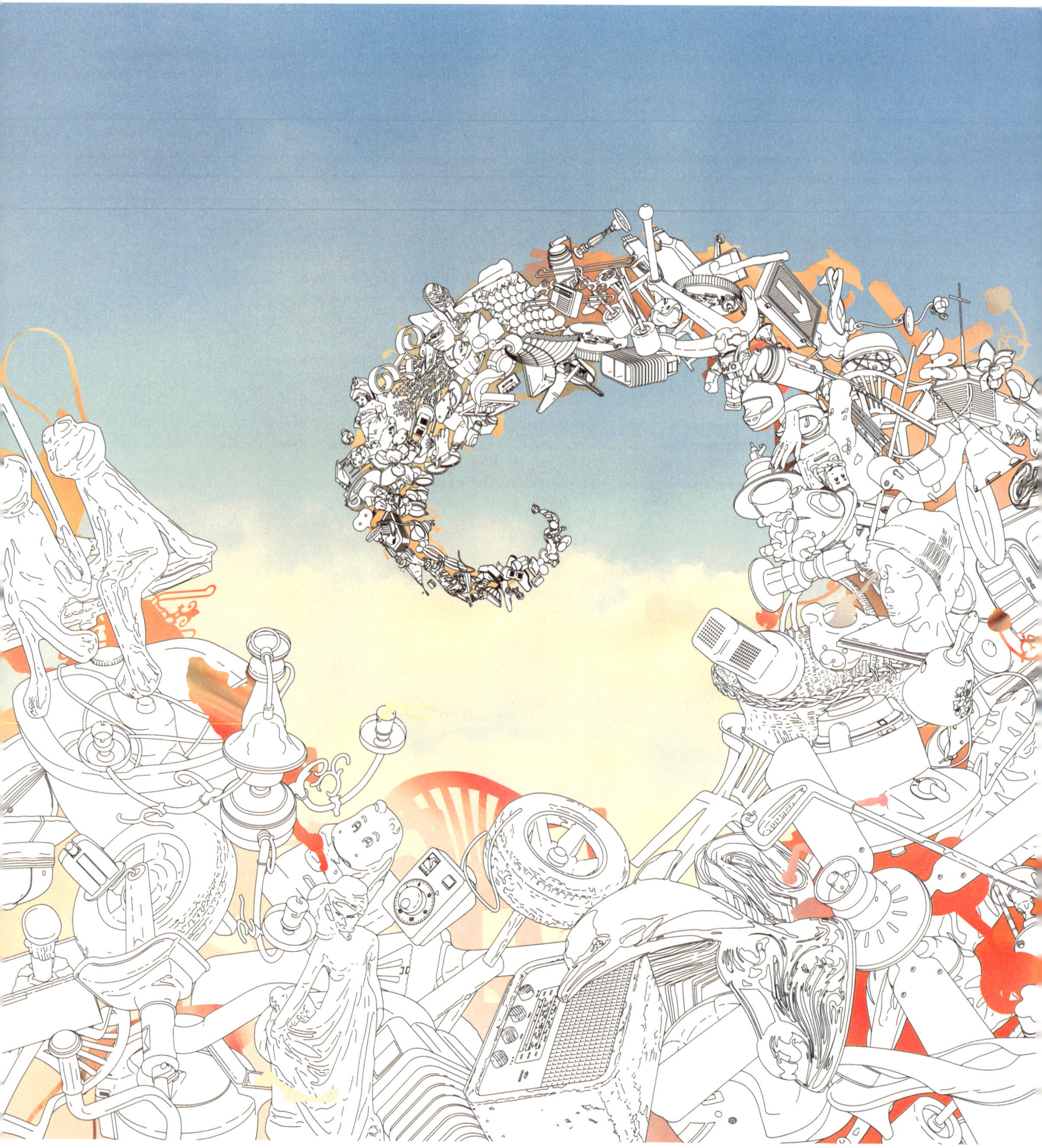

the personal? There can be, the level of personal expression can at times be limited by the client. The most successful (and enjoyable) projects allow me to bring something to the table; I enjoy working with art directors that ask me use my head as well as my hands.

You're probably best known for your work with the London Design Museum and Wallpaper* magazine. It was great to be involved in the new identity for the Design Museum. This was art directed by GTF and the identity was created using objects that represent all the practices and movements in the design world. It is one of the jobs I'm most proud of simply because the forms worked so well for what was required, while allowing me to indulge myself. And for *Wallpaper** magazine, the *Navigator* maps were illustrations created on a given location by the magazine, to give the reader not only a map but an added interpretation to the key sites of interests in the city. **You've also done sleeve work for the Chemical Brothers, Athlete and Two Culture Clash. Very different styles, could you talk a little about each one?** The sleeve work for the Chemical Brothers was art directed by Tappin Gofton. The campaign was based on revolutionary posters with a social message – the human. Athlete was art directed by Blue Source and the campaign was created using elements observed and drawn from the band's locality. Objects from the local market amass and spiral out as the campaign develops. The album artwork for *Two Culture Clash* (art directed by Tom Hingston Studios) set out to reflect the colourful world, exotic and carnival-like nature of the music created when UK musicians 'clashed' with their Jamaican counterparts. **Your work is often very detailed. What are your thoughts on ornament and decoration in your design?** There is a reason for the elaborateness of certain pieces; they are there to add a greater depth and richness to the whole, besides looking busy and decorative. I like rich and complex things but not superfluity – that's just a poor veil for little substance. **'Flow' is a great example of the ornamental; can you tell us more about this project?** This is a wallpaper design. It was primarily a study of lines

'The whole notion and process of taking a problem, analyzing and interpreting the 'answer' is really gratifying (assuming the pieces fall into place). It's like a game, using your imagination, drawing and having fun'

Far left
Vehicles And Animals
2003
CD cover art for Athlete.
Art directed by Blue Source

Left
Design Museum identity
Art directed by GTF

Following spread
Flow
Wallpaper design for Maxalot's *Exposif* collection

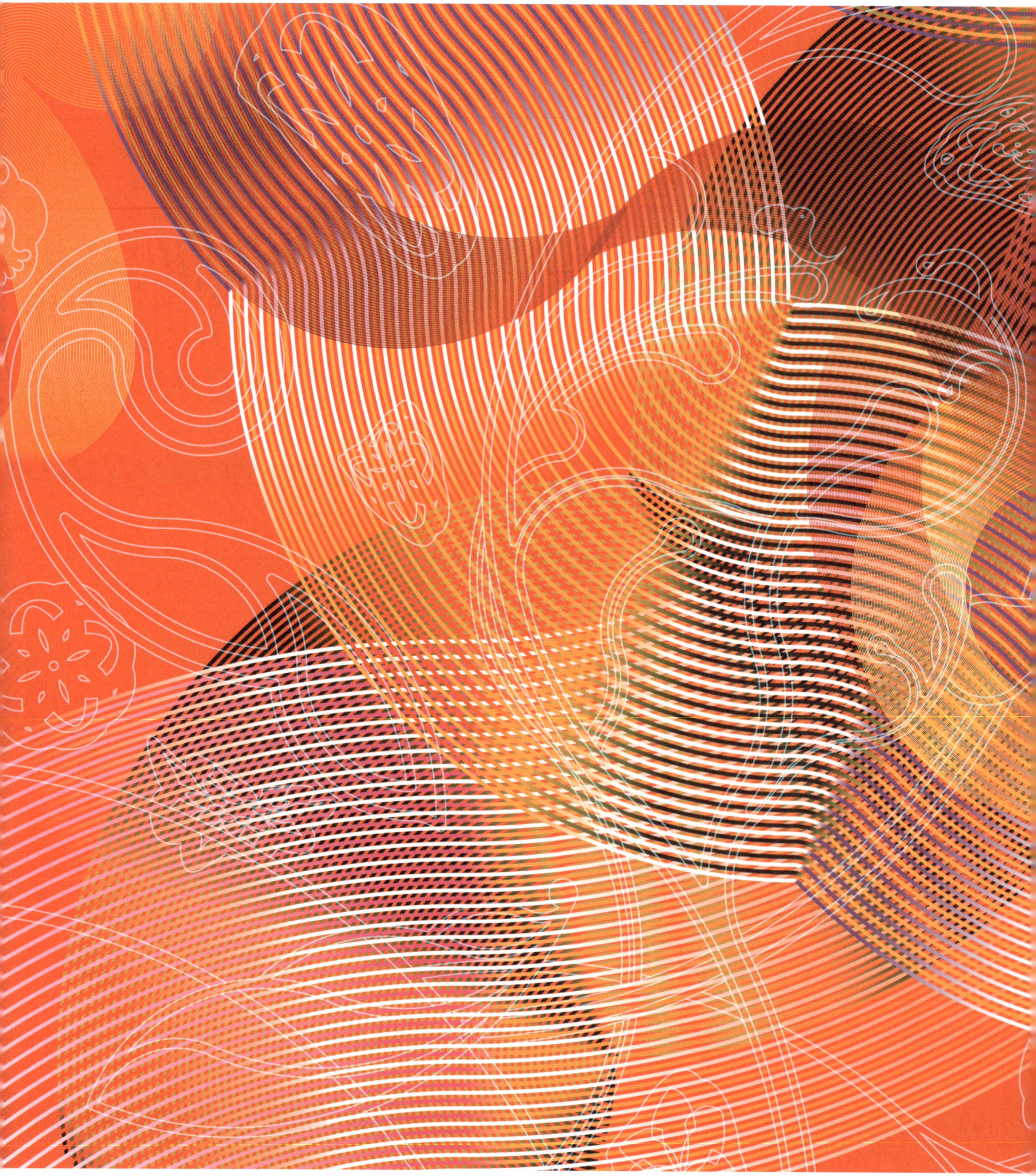

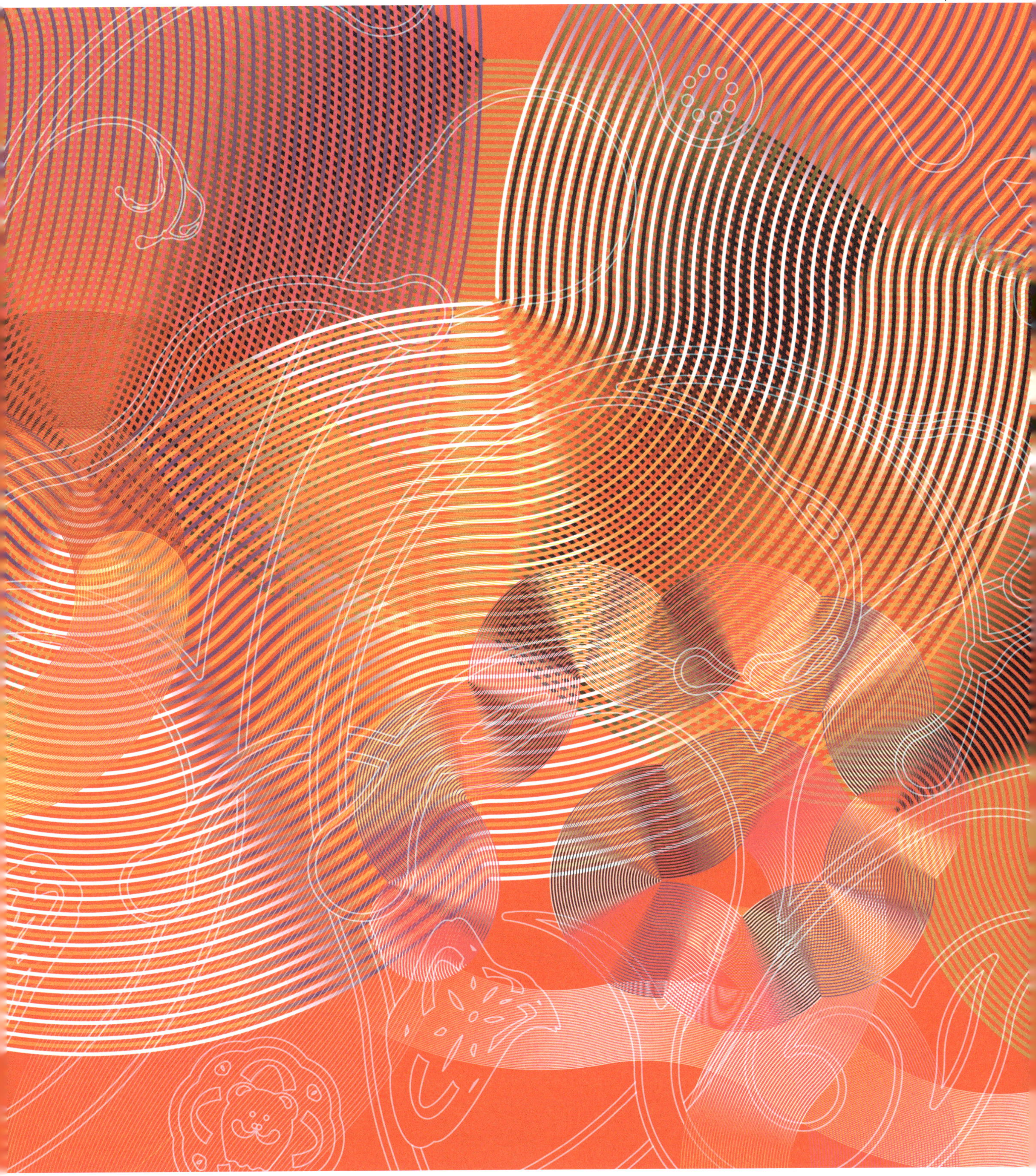

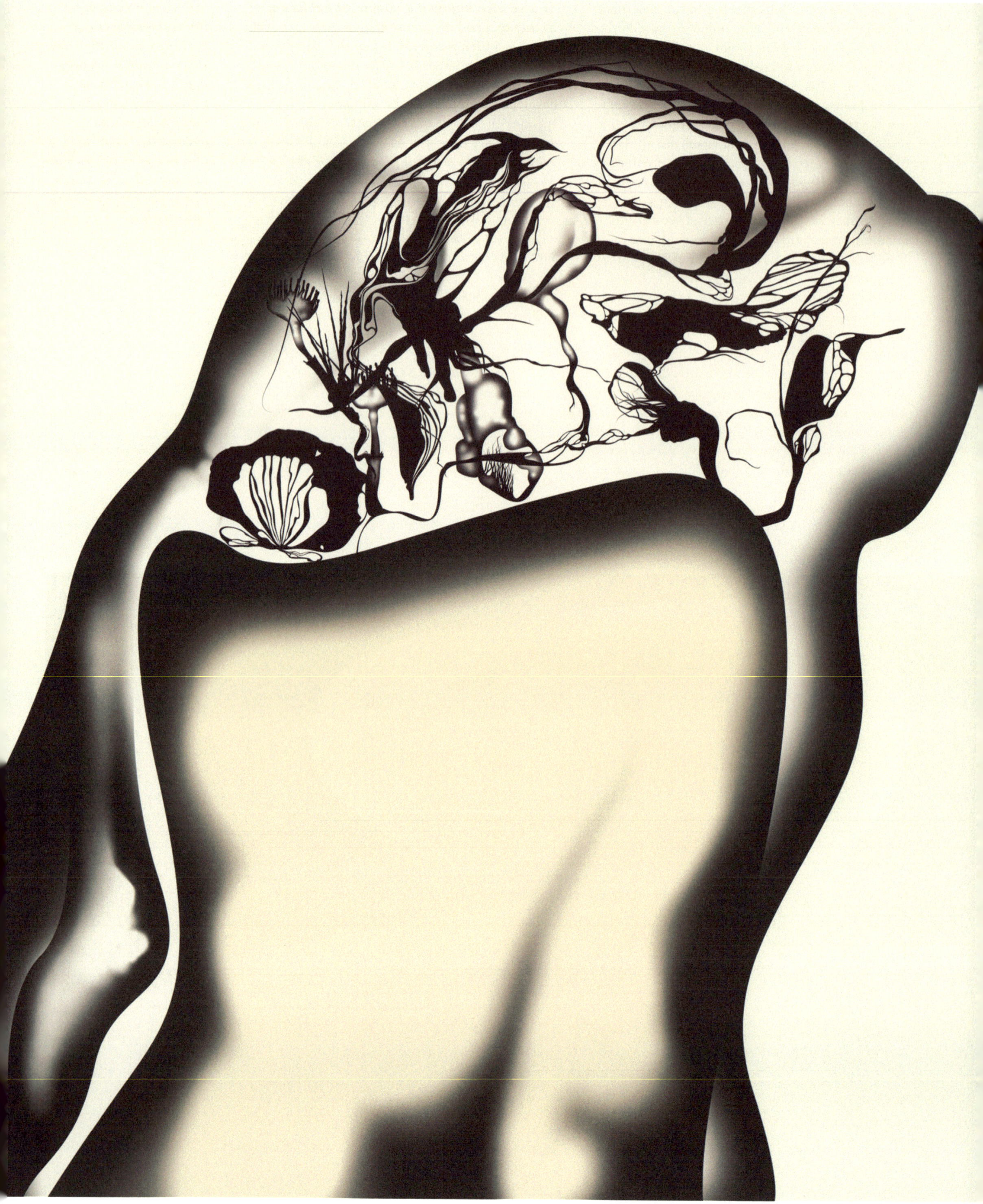

and an experiment into drawing on the Mac that turned into something more immersive which the large format allowed for. I wanted to bring flowing elements together to create a piece with lots of movement, while keeping it very abstract. The colour palette that was used was chosen because it was a range of colours I'd not worked with for a while at the time. (These wallpapers are available for purchase – see www.maxalot.com for details.)

The 'Head Heart & Hips' book features a new and very different style from you. These are personal works – explorations, observations and drawings for the Big Active book. I have been thinking about new ways of drawing with a computer for a while and this project presented itself as the perfect platform to take them further. I also wanted to try to capture a moment, a feeling or atmosphere by digital means other than just visually rendering an image. The first image is a test in capturing the grace and voluminous qualities possessed by jellyfish and gossamer like materials. The second drawing is simply a collection of observations from everyday phenomena looking at glass, fluids, smoke, movements and materials etc. The other two are studies about fluids, which are qualities I find very engaging. The fluid movements are very different. One image is peaceful and the other is troubled, but both are 'quiet' and slightly brooding – still but with inner movement.

You've also enjoyed a couple of exhibitions in Japan. I had my first solo show in Tokyo earlier this year which was great, before that there was the *Versus* exhibition (a collaboration of UK and Japanese artists). *Through the Looking Glass* was developed for the *Versus #2* exhibition in Tokyo. It's a series of 16 pieces that started with a personal study and interpretation of Louis Carroll's book.

What projects are you planning for the future? At the moment I'm moving away from editorial commissions and moving into other mediums. I've just completed my first two textile designs and a design for a *Be@rbrick* toy (both through the Japanese company Medicom) and my first Penguin book cover. There is also a bank job in progress (supplying illustrations, not robbing), a project with wallpaper printers Cole & Sons and another music campaign with Tappin Gofton.

www.kamtang.co.uk
www.bigactive.com

'There is a reason for the elaborateness of certain pieces; they are there to add a greater depth and richness to the whole, besides looking busy and decorative. I like rich and complex things but not superfluity – that's just a poor veil for little substance'

Left & below
New illustrations for
Head Heart & Hips
2005

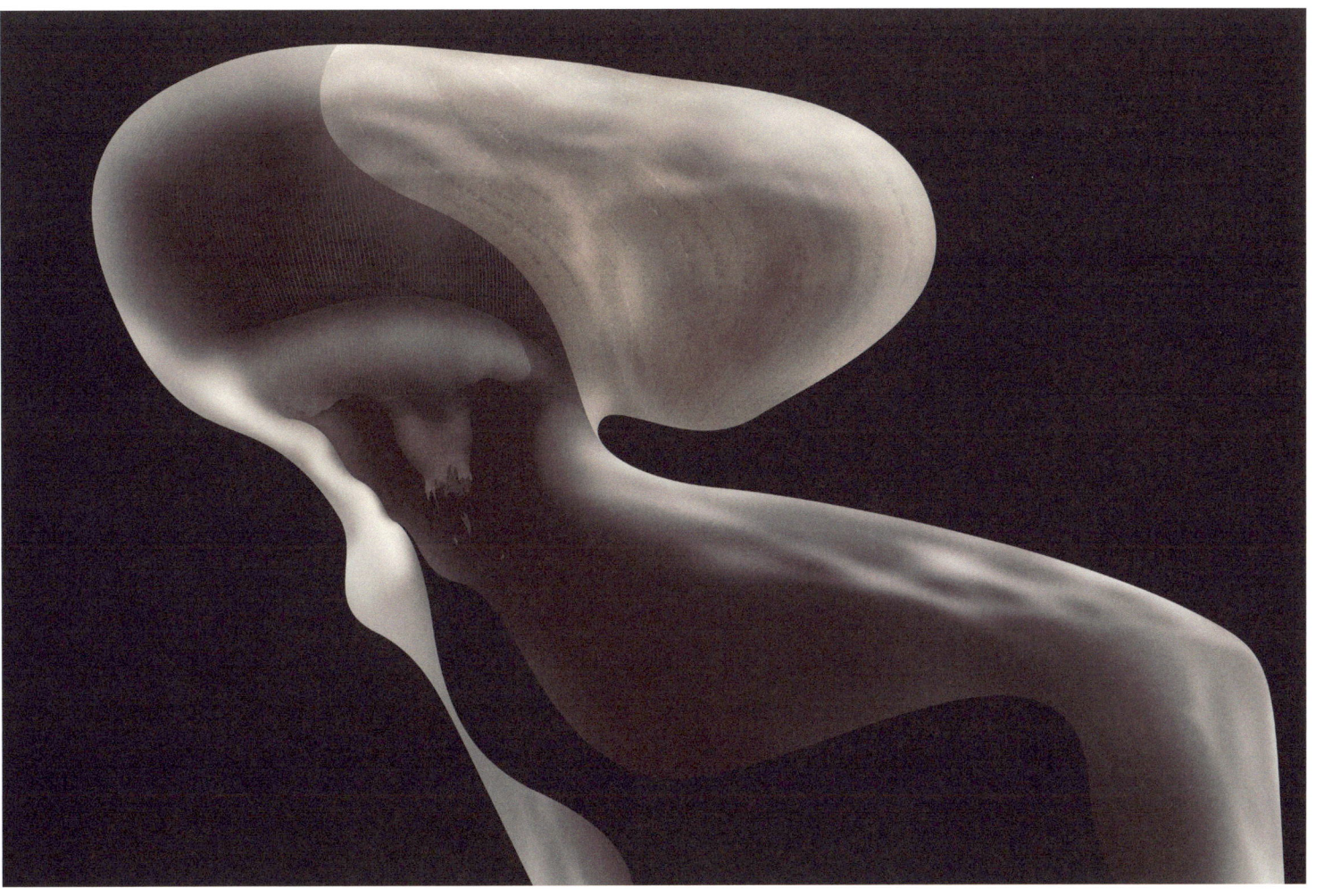

Wallpaper [for Places and Spaces]
Absolute Zero Degrees

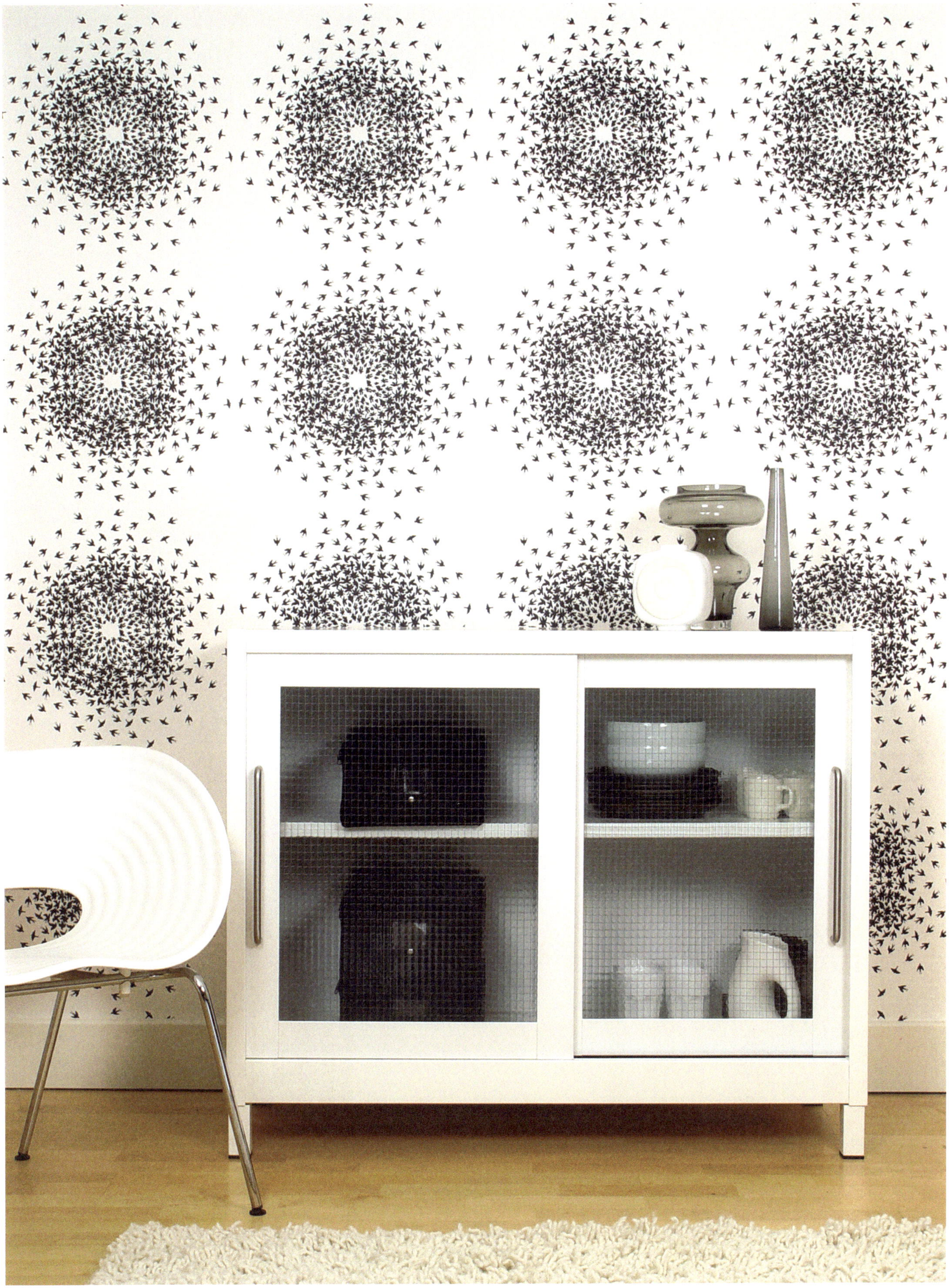

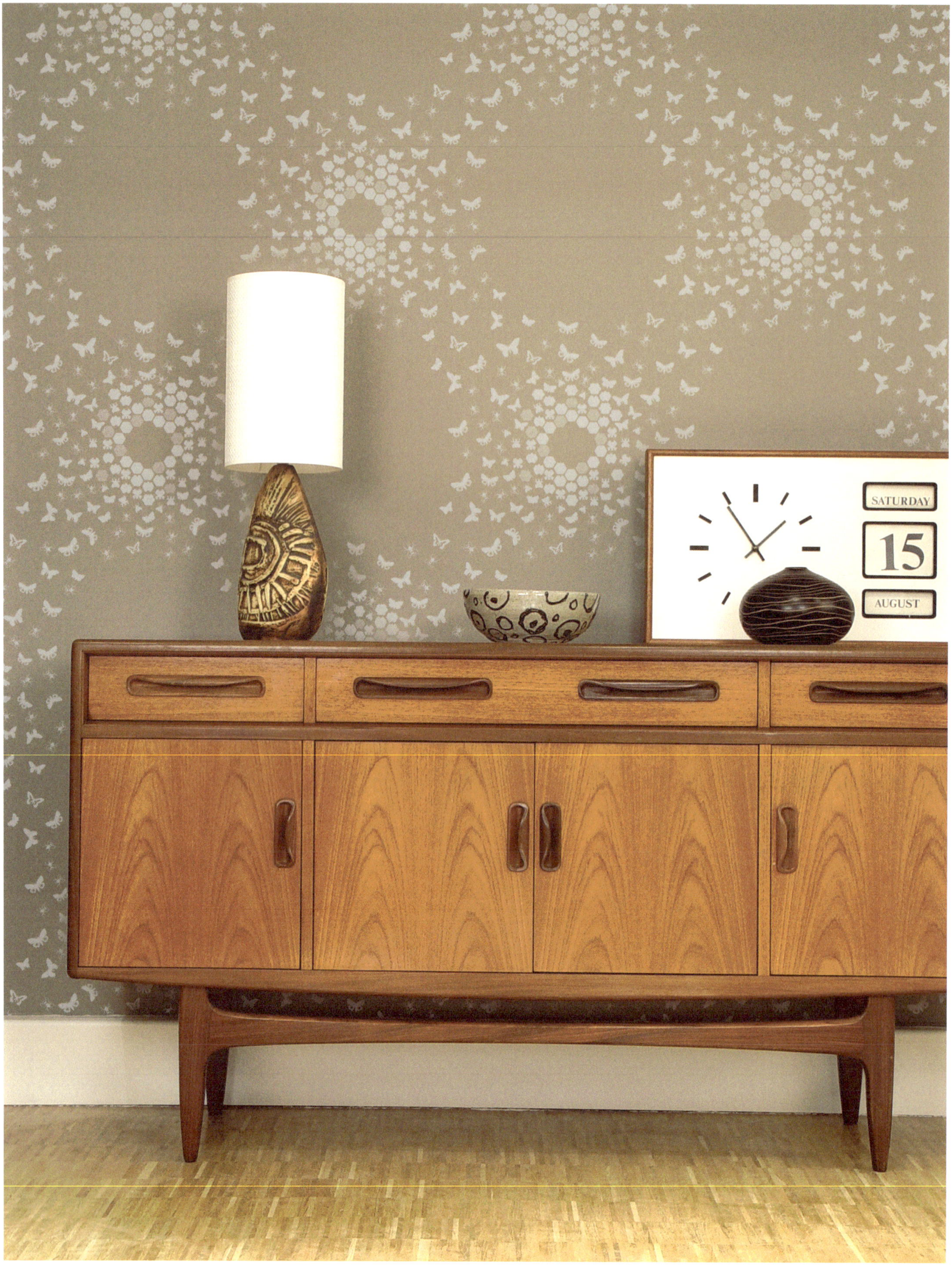
SATURDAY
15
AUGUST

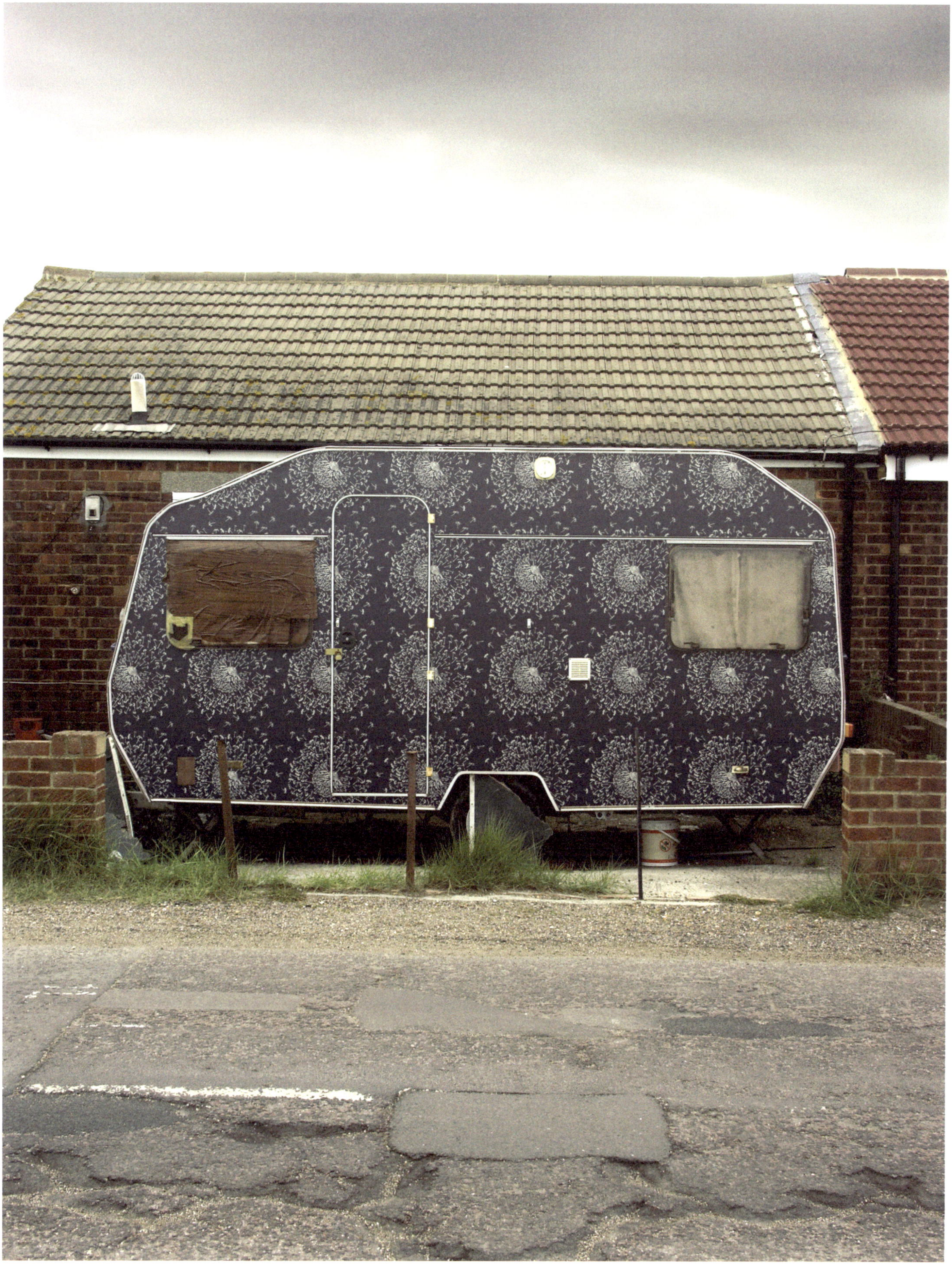

62–65
(preceding pages)

Keith Stephenson / Absolute Zero Degrees

Range of wallpaper [designed for Places and Spaces]
2003–2005
The 'Swallows', 'Bees' and 'Dandelions' wallpapers were designed for London-based furniture retailer, Places and Spaces. The theme of the range is 'natural transformation'. Each design has natural elements morphing, Escher-like, into another: leaves turn into birds, dandelions become dragonflies. The wallpapers are intended to work in a broad range of contexts – they occupy the space between graphic and decorative. There is a duality about the production technique. Drawn freehand directly onto the computer, they are produced by traditional methods using chalk-based colour that creates a rich texture.

Keith Stephenson is founder and Head of Design at London-based design studio, Absolute Zero Degrees. Pattern and decoration play a big part in their design solutions for both independent and corporate clients. They are currently writing and designing two books in the *Communicating with Pattern* series for Rotovision: *Stripes* and *Circles*. The series explores the graphic language of pattern and its use in contemporary design, featuring work by Peter Saville, Karim Rashid, Ben Kelly, Paul Smith and agnès b. The books will be published in Spring 2006.

Interior images by Jonathan Warren / Keith Stephenson
Location images by Ian Rippington

keith@absolutezerodegrees.com
www.absolutezerodegrees.com

In what context was your work produced? Post 9/11 there just seemed to be this overwhelming desire for comfort and I started to think about 1920s domesticity. I think that feel comes across in the work. They are a little bit escapist, I suppose. *Is there such a thing as over design?* Yes, though this shouldn't be confused with ornament – they are different things. Even the most minimal piece can be over-theorised and over-designed. *Does form always follow function?* It's a good principle to start with, but everybody craves an element of personalisation. Look at the interiors of Ray and Charles Eames' house. The architecture is simple and honest, but they don't keep it sparse – they fill their space with an eclectic mix of personal objects. These days their pieces are always displayed in a minimalist setting, but modern loft dwellers would be shocked to see these original photos of the furniture covered in rugs and knick-knacks. *On a scale of 1 to 10 – where 1 is fanatical minimalism and 10 is gilded rococo – where would you place your work? Why?* 5 – dead centre. I set out to create something very decorative but very graphic. The wallpapers can be styled equally successfully with mid-twentieth-century modern furniture or a Louis XIV chair.

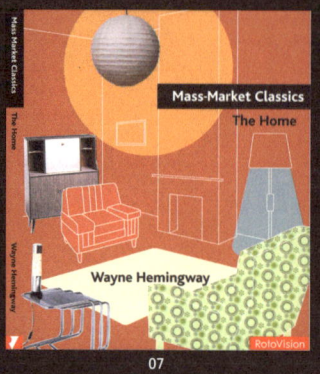

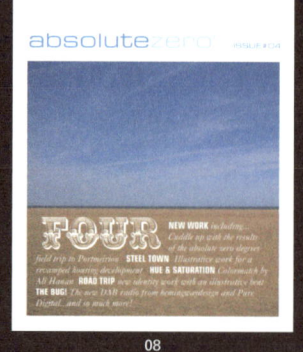

00

01

02

03

04

05

06

07

08

00
Keith Stephenson

01
Pharmacy
2003
Brochure cover. Identity, seasonal prints and promotional material design for active sports label from White Stuff

02
Pharmacy
2003
Specific garment spread of promotional seasonal brochure.

03
Pout
2005
POP material for Pout Bustier, bust enhancing cream

04
Pout
2005
Promotional material for Pout's Autumn/Winter cosmetics collection, Twinset and Pearls

05
The Birchin
2004
Brochure cover. Property marketing material, for Manchester conversion development

06
The Birchin
2004
Page 3 of marketing brochure for apartment block development in Manchester

07
Mass Market Classics
2003
Design and illustration of Wayne Hemingway's celebration of everyday design. Published by Rotovision

08
Absolute Zero° Issue #4
2004
The cover of our fourth in-house promotional magazine, includes recent projects, field trips and recent press. Photography: Keith Stephenson

Birgit Amadori

68–73
(following pages)

I was born and raised in Germany, where I also went to art school and earned my degree in 2002. I freelanced for a while and then packed my bags to come to California in 2004. Here I am, still freelancing for clients from all over the world but also having a strong connection to my home country. When I am not drawing, I like to go to the beach for a swim or run to think about new works and designs.

birgitamadori@gmail.com
www.amadori.org

What is your work about? Any central themes? Beauty, details, hair, lips, patterns, the ideal Bezier curve. *What medium(s) do you work with?* Adobe Illustrator. *Computers, more or less?* More. *What would you say are your influences? And main sources of inspiration?* I started out loving Art Nouveau. I get inspired by people who are really good at using the software's full capacity along with a sense for beauty. *What kind of work do you really like? What turns you on as an artist?* It's bad but I really like best works by other people who work with the same medium. I don't have much connection anymore to abstract paintings or abstract sculpture for example. It turns me on when I see somebody who has perfected his/her skills, and shows the result with self confidence. *Do you make a distinction between commercial and non-commercial work?* Definitely yes. *Do you manage to make a living out of your artwork?* Sadly, no. I have too many bills to pay, and being the starving artist is not my ideal lifestyle. *Who would you never, under any circumstances, do work for?* Eminem.

Project Fox
2005
Client: Volkswagen
Photography: www.diephotodesigner.de

As part of a campaign when launching the new VW Fox, Volkswagen invited 20 designers from all over the world to completely redesign a hotel in Copenhagen, Denmark. I was assigned three rooms. Two of them were assigned my 'blue theme' (King's Court), one the 'red theme' (King's Forest). In coordination with the event managers, we were able to design the complete interior area including carpet, wallpapers, curtains and bedsheets, and to choose appropriate furniture. The hotel opened doors for everybody in spring 2005. I even was able to spend a night in one of 'my' rooms.

00
Birgit Amadori

01
Amadori_and_Asuma
A collaboration with an illustrator from Japan, just for fun

02
Dogs
Originally made for a poster contest, and because I am crazy for Borzoi dogs (but I don't have a dog. Only a hamster...)

03
Domino
08.2005
From my portfolio

04
Encounter
One from a series about the Japanese folktale *The Crane Wife*

05
Starmaker
This one was made for the *Drench Award 2004* competition

06
Real Love
2004
Part of a series that illustrated Japanese slang words, exhibited at the Japanese film festival *Nipponconnection* in Frankfurt, Germany

07
Silverfox
From my portfolio

08
Untitled

Project Fox
Birgit Amadori

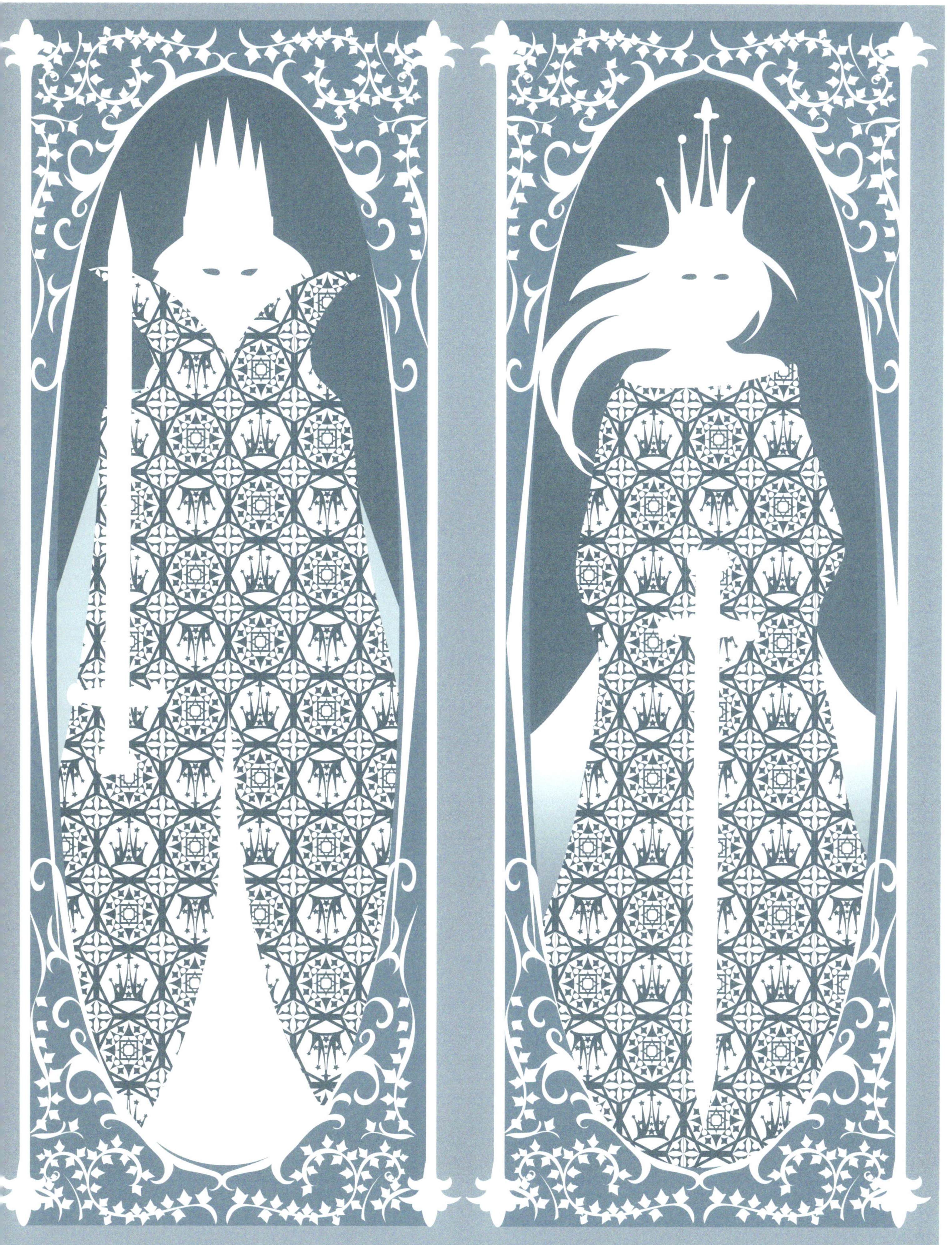

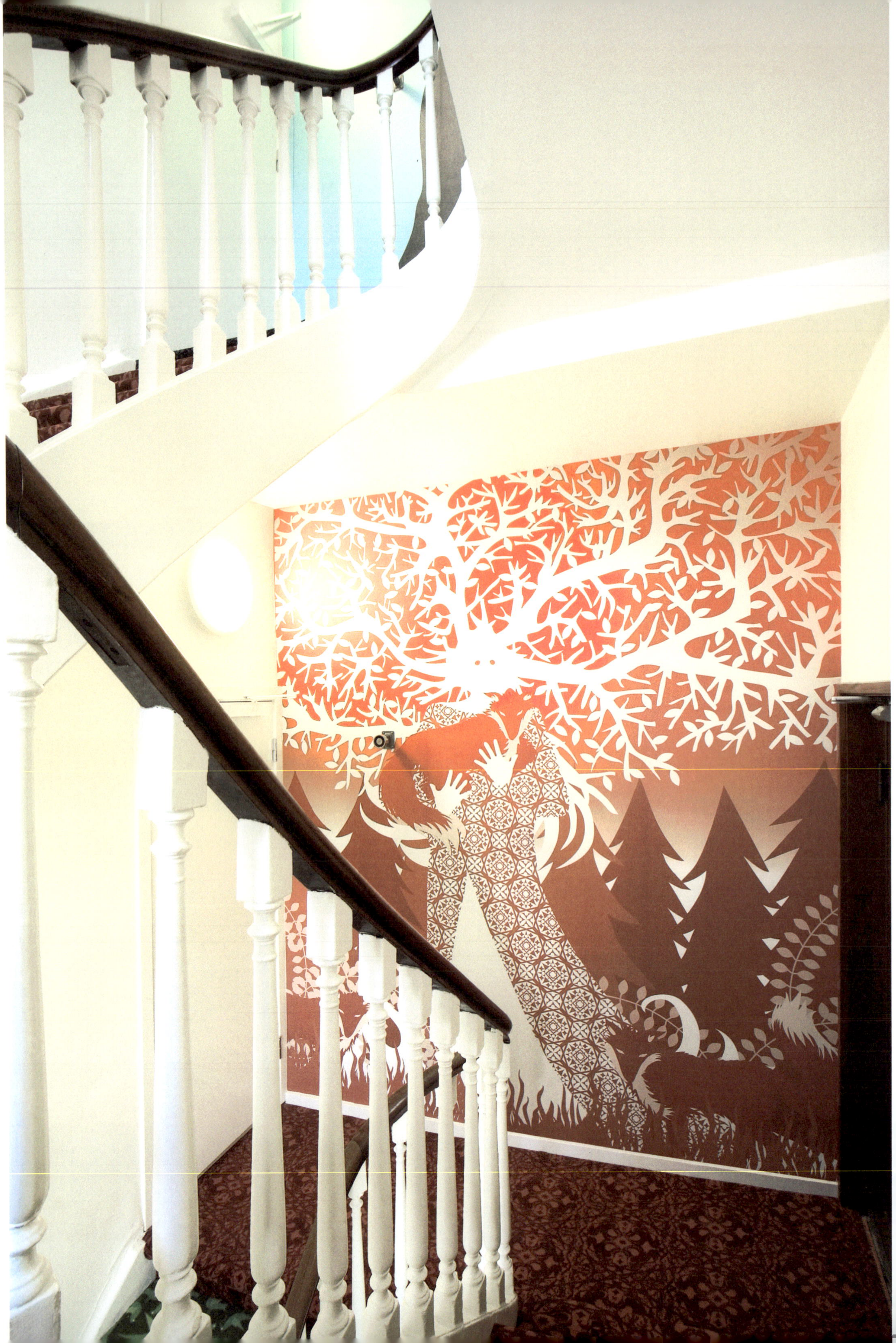

71

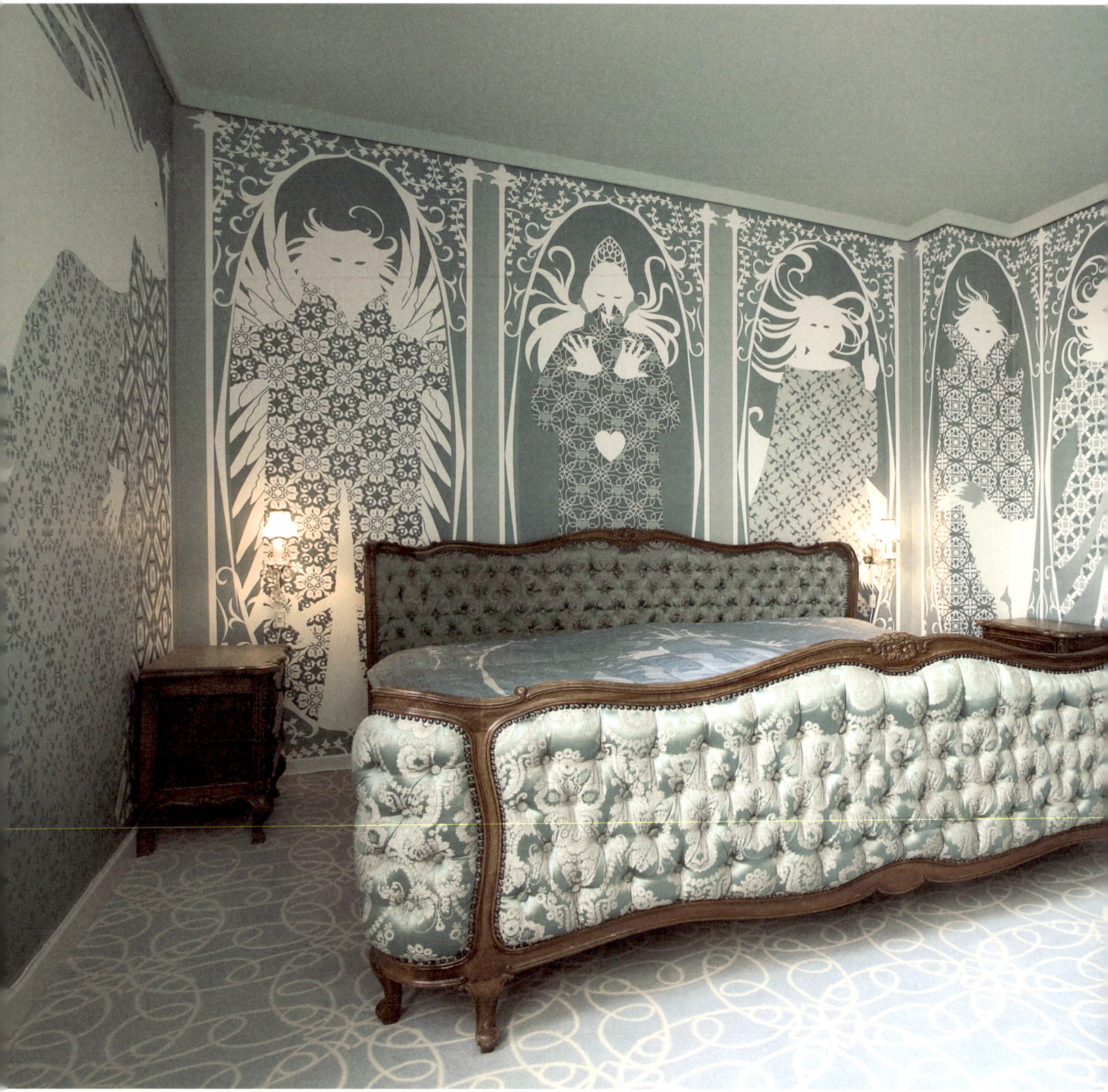

73

74 *Blister*
Aya Ben Ron

75

74–75
(preceding pages)

Aya Ben Ron

Blister
2002
The work is made out of paper cut-outs which are glued one on top of the other in 7 layers, in a way that resembles 3D pop-up.
The images, which were taken from scientific and medical text books, shows different situations of illness or crisis of the body. After being digitally redrawn with clear and even line, the images were arranged in a geometric, kaleidoscopic structure which looks like the shape of mandala.

I grew-up in Haifa, Israel. At 1989, I started my 4 years studying art at Beit Berl College, School of Art. I worked as a graphic designer of Hed-Artzi, a music label, and as an illustrator at daily newspapers and continue working on my art. When I had enough money I quit my job and left to London to do my MA in Fine Art at Goldsmiths College. I lived in London for 4 years, doing my art and now I'm in Tel-Aviv, doing the same thing.

artistindex.co.il/ayabenron

What is your work about? Any central themes? My work is trying to look at aspects of extreme body states and experiences in a way that forms a structure which seems to be organized and understandable. ***What kind of work do you really like? What turns you on as an artist?*** Some works by the Chapman brothers are really moving for me, though I'm not sure I know why. In the same way, the look and violence in Miike's films fascinates me. ***What is the most interesting book you've read or the most interesting film you've seen in the past year?*** The lucid way Elfriede Czurda in her book *Die Schlaferin* deals with love and cannibalism made me think a lot about things I see in my work and in real life. ***Is there such a thing as over design?*** Most design is over design. ***On a scale of 1 to 10 – where 1 is fanatical minimalism and 10 is gilded rococo – where would you place your work? Why?*** I would go towards ten. I'm more fascinated by temptation and glamour, and I find it more in the rococo than in the minimalism. ***Computers, more or less?*** Much more.

00

01

02

03

04

05

06

07

08

00
Aya Ben Ron

01
Pad
2003
250cm × 250cm
A floor piece. Technique: black & white drawing engraved in PVC

02–05
Seasons
2002
73cm × 86cm
This series of 4 pieces is inspired by 4 multi-layered copperplate engravings entitled *The 4 Seasons of Humanity* (1680) which present a cross section of the history of medicine and science up to the 17th century. Each piece contains approximately 7 layers, which are glued one on top of another to create a 3D pop-up effect. Technique: print on paper, foam tape, 7 layers

06–09
Particle
2000
100cm × 100cm
Technique: print on clear transparency. Hung from the ceiling and set 6 inches away from the wall to create a reflection on the wall

Catalina Estrada Uribe

78–81
(following pages)

I was born and raised in the countryside near Medellin, Colombia. There, I graduated with honours in graphic design. Some years ago I moved to Barcelona where I graduated in 'plastic arts'. I work as a freelance graphic designer and illustrator. I also teach illustration at IDEP (a graphic design school in Barcelona) in the graphic design and professional illustration areas. At the same time I work on my personal art projects.

www.catalinaestrada.com

What would you say are your influences? And main sources of inspiration? I get lots of influences from latin american and folk art, I guess colombia and the memories of my childhood in that country are my main sources of inspiration. **What kind of work do you really like? What turns you on as an artist?** I love folk art, art nouveau, modernism, arts and crafts. **Is there such a thing as over design?** Not for me. **On a scale of 1 to 10 – where 1 is fanatical minimalism and 10 is gilded rococo – where would you place your work? Why?** 8. Although it is obvious that my work is not minimal, I work with ornaments but not for them. **Computers, more or less?** Just the way it is.

1001 Nights
2005
I always combine graphic design, illustration and art in almost all my work. I guess it is all a reflection of what I have experienced in my country and now that I live abroad I realize how much I miss all those things: the colourful green, the beautiful landscapes, the amazing flowers, the trees, so many kinds of plants, the animals, the memories of my childhood, the incredible contact with nature I was lucky to have during all my childhood. Also the people and their stories, the literature, the tales I was told, the beautiful music of that place, the time I spent with the people I love. I guess most of my work is all about that.

00
Catalina Estrada Uribe

01
Casa Viva

02
Humming Bird

03
Little Red Hood

04
Love

05
Popular de Lujo

06
Self portrait

07
Untitled

08
Wedding book cover

1001 Nights
Catalina Estrada Uribe

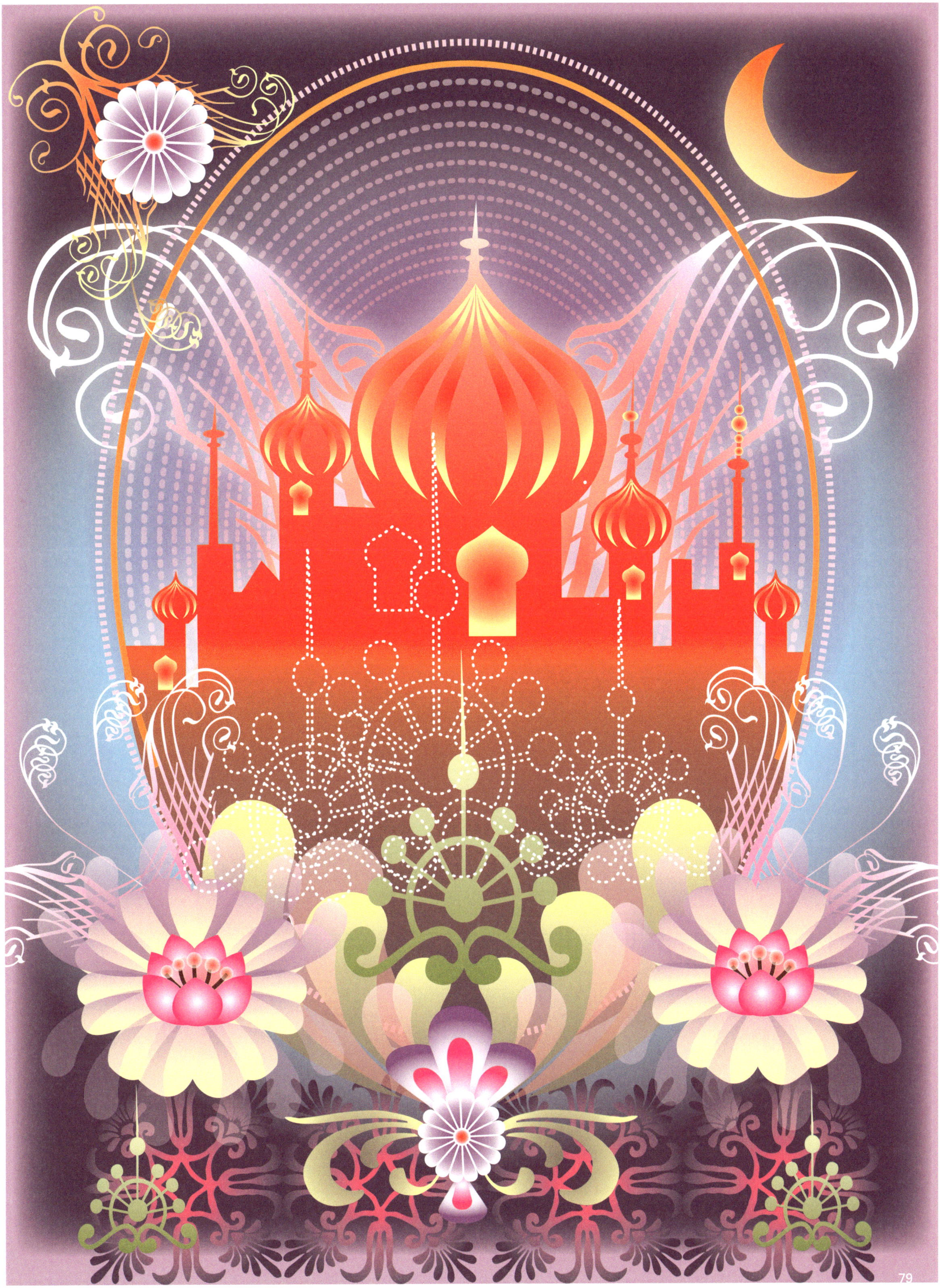

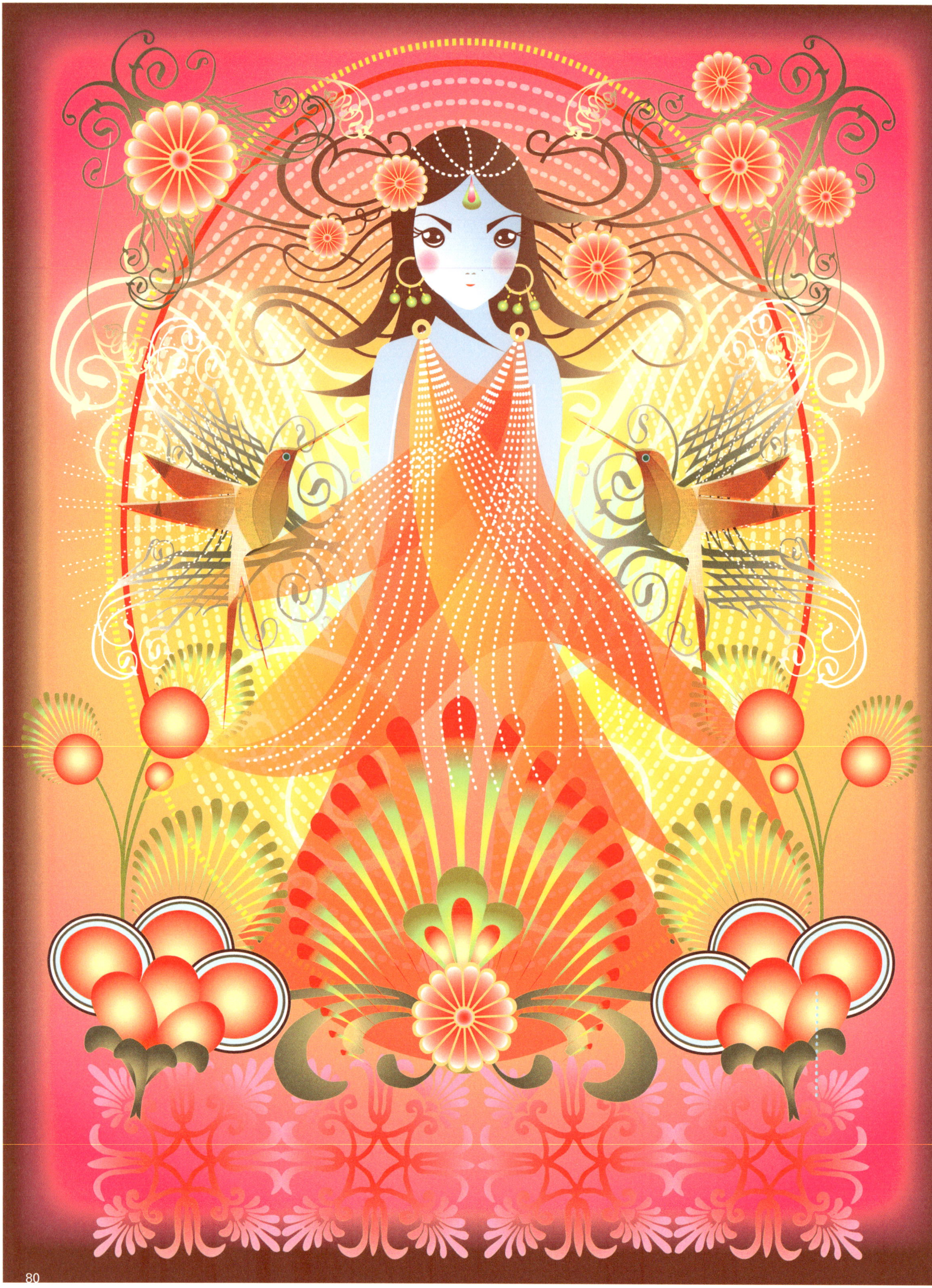

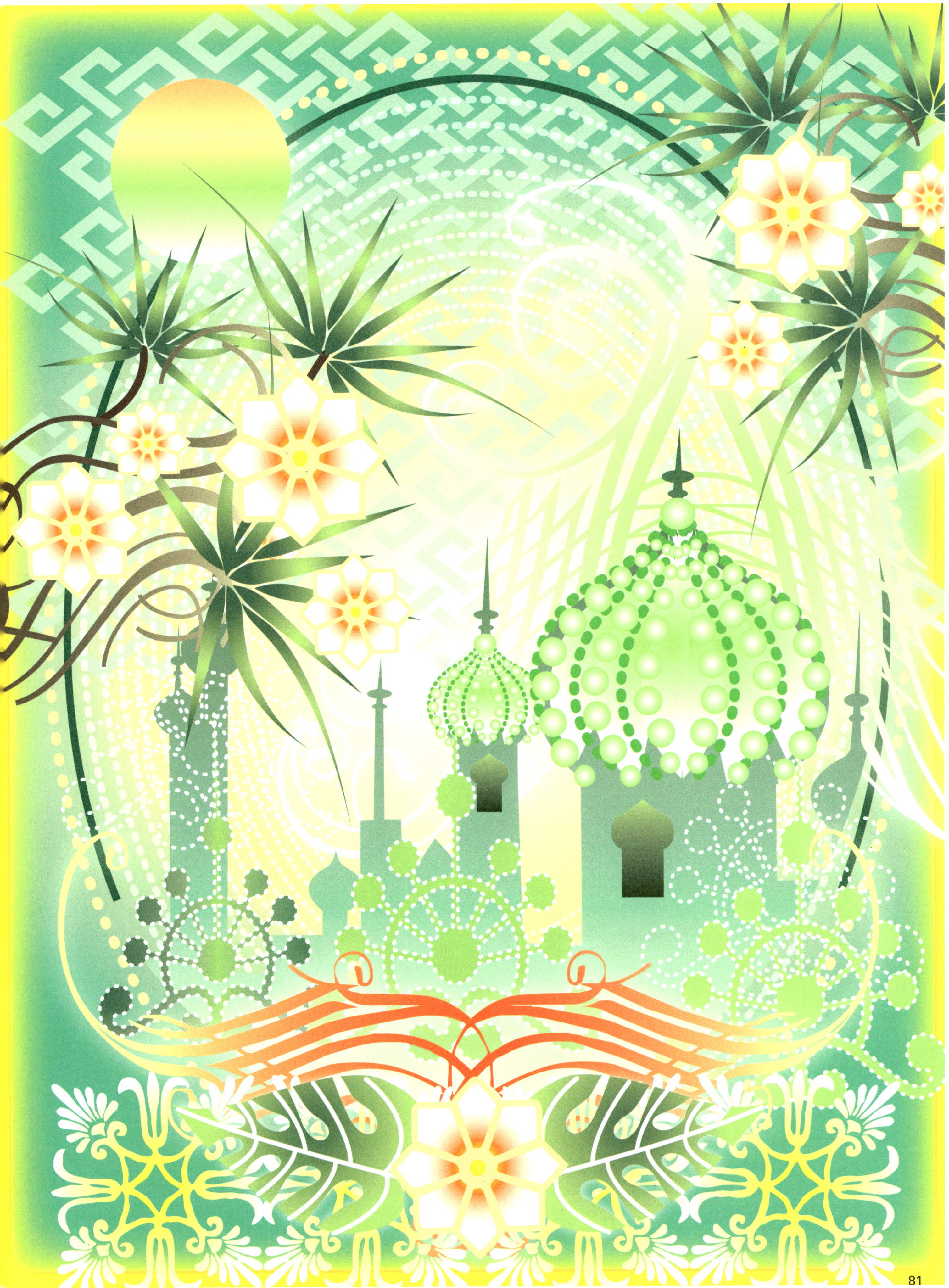

Leaves and Flowers
Federico Galvani

83

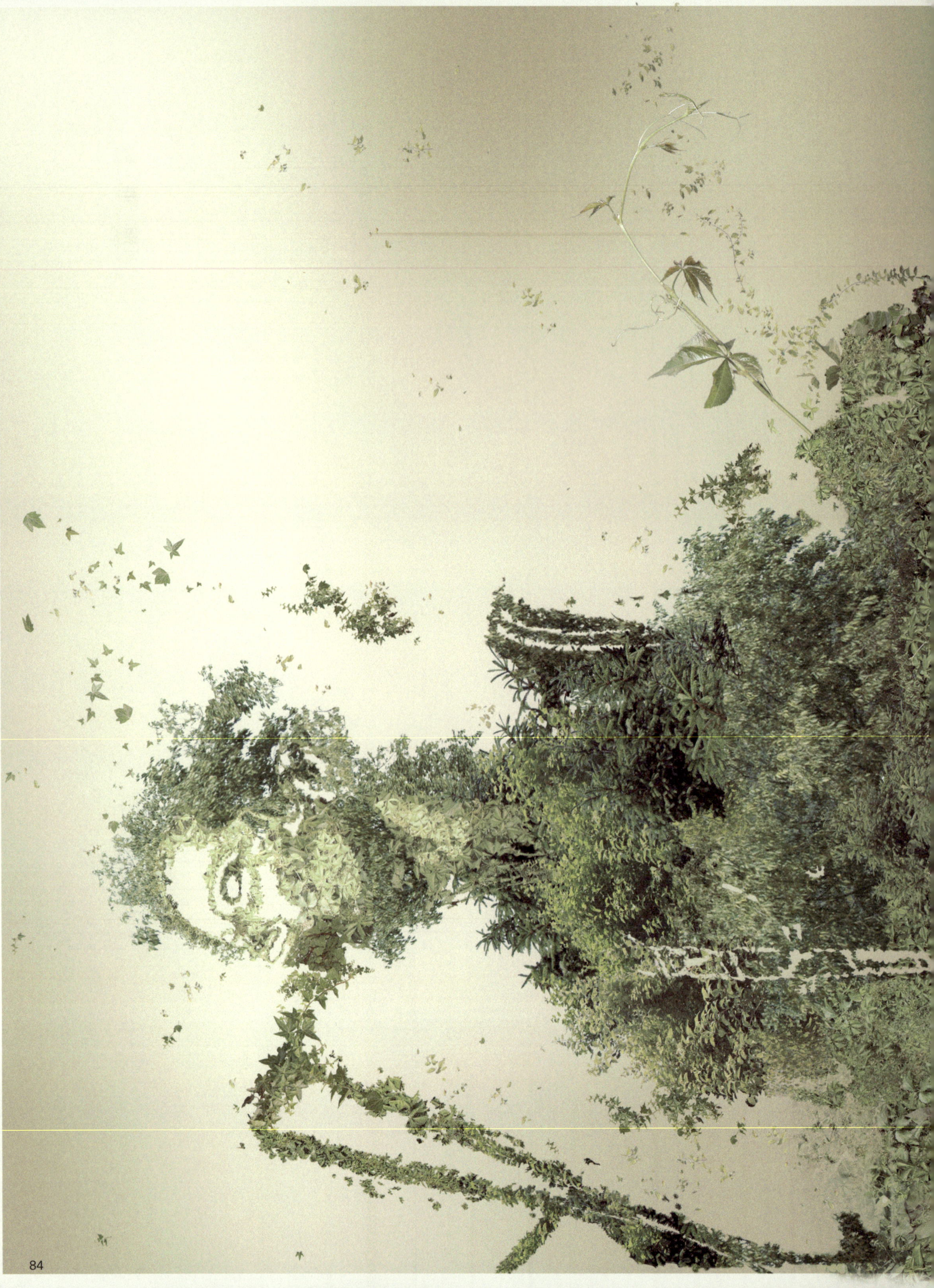

*82–85
(preceding pages)*

Leaves and Flowers
03.07.2005
Music is decoration for life as much as a movie soundtrack. I wanted to draw these two lifeforms that decorate music, as music does in a music video.

Federico Galvani
from Happycentro+Sintetik

I live and work in the lovely town of Romeo & Juliet. Since 1998, I share the experience of Happycentro+Sintetik project with a bunch of friends. I love my sweetheart Chiara (forever), I have a brother, a sister, three nephews, many friends, an old blue car with a broken CD player in it, the same red Pumas since 10 years, a website, a passion for cheese and wax records, a green cantina in which I used to play my music, a bad English, a baby face, a father somewhere still looking after me. And all of this decorates my life.

federicogalvani@happycentro.it
www.happycentro.it

What is the most interesting book you've read or the most interesting film you've seen in the past year? The most interesting book I've read is the 'Universal Atlas of New Wave Music', published by Giunti. I think the movie could be 'The Warriors'. *Do you manage to make a living out of your artwork?* Of course I do. *Does form always follow function?* Not when form has just to amaze. *On a scale of 1 to 10 – where 1 is fanatical minimalism and 10 is gilded rococo – where would you place your work? Why?* 11 gilded rococo, because you can say a work is great if there's a lot of effort behind to make it. *What is your definition of ornament?* The colour of the flowers, the different gradation of the skin makes everything and everyone unique. *Wallpaper or paint?* Wallpaper. *Who would you never, under any circumstances, do work for?* I will never make an inscription on a tombstone. *Computers, more or less?* Less. *If money and time were no object what would your ideal project be? What would you most rather do?* Maybe a book about the printing process. It's been one of my dreams since I finished school. I would like to do something for good.

00

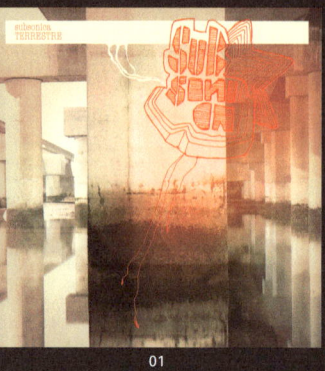

01

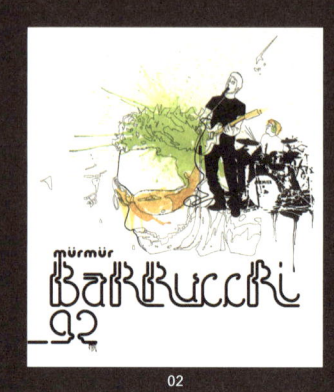

02

03

04

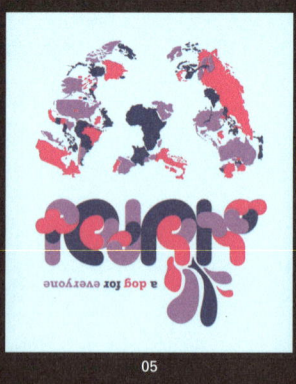

05

06

07

08

00
Federico Galvani
Two of my four eyes

01
Subsonica
CD cover of an Italian rock band who played to 85,000 people in the first 12 concerts of their new tour. www.subsonica.it

02
Mürmür
CD cover of the band of two great friends of mine

03
Radio New York
Concert poster

04–05
Pedrho
Concept design for an italian fashion brand.
www.pedrho.com

06
My personal vision of paradise
Artwork for the French magaine *La Trentaine Sympathique*

07
Copa Classic
Concept design for a Dutch fashion brand.
www.copaclassic.com

08
Piston Pink
Concept design for an Italian fashion footwear brand

Giuliano Garonzi
from Happycentro+Sintetik

Giuliano was born in 1974 and raised in Verona. He lived in a 90m² apartment with his father and shared a bedroom with his older brother. The grey and pink building was located on a street named after the talented Italian typographer, Bodoni. On the left side of the road were the apartment blocks and on the right the printing works of Italy's largest publishers. Giuliano remembers how on summer nights the air was filled with the noise of the offset printers, running at a speed of 15,000 copies an hour. Giuliano knew all along that having grown up on that street, so close to the printers, educated by a graphic designer father and having a brother who worked in graphic arts as a room mate, he stood absolutely no chance of becoming a cook instead of a graphic designer. Today, Giuliano is now part of the multi-disciplinary design studio Happycentro+Sintetik in Verona, working with design, photography and filming. In summer 2005 he started a lively collaboration with the design magazine Xfuns.

Was there a defining moment when you decided to become a visual artist? The day I decided to not become a cook. It was a Sunday. I was 14. *What medium(s) do you work with?* Print and television. *What would you say are your influences? And main sources of inspiration?* Stella, the northern light, the midnight sun, my house in Tavernole, my bike, my father, Diego Armando Maradona. *What is the most interesting book you've read or the most interesting film you've seen in the past year?* 'Interismi' by Beppe Severgnini. It's a book about love for a football team. 'Star Wars'. But the original trilogy, of course. *On a scale of 1 to 10 – where 1 is fanatical minimalism and 10 is gilded rococo – where would you place your work? Why?* I place my work at 5. I don't know why, I like to live in the middle of everything. *Wallpaper or paint?* Paint. *Computers, more or less?* Less. But I still need mine. *If money and time were no object what would your ideal project be? What would you most rather do?* Design a book about football. Make a movie about football. Be a professional football player.

88–91
(following pages)

What are all these lines for?
06.2005
It's all about lines.

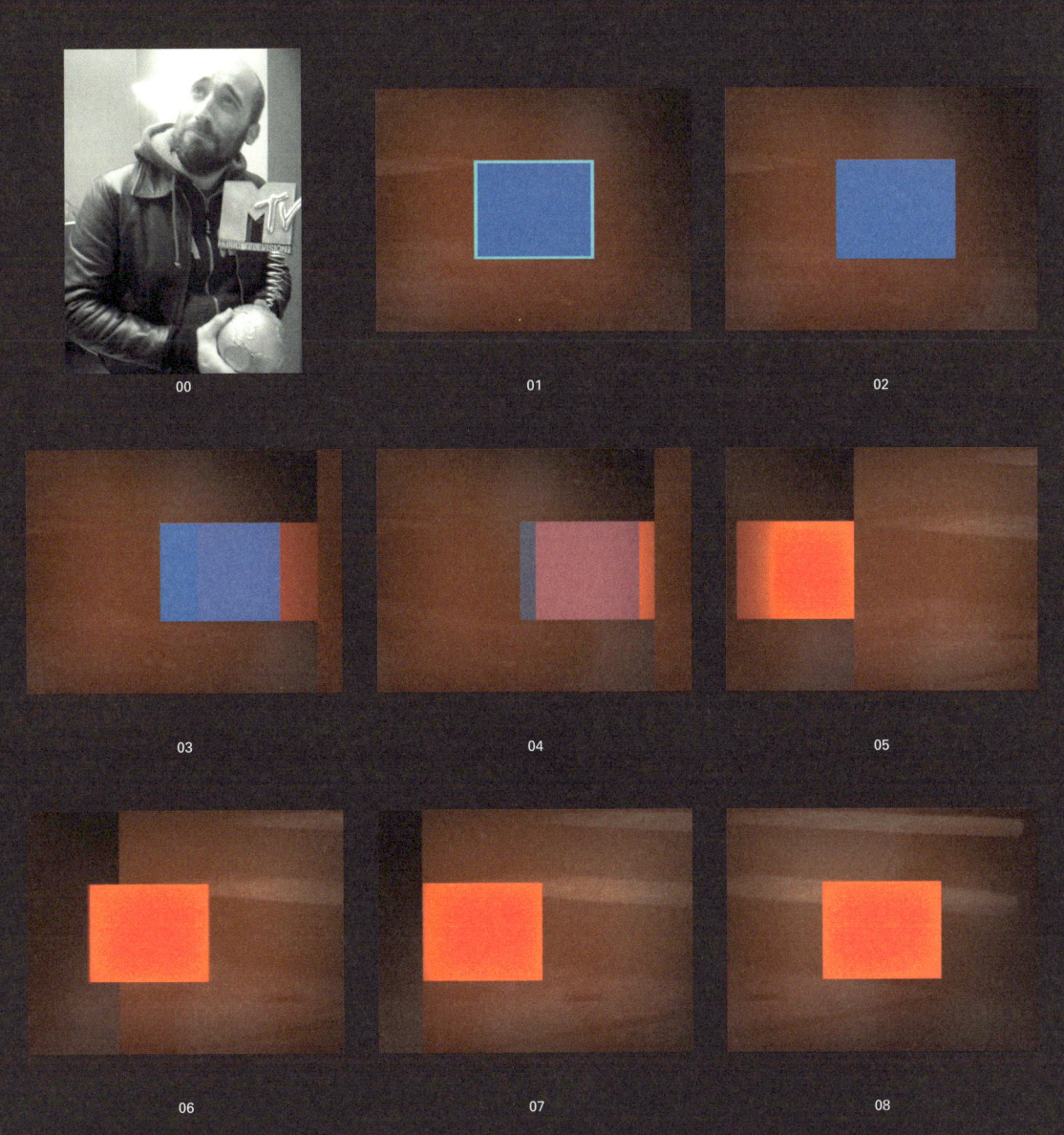

00
Giuliano Garonzi

01–08
Subsonica, tour 2005
Frames from one of a total of 5 animations (15 secs each), running on 5 large screens during the band's performance

88 *What are all these lines for?*
Giuliano Garonzi

03:

03: these things

"blue

Sullivan
Tom Griffiths

KV
AT

92–95
(preceding pages)

Tom Griffiths

Sullivan
This giant typeface was devised to address problems I have with architectural-scale graphic design and typography. A typeface scaled up and applied to drab, minimal walls always looks cool and funky when the space is photographed for a magazine spread; close up, however, the effect can be de-humanizing, dwarfing the viewer. There is a need for a typeface which works like architecture – at both macro and micro scales.

Who are you? A twenty-seven year old English immigrant who moved to America ten years ago. Six months ago I joined two fellow designers, Brendan Dugan and Jessica Green, who had started a company called 'Art and Enterprise' – at the same time, I'm finishing my Masters at Yale. *Where do you come from?* London. *Where in the world are you?* New Haven / New York. *Where would you rather be? What is your favourite city?* New York – soon I'll be living there permanently. *What's your background?* Pratt Institute/Yale School of Art. *What is your star sign?* Come on now, get a grip. *What is your definition of ornament?* Not a definition, but several ways of considering it… Ornament humanizes surface through the importation of natural forms. Rhythmic foliated patterns are to be found on the objects of every civilization. Ornament serves as an interface between a culture's inanimate utilitarian objects and its citizens. The urge to ornament is innate. From the eye painted on the prow of the primitive canoe to the eagle airbrushed on the hood of a Chevy, we add emotional and aesthetic meaning to functional objects by the use of color and pattern.

The Modernist mantras of 'truth to materials' and simplicity of form are lies concerning the true nature of nature. The building blocks of the universe are simple, yet the direction of the cosmos is towards ever-increasing complexity. Ornamentation, both in its de-materialization of surface and its expanding lexicon of signifiers, is a closer approximation of reality than Modernist austerity; ornament's rhythms of vegetal growth imports the outside to the inside, while its access to the realm of our imagination externalizes what is within us.

Ornamentation is about contradiction within order; it enables ambiguity and paradox. I've noticed that too much devotion to Modernism can give one blinkers, a narrowing of the intellectual horizons. The trend in contemporary product design is towards an iPod smoothness of form – in marketing, sleek and simple are visual synonyms for cool – but in the final analysis, we may find ourselves impoverished by a visual code which reduces our ability to appreciate the eccentric and foreign.

00 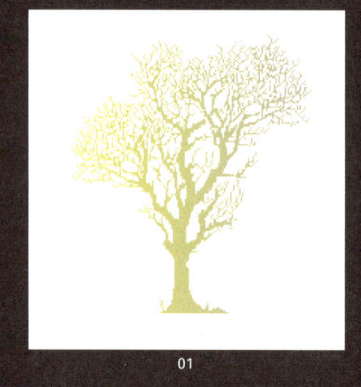 01  02
03 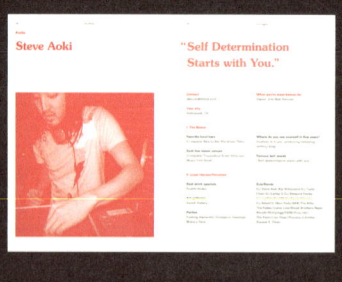 04  05 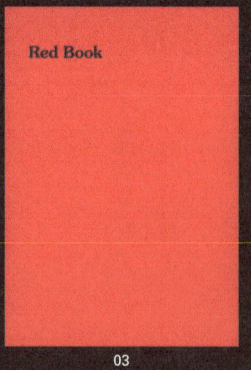
06  07 Artspace 2005 Benefit Auction 08 

00
Tom Griffiths
All projects designed in association with Art and Enterprise

01–02
Look showroom environmental design
A modular system of supergraphics. Thematically the designs are based on the dichotomy of nature and technology

03–06
Red Book for Red Stripe Beer
A clubbers' guide to cities across America. Photography by Mark Hunter

07
Yale ISP Global Flow of Information conference graphic identity system (detail)
Rather than one logo for this event, this kinetic mark changed for every promotional application

08
Typeface
Annual Artspace Auction in New Haven

Hjärta Smärta

Hjärta Smärta are Samira Bouabana and Angela Tillman Sperandio. Since they started working together with graphic design and illustration in 2001, they've been commissioned by major Swedish advertising agencies such as TBWA / Stockholm and Storåkers McCann, made catalogues for exhibitions, editorial illustrations, wallpapers, bookcovers and posters for music and theatre events. Currently they're participating in the exhibition *Concept Design* at the Swedish National Museum.

office@woo.se
hjartasmarta@woo.se
www.woo.se

What is your work about? Any central themes? S: Mix-ups. A: The wrong thing at the right place and vice versa. *What medium(s) do you work with?* S: Pen, scissors, computer, camera. A: Head, hands, computer and chance. *What would you say are your influences? And main sources of inspiration?* S: Old avant-garde, old books, old magazines, new fashion. A: Listening to people telling stories and listening to the radio. *What kind of work do you really like? What turns you on as an artist?* S: Failed objects. The kind of hobby work people do that don't turn out like they want and end up in flea markets. A: Humour. *When are you most aware of design?* S: When I work. A: I'm not sure if I am aware of design. *Does form always follow function?* S: In some sense. A: I have forgotten the meaning of that expression. *What styles do you most identify with?* S: Stylish styles. A: I leave that for someone else to define. *Computers, more or less?* S: Less. A: More.

98–101
(following pages)

Various works
2001, 2003

00a
Samira Bouabana

00b
Angela Tillman Sperandio

01
Earring font

02
Wallpainting Elverket

03
Pain
Illustration for the Swedish Pharmacy *Pain*

04
Pain
Illustration for the Swedish Pharmacy *Pain*

05
Scandinavian Sparks
Art catalogue

06
Miss Universe
Book

07
Femkamp
Book

Various works
Hjärta Smärta

Left:
Lamp with stickers
2003

Right, below:
Window with stickers
2003
Window decorated with sticker leftovers.

Following pages:
Wallpapers made of scribbles
2001
We have taken photos of scrawls in public areas such as toilets, parks and bars and transformed them into patterns. From a distance they look just like classical wallpapers but if you look closer you'll discover the scribbles.

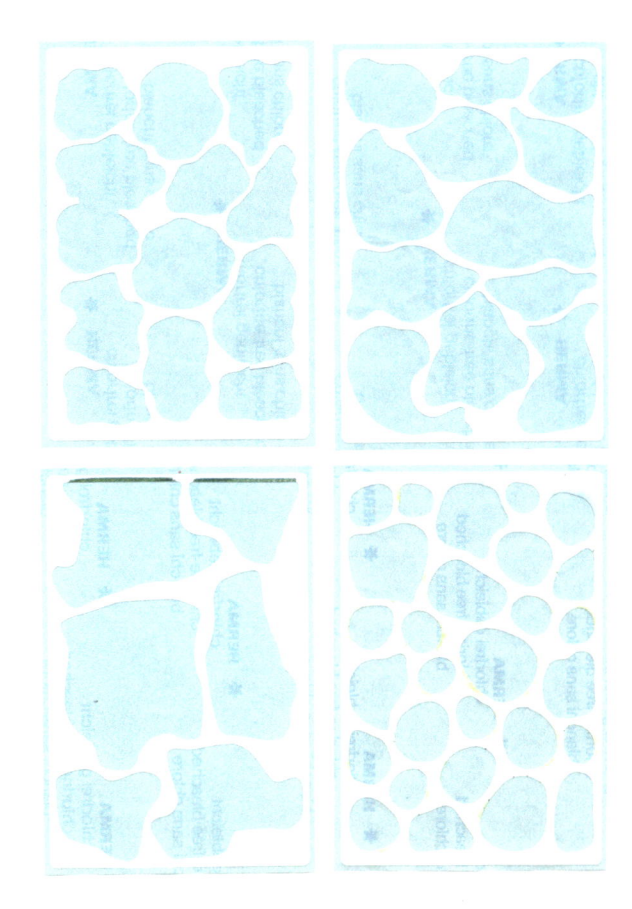

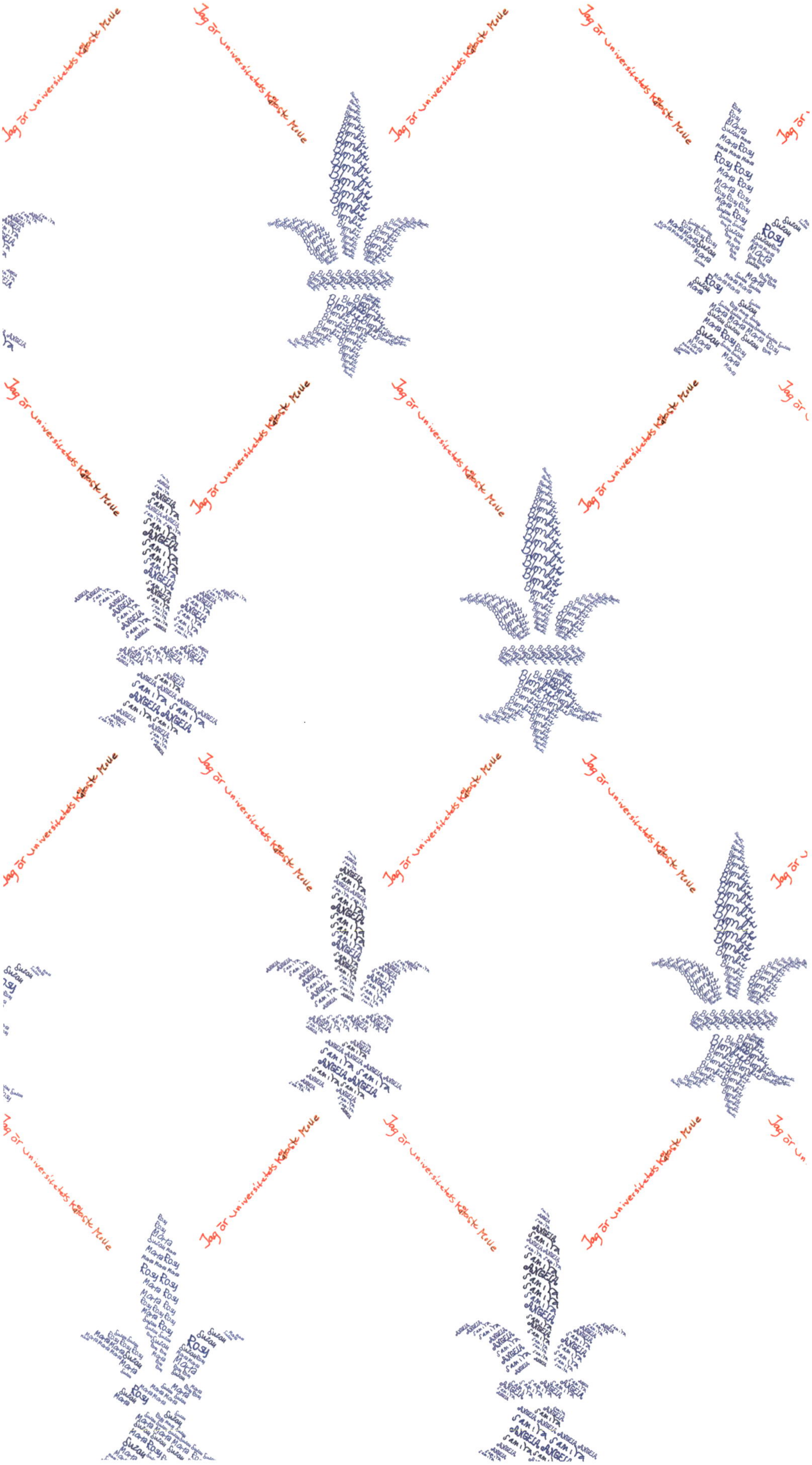

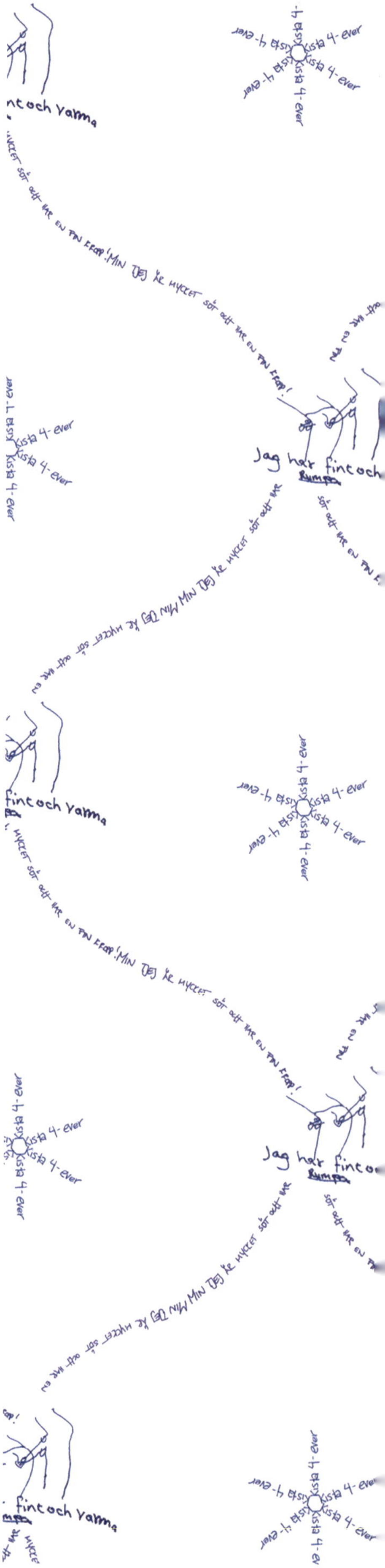
Kista 4-ever

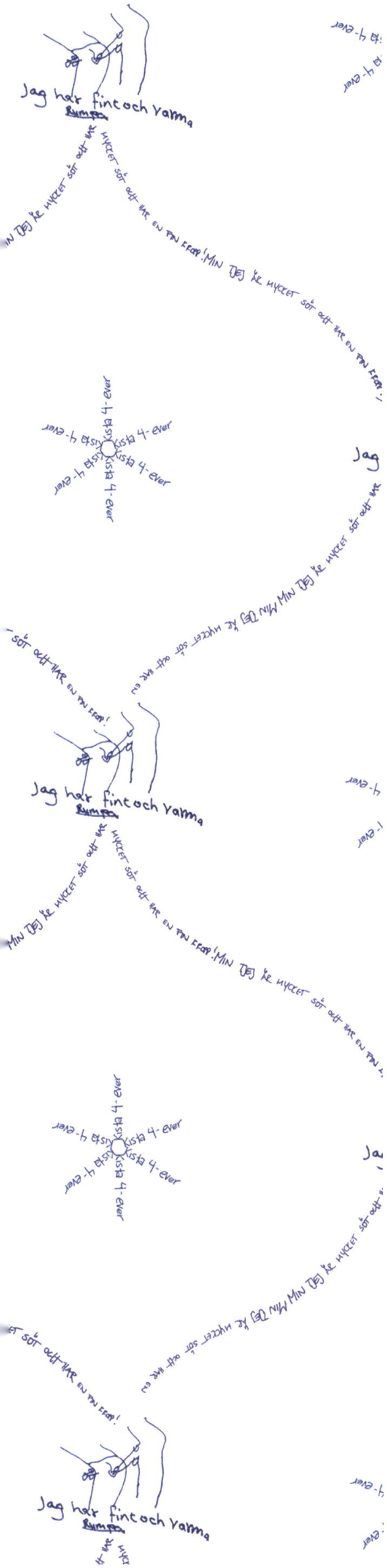
Jag har fint och varma
Rumpa
sista 4-ever

HÄR RÖKER VI MARIJUANA

Collected works
Yoko Ikeno

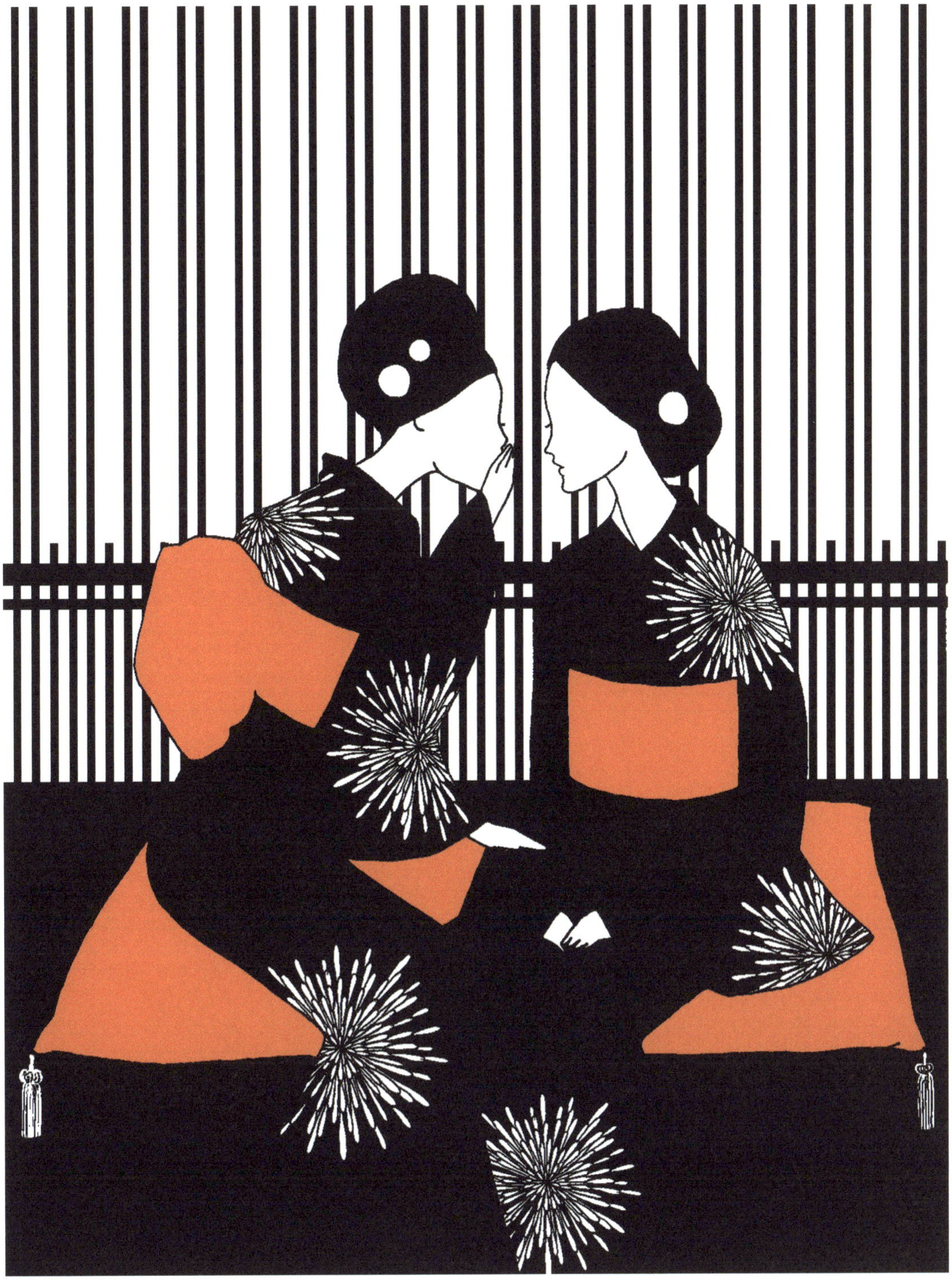

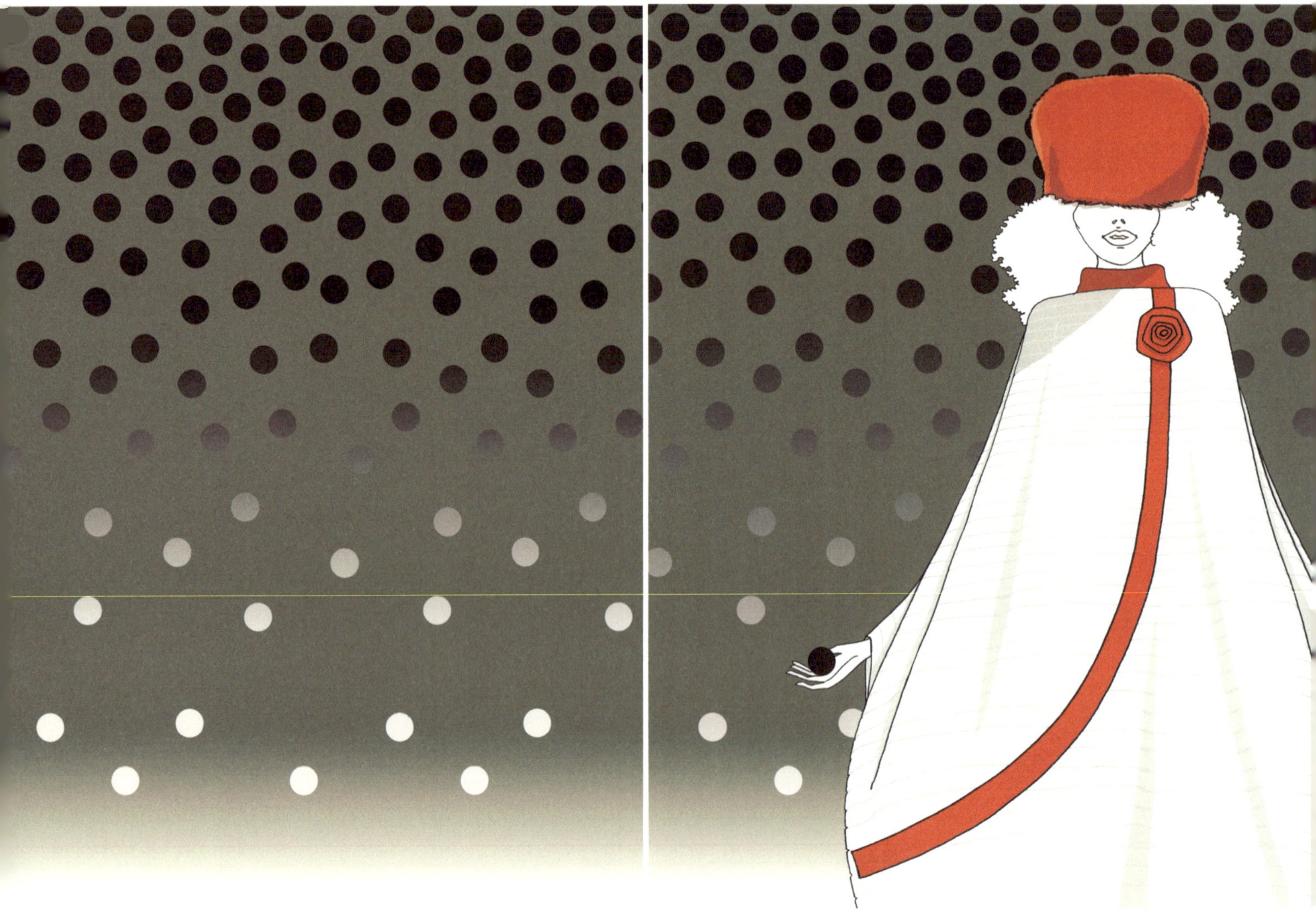

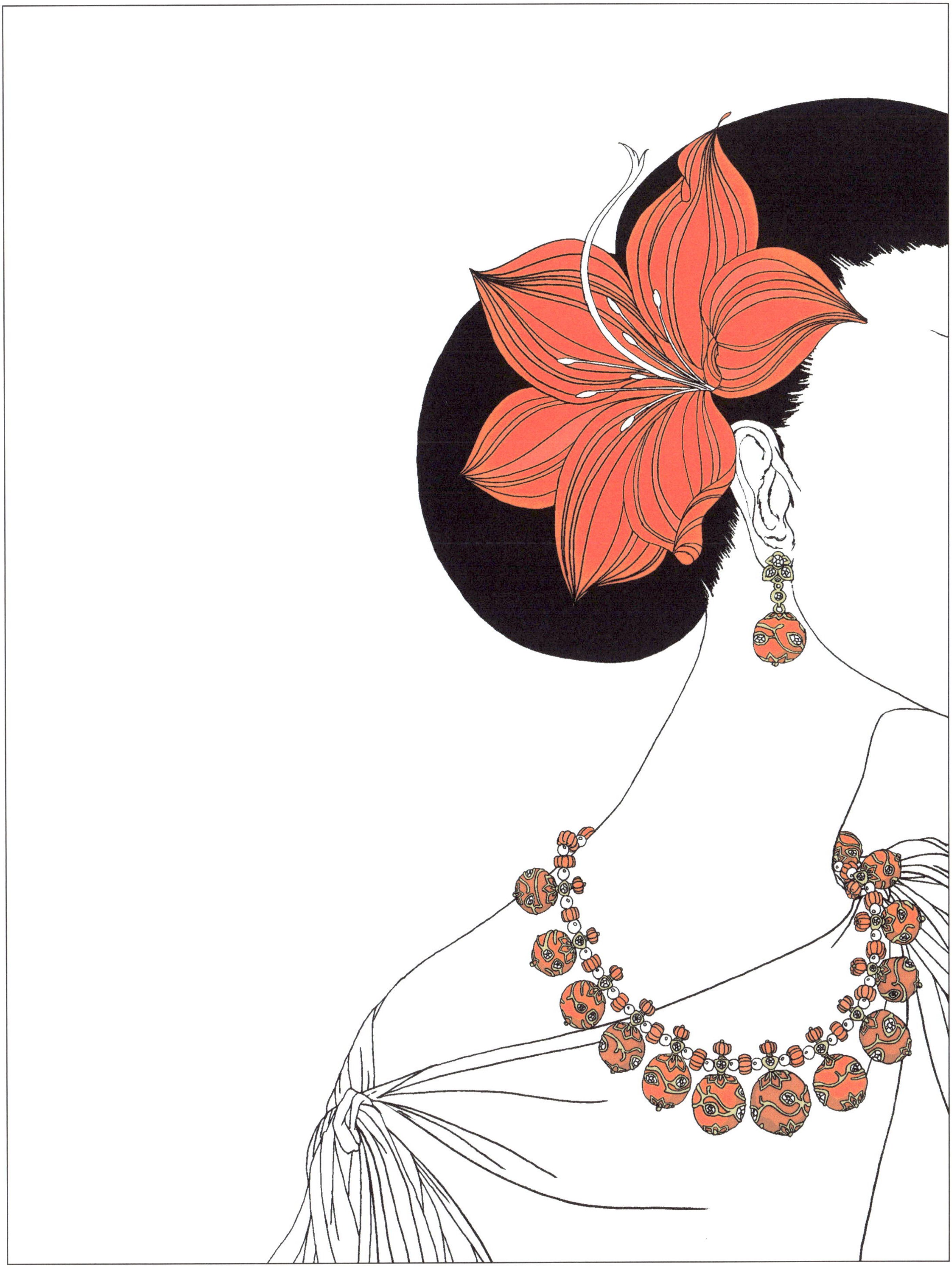

Blossom

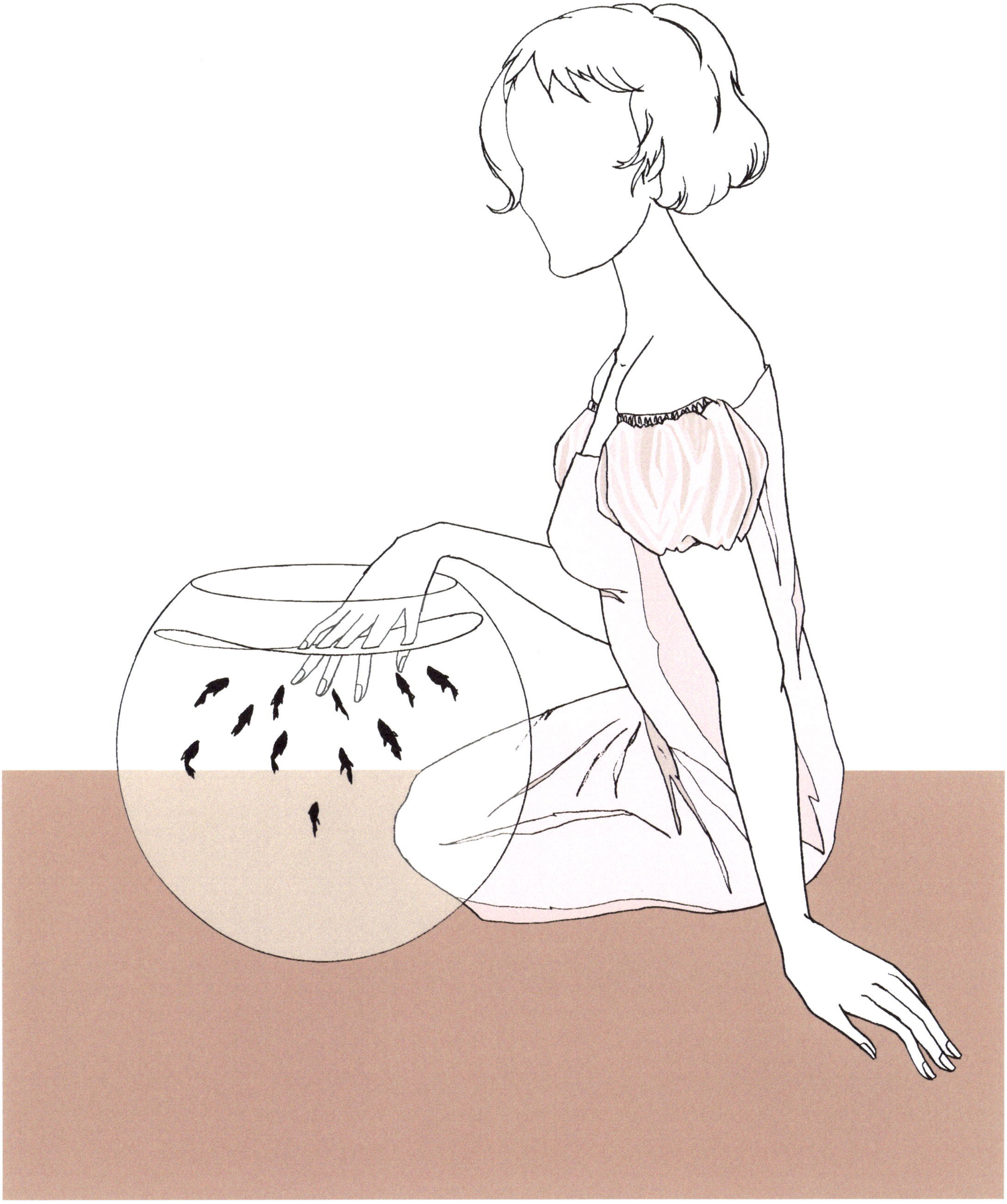

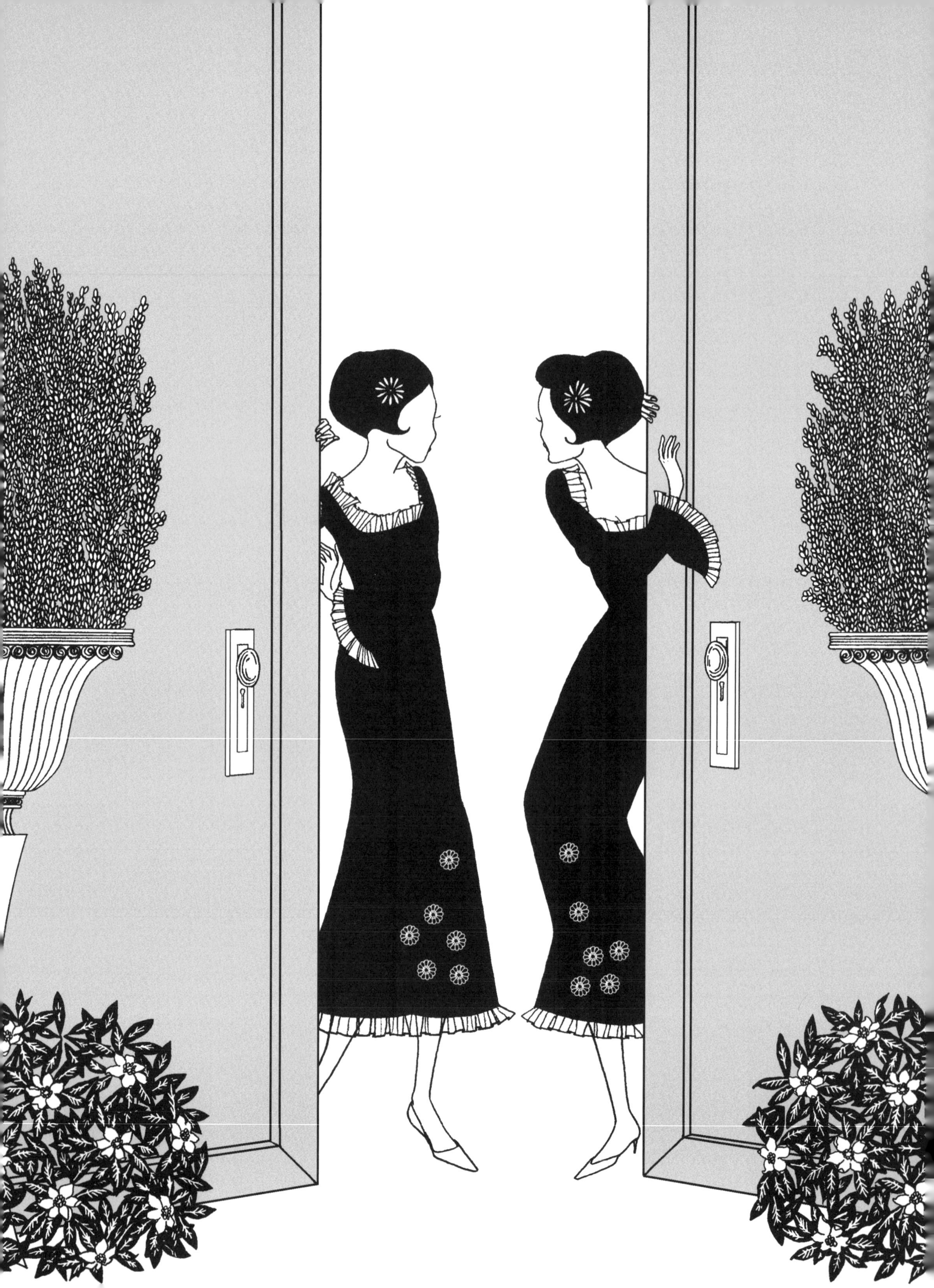

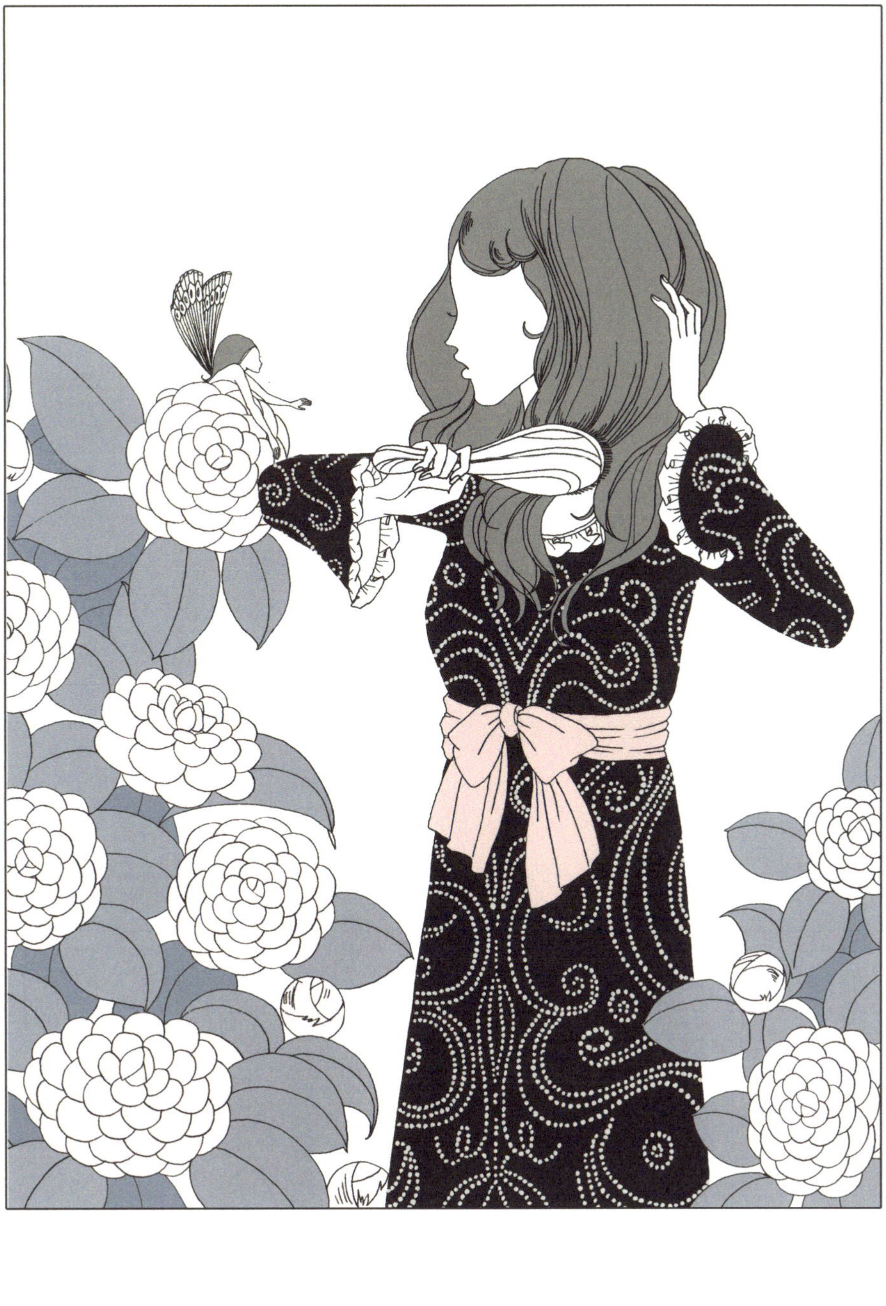

*102–109
(preceding pages)*

Yoko Ikeno

Collected works
These are collected works from commissions I have worked on over the past few years.

Born and raised in Japan outside of Tokyo, Ikeno spent six years in Milan and Paris assisting a fashion designer and working on personal art works. Ikeno moved to New York in 1998. She is a self-taught artist. Her work is enriched by the many influences of different cultures including her own background in Japan. Her work celebrates and fuses the classic and the modern, nature and human culture.

Yoko Ikeno is represented by Art Department New York & Agent Form Stockholm

stephaniep@art-dept.com
ebba@agentform.se
www.yokoikeno.com

Where do you come from? Japan. *Where in the world are you?* New York City. *Where would rather be?* I am very happy to be here. *What is your favourite city?* Chigasaki, my home town. *What's your background (training, education, other)?* I studied languages at university in Tokyo. *Was there a defining moment when you decided to become a visual artist?* It was a natural progression. *What is your work about?* Celebrating the beauty of what is around at any moment. *What is your definition of ornament?* The form rising over the function. *Wallpaper or paint?* Paint. Wallpaper in the right amount in the right place. *What styles do you most identify with?* Classical. *If money and time were no object what would your ideal project be?* I would like to draw all the chairs I have collected in my house.

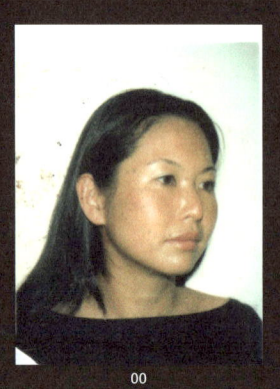

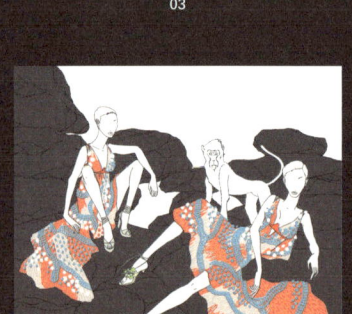

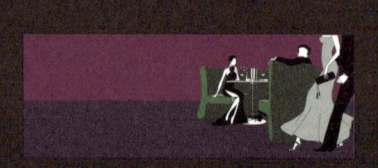

00
Yoko Ikeno

01
C
2003
Personal work

02
Banquet
Personal work

03
Fortune cookies
2004
For Bloomingdales USA

04
Jewel 1
2004
For Italian Vogue Gioiello

05
Jewel 2
2004
For Italian Vogue Gioiello

06
Rock
2004
For Italian Vogue Pelle

07
Run
2003
For VH1 Fashion Awards

08
Swing
2004
For Italian Vogue Pelle

Yumiko Kayukawa

Yumiko Kayukawa was born in the small town of Naie in Hokkaido, Japan. The panoramic beauty of her surroundings and feelings of communication with the native animals inspired her to paint the things around her. As a teenager she also fell in love 'with the energy and giddiness' of American pop-culture through her exposure to rock & roll, film, and fashion. By the age of 16, she had debuted into the art world with a comic book (manga) feature. After graduating from art school, she continued to paint, but struggled with truly expressing herself in her art. Fortunately, this frustration took a dramatic turn during a visit to Seattle where Yumi painted a picture at the request of an American friend. In comic book style, two girls sit entwined atop a mushroom, Japanese symbols and American pop art styles melding together in lively colour and bold lines. Yumi now realized her art persona – sagacious Japanese tradition in synergy with the jubilant irreverence of American pop culture.

yumiko@sweetyumiko.com
www.sweetyumiko.com

Where do you come from? Sapporo, Japan. *Where would rather be? What is your favourite city?* Seattle and Sapporo are my favourite cities. *Was there a defining moment when you decided to become a visual artist?* Painting and drawing is in my nature – since I was a little child. Beeoming a visual artist is not something I planned. Fortunately I had a chance to have a show in the US, at *roq la rue* gallery in 2001. After this my art career grew little by little in a very natural way. I'm really happy about it, because I never expected to make my living as an artist. *What would you say are your influences? And main sources of inspiration?* Music and movies; especially rock & roll culture. Also Japanese pop culture and yakuza (mobster) films from the 60s and 70s. *Do you make a distinction between commercial and non-commercial work?* Of course I need to make a piece in consideration of the request / opinion of the client if it's a commercial illustration job. But 99.99% of my work is for gallery shows, so I don't need to think about it and I get to make whatever I want.

112–115
(following pages)

Page 112
Psycho Kinesis (Nenriki)
Acrylic on illustration board
15" × 21"

Page 113
Bath (Ofuro)
Acrylic on illustration board
15" × 21"

Page 114
Squeeze (Sukuiizu)
Acrylic on illustration board
15" × 21"

Page 115
Cowbell (Kauberu)
Acrylic on illustration board
21" × 30"

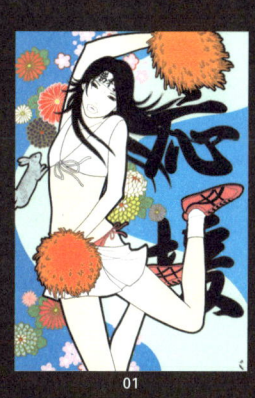

00
Yumiko Kayukawa

01
Cheering (Ouen)
acrylic on illustration board
21" × 30"

02
Little Kitty Heaven (Nekochan Tengoku)
Acrylic on illustration board
21" × 15"

03
Tatami Room (Tatami Ruumu)
Acrylic on illustration board
30" × 42"

04
Three Straight Holidays (Sanrenkyuu)
Acrylic on illustration board
15" × 21"

05
Trap (Wana)
Acrylic on illustration board
21" × 15"

112 *Various works*
Yumiko Kayukawa

お風呂

スクイズ

カウベル

116 *Isle III, Isle I*
Jung Kim

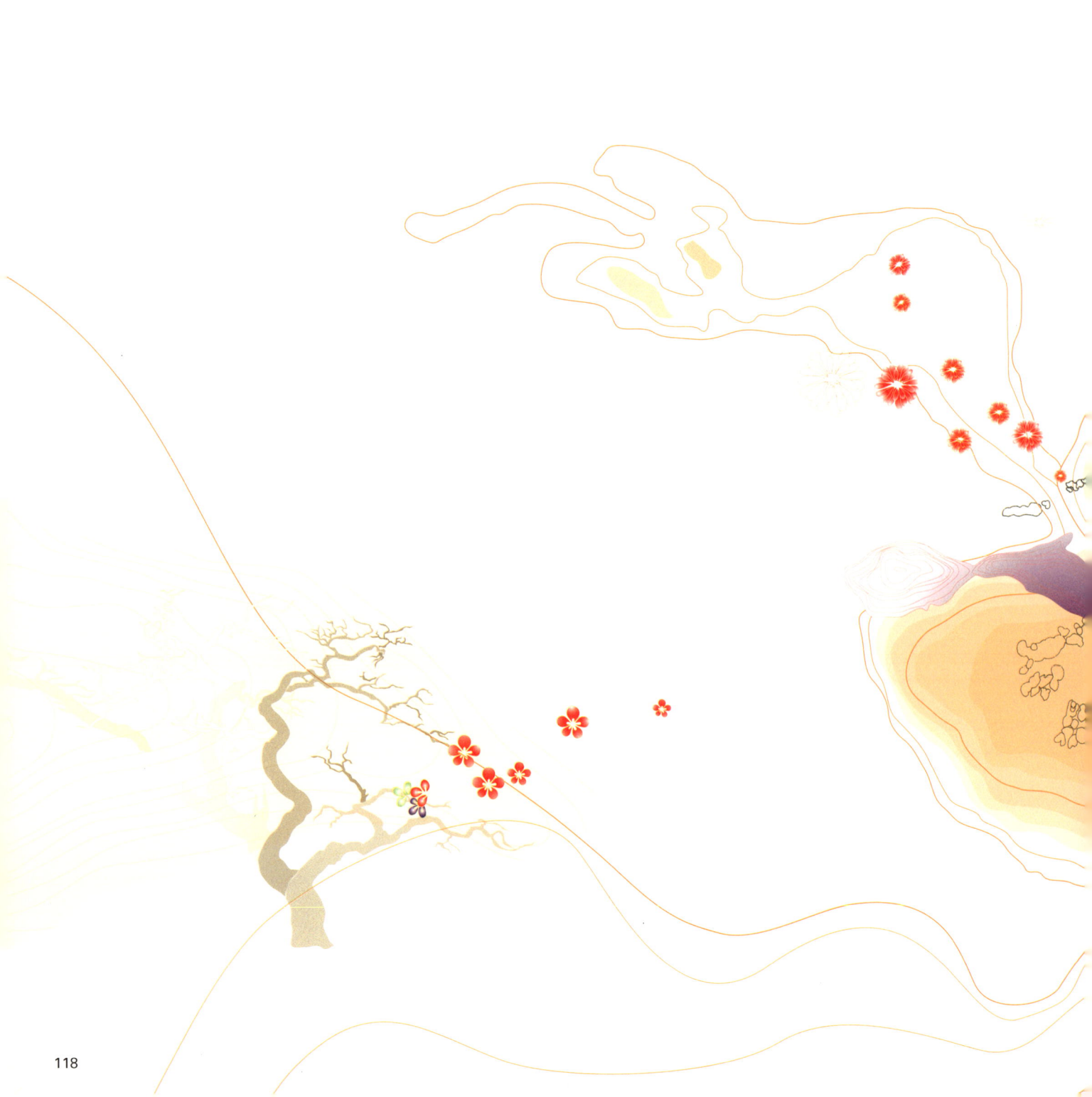

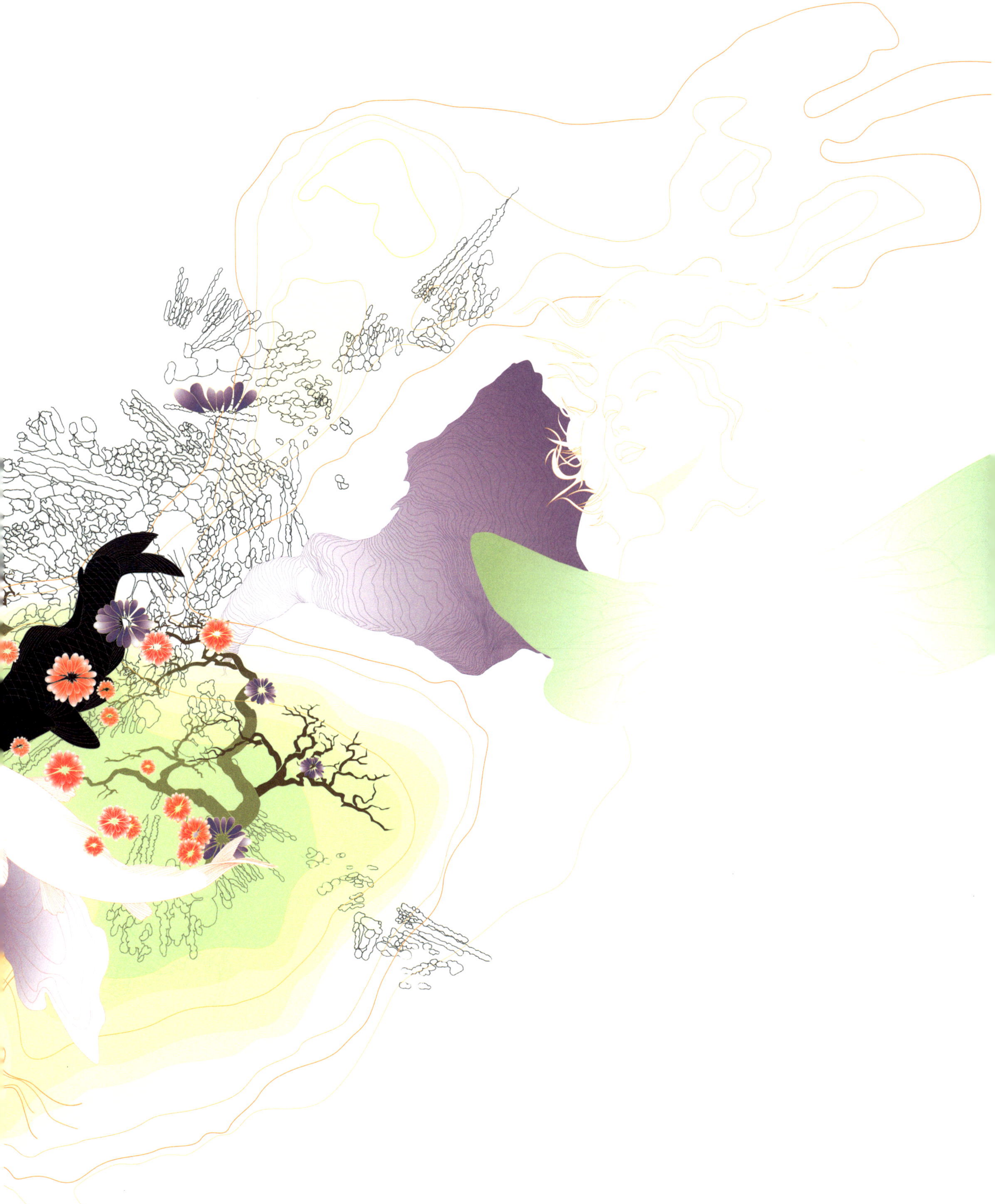

116–119
(preceding pages)

Jung Kim

Isle III, Isle I
For the last two years, I have been working with the central theme of an illusory landscape that only exists in a psychological terrain. The work evolved from ideas inspired by a Korean film titled *Flower Island*. In the movie, three women who desperately need an escape from reality find their way to an idealized island. Upon reaching the island, they come to find that it is just like any other place. Each woman finds their own way to disclose their physical and emotional burdens. The island is an unattainable ideal. *Isle* is my version of a utopia where pathos transcends as I work through a meticulous process of creating the terrain. Beginning with *Isle I*, I have been developing a series of work that shares a common theme over time. *Isle III* is the most recent work in the series.

Jung Kim's recent works of non-linear visual narrative take form as abstract and poetic landscapes where she explores symbols that embody the presence of beauty. A series in its becoming, these pieces represent two years of work under the umbrella of one idea; transcending pathos, lifting oneself above sadness through the contemplation and meditation of visually elaborate meticulous work. 'She sees beauty in every existence. I am becoming her. I see beauty in pain, in the past, in the dark memories, and in my life.' Born and raised in Busan, Korea, Kim relocated to the US in 1994. She earned her BFA in graphic design from the University of Hawaii, and her MFA in 2D Design from Cranbrook Academy of Art. She has recently concluded a term at MASS MoCA, and is currently working for the Rubell Family Collection contemporary art museum in Miami.

boopi55@hotmail.com
Biography by Nick Austin

What would you say are your influences? And main sources of inspiration? I get inspiration from very ordinary scenes. I was once inspired by a pile of dust that had collected on an old window sill. Its particles formed a really beautiful pattern that had a story about time embedded in it. Almost everything has a degree of beauty built into it when you get into the micro level. *What kind of work do you really like? What turns you on as an artist?* I am particularly drawn to the extremely delicate and the extremely meticulous. *Does form always follow function?* Form also creates function. Ornament is one of them. *On a scale of 1 to 10 – where 1 is fanatical minimalism and 10 is gilded rococo – where would you place your work? Why?* I identify more with rococo's intense color, visual elaboration and complex imagery. *What is your definition of ornament?* Something visually pleasurable on a surface level. A commonly accepted stylistic conceit, although that doesn't mean it is devoid of content. *Computers, more or less?* More. New tools can always add a new layer to one's work. *What would you rather have: More of… Less of…?* More imagination, less fear.

00
Jung Kim

01
Isle II

03
MooRungDoWon (left panel)

04
MooRungDoWon (right panel, detail)

05
Subversive Urge from Slash

06
Usual Hope Unusual Day

Kiyoshi Kuroda

Kiyoshi Kuroda was born in Tokyo in 1975. After completing graduate school at Tama Art University, he gained experience at a design firm, and has been working independently as an illustrator and designer since 2003. In his often monochromatic style, Kiyoshi uses plant, insect and animal motifs in his designs. Along with regular personal exhibitions, he has also been featured in various magazines (Dazed & Confused Japan, Studio Voice, Saizo, SAL magazine, PS, F-mode…) as well as work for CD covers, T-shirts, PlayStation and JAL.

komatsu@shigotoba.com
www.kiyoshikuroda.jp

Was there a defining moment when you decided to become a visual artist? When I opened an insect picture book in childhood. *What is your work about? Any central themes?* Since I was a little child, I have been glued to pictorial books of animals and plants. In the beginning I think I was simply attracted to their interesting structure and beauty. Then, since I started creating my own works, I have become more fascinated by the contrasting elements co-existing in beautiful animals and flowers, such as beauty and the feeling of violence and malice. My work expresses and emphasises such seemingly contradictory elements. *What would you say are your influences? And main sources of inspiration?* I am often inspired by the scenery – the sky, plants, man, colours and my surroundings that I see with my own eyes, as well as those in photos or books. Naturally, I think my sense of beauty is deeply influenced by the environment in which I live. Specifically, as a Japanese person, born and raised in Tokyo. To me, the aesthetic sense nurtured in this cultural environment is very important and something I value in my artistic expressions. *Computers, more or less?* Computers.

122–127 (following pages)

Page 122
Latent Insect

Pages 123–125
Latent Insect
Photography: Kio Yoneda (AVGVST)
Stylist: Megumi Date
Make-up: Chihiro (suomi)
Model: Carolina (FRIDAY)

Pages 126–127
Plus+
Exhibition with Hisashi Narita

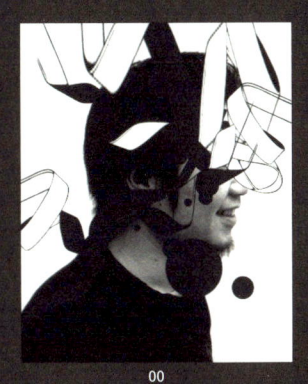

00
Kiyoshi Kuroda

01
Latent Insect
9–19.05.2005
at Guardian Garden

02
Plus+
Exhibition with Hisashi Narita in Kyoto

03–05
Illustrations

Latent Insect / Plus+
Kiyoshi Kuroda

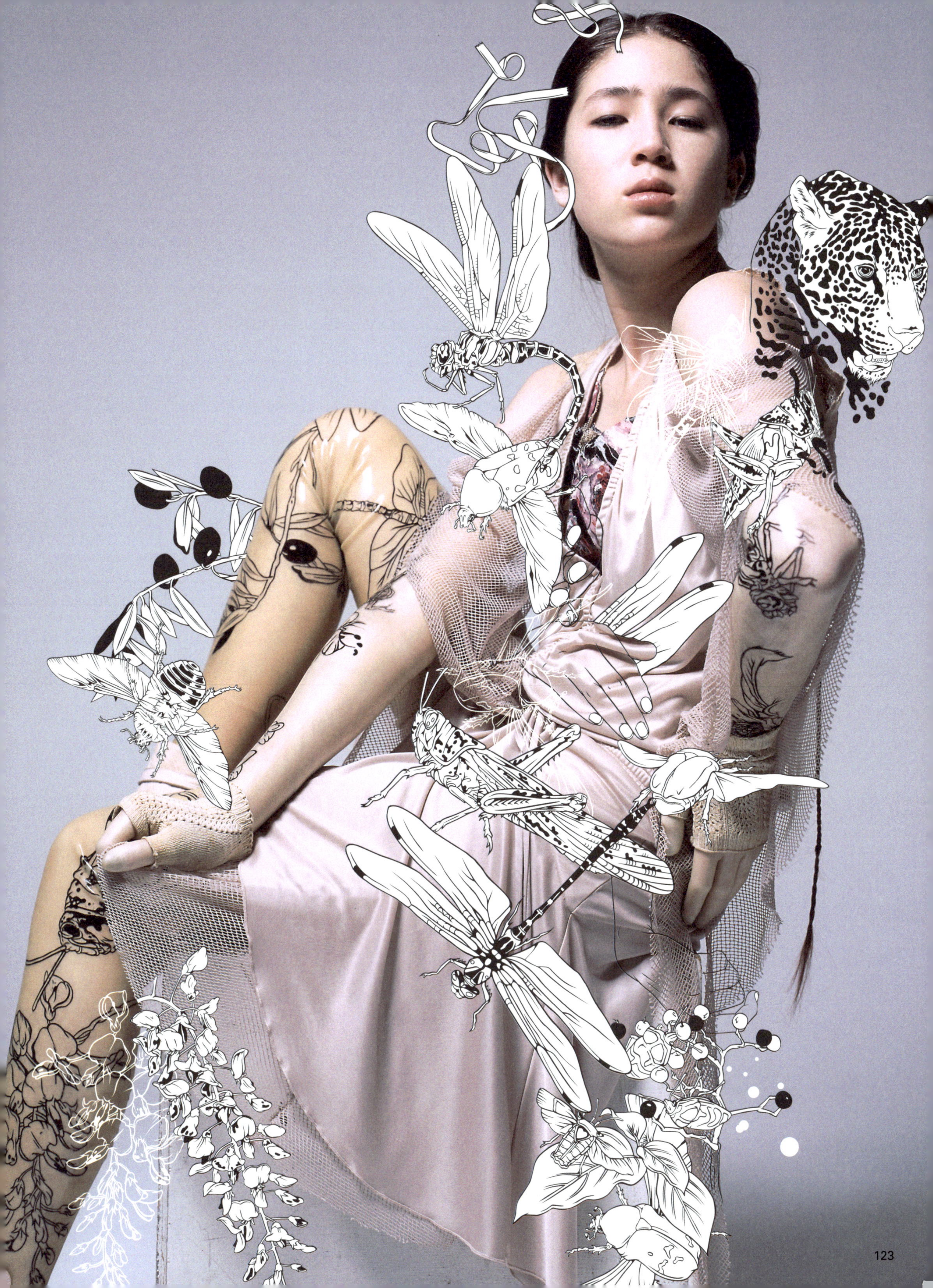

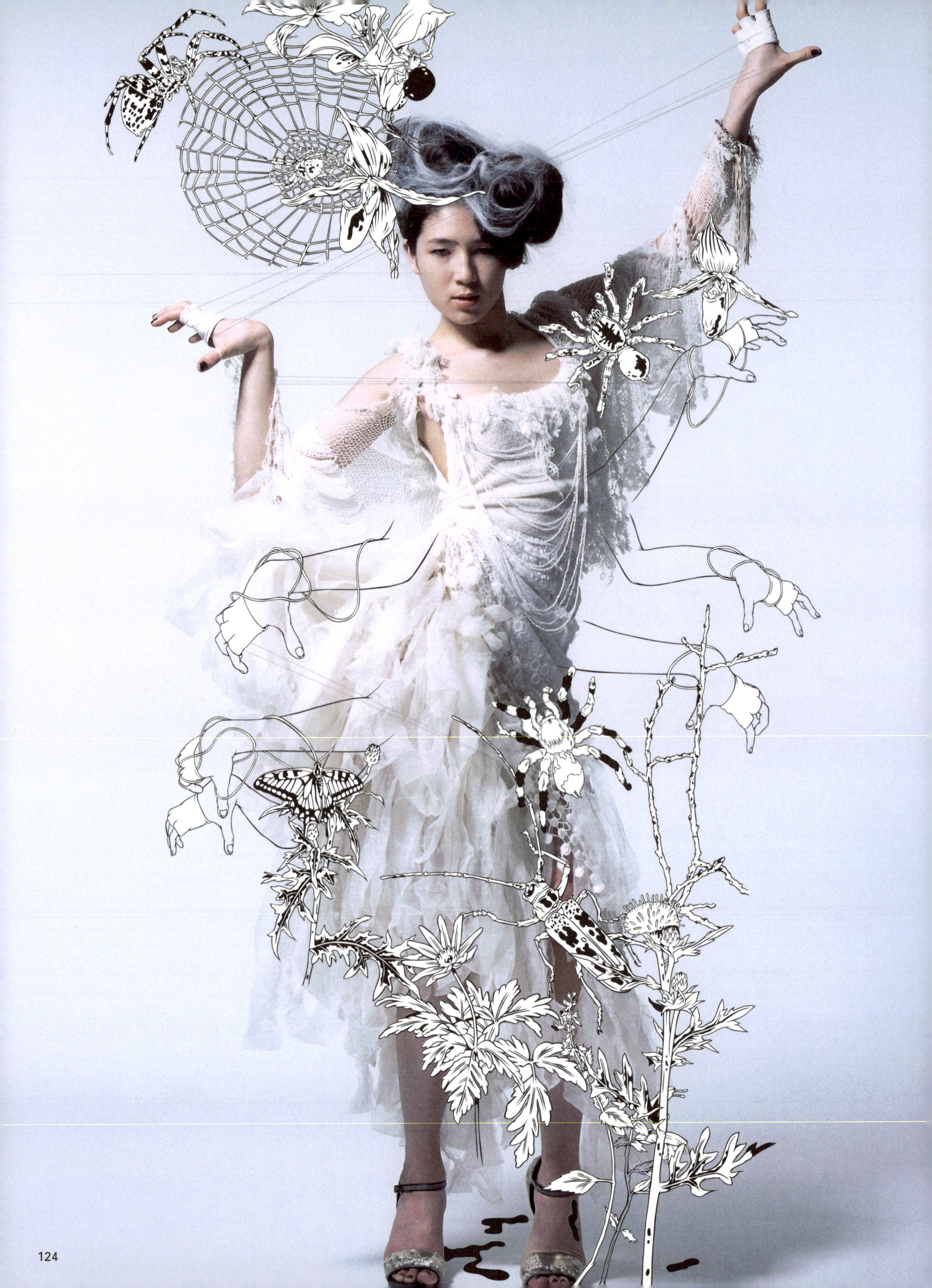

125

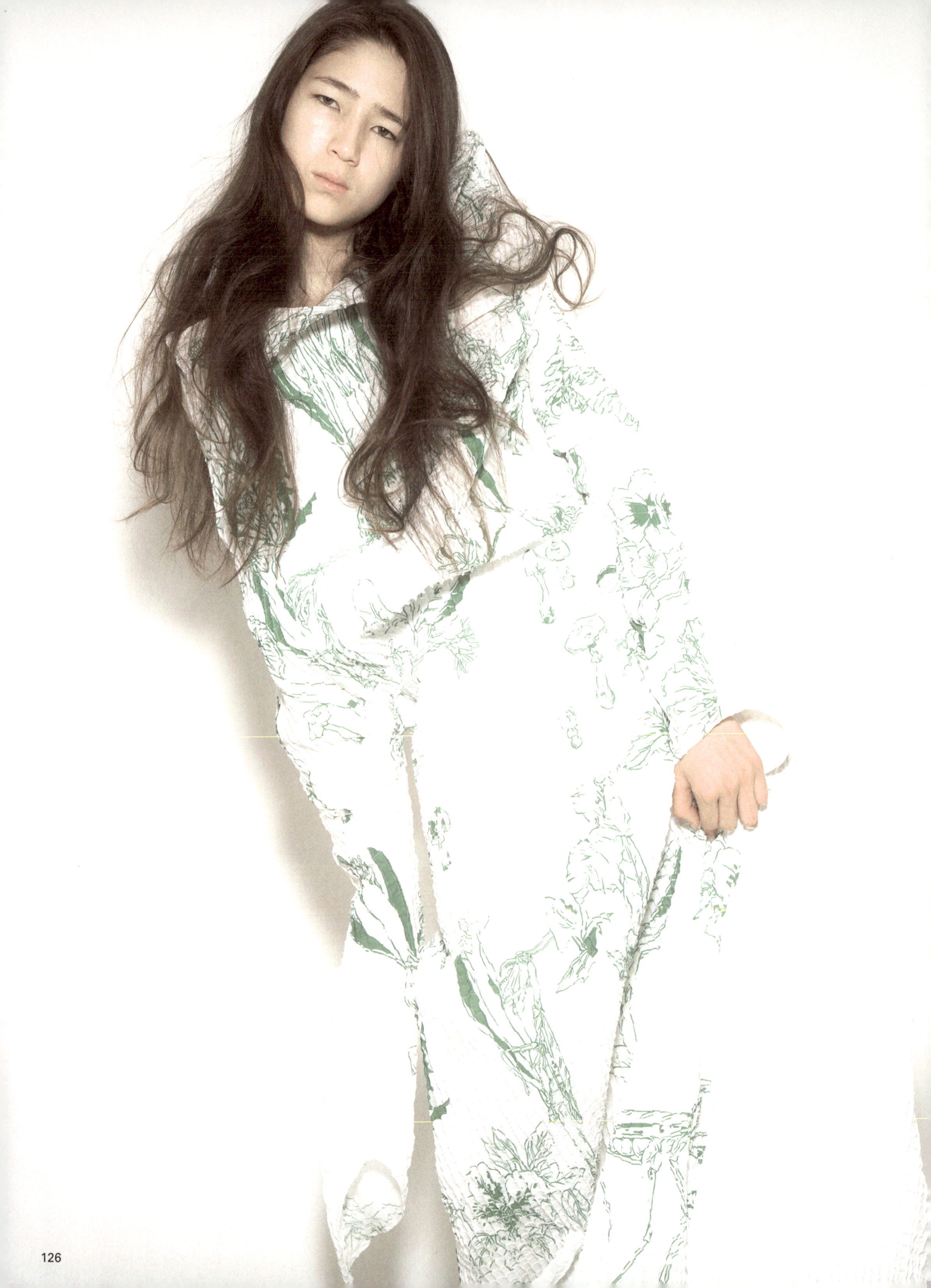

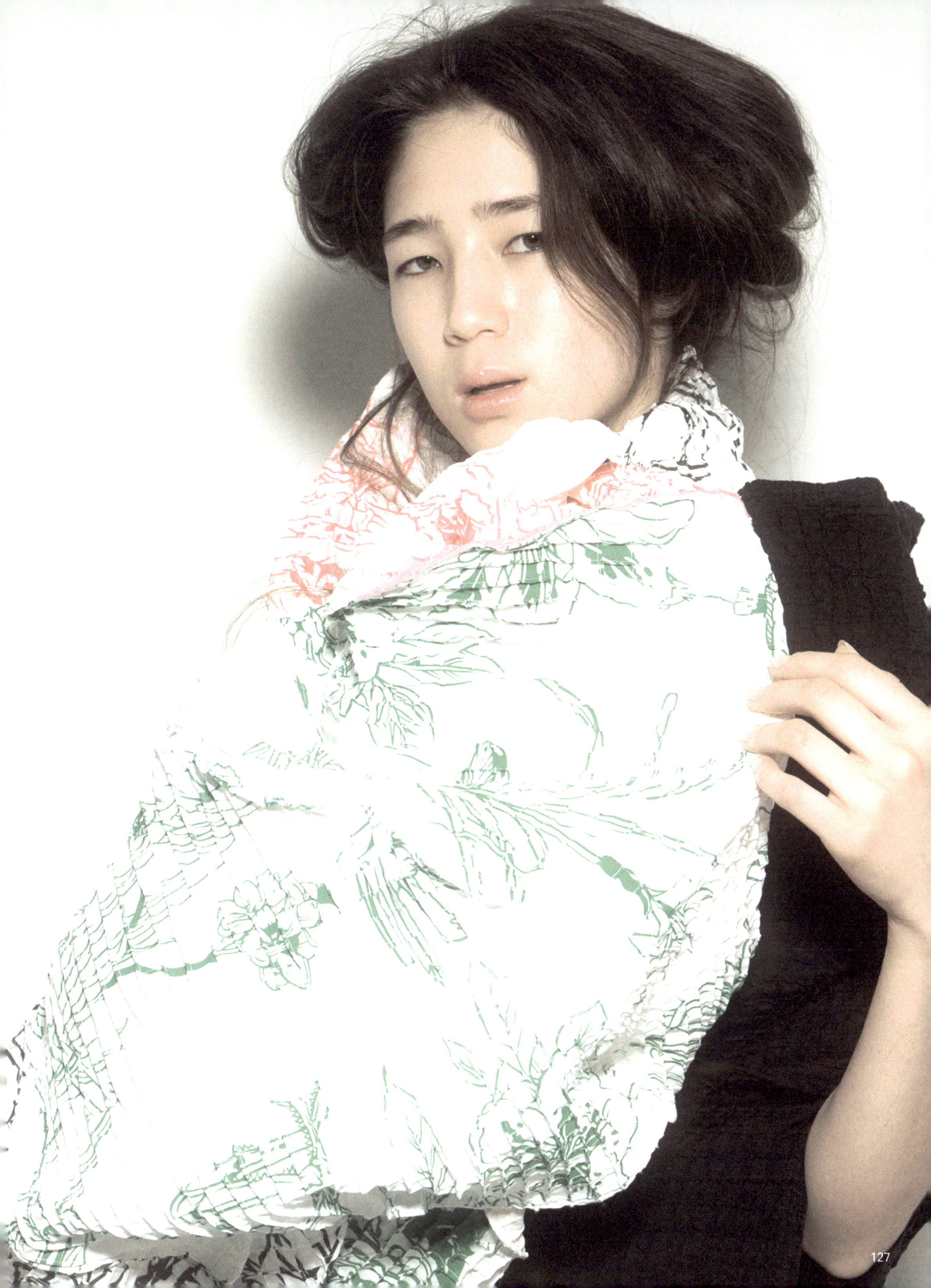

Scrap Car
Lucy McLauchlan

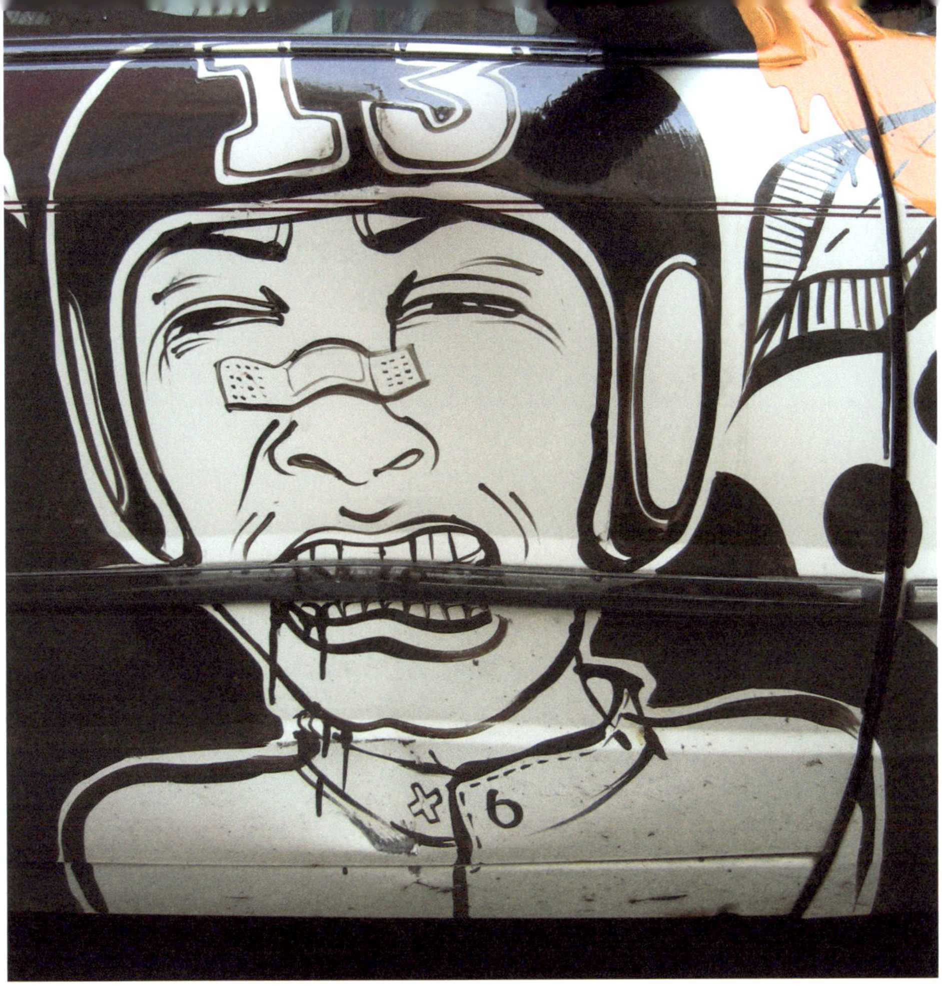
13

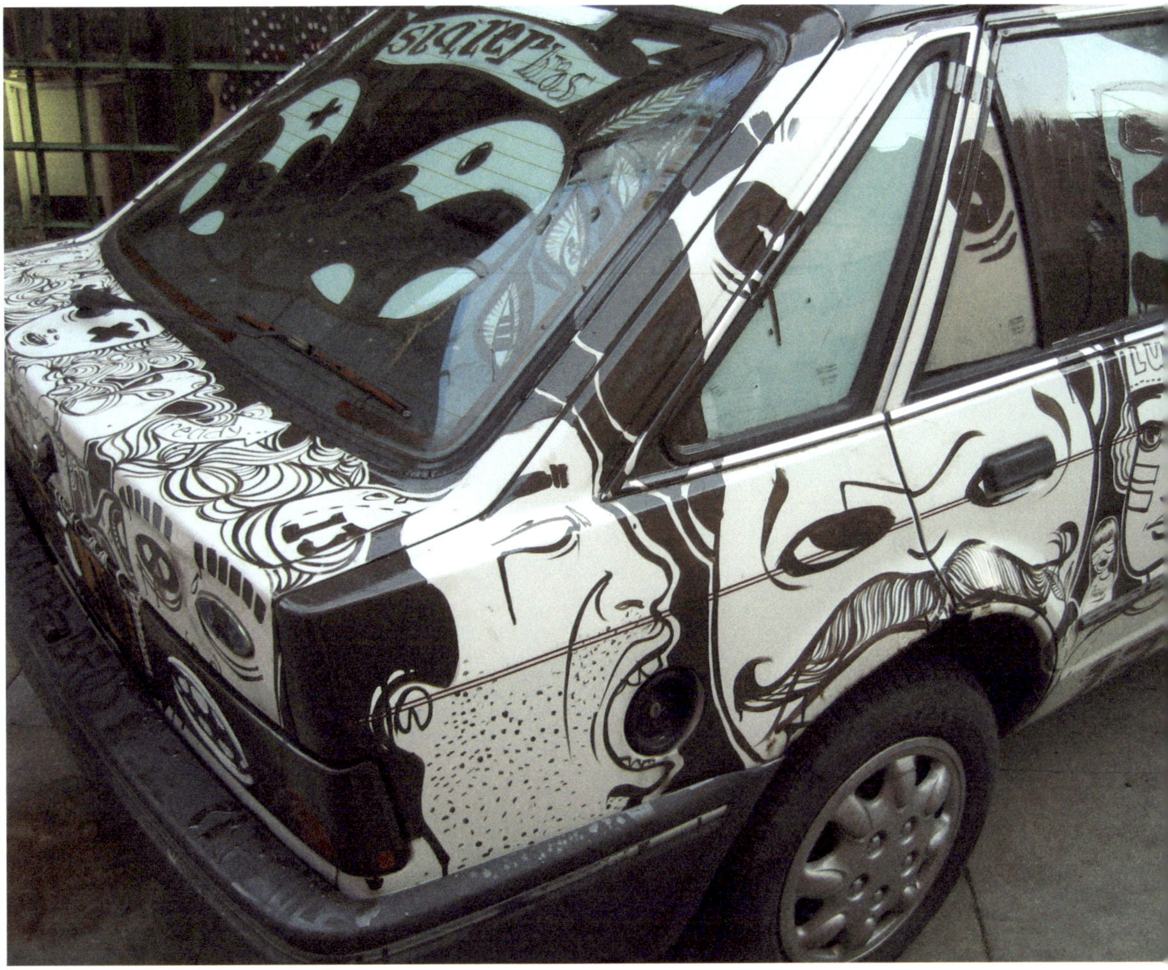

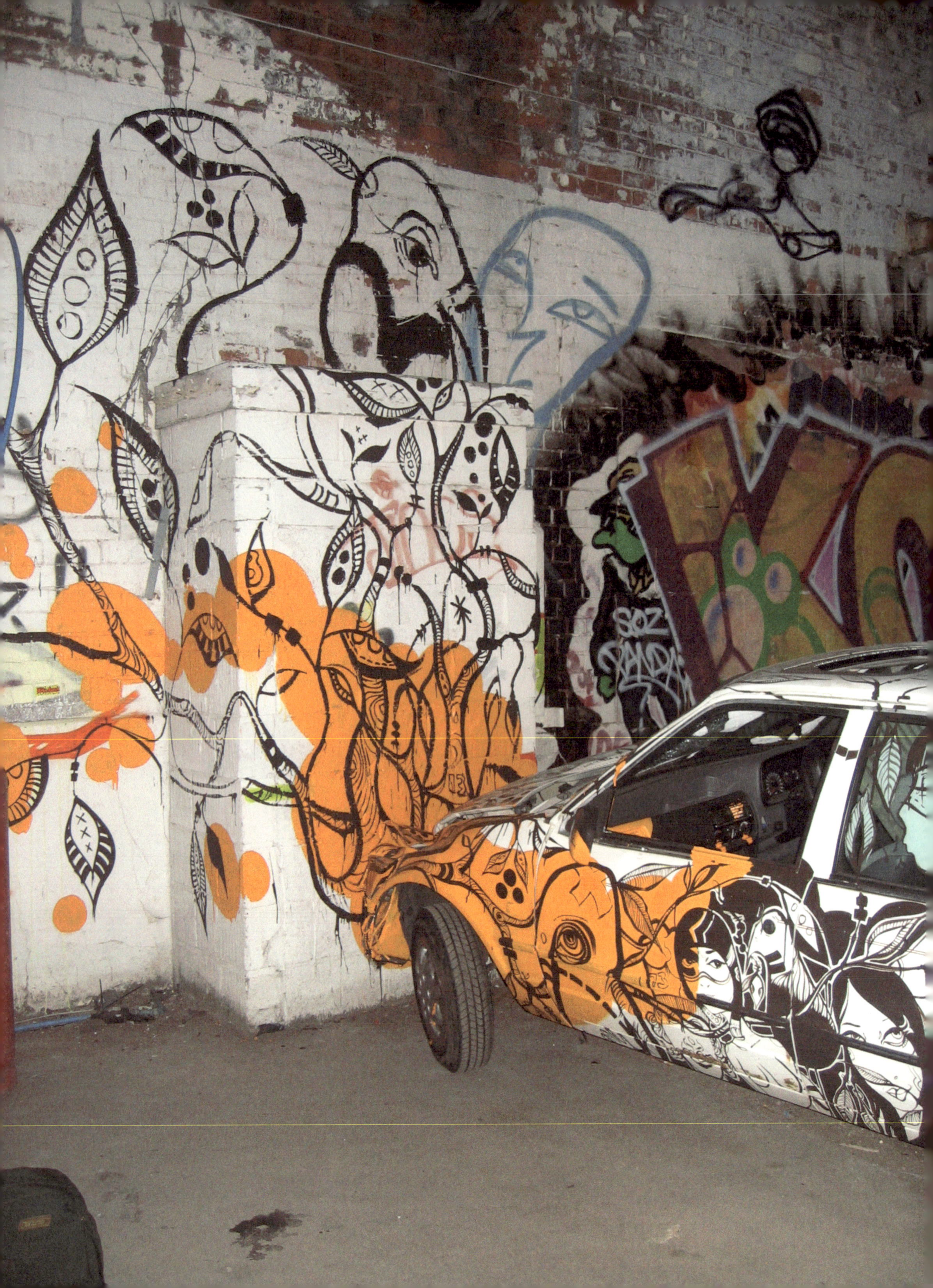

131

*128–131
(preceding pages)*

Lucy McLauchlan from Beat13

Scrap Car
07.2005
Painted by Lucy for an art installation at the music and arts Supersonic Festival, Birmingham.

Who are you? Lucy McLauchlan. *What is your star sign?* Taurus. *Where do you come from?* Brum [Birmingham], UK. *Where in the world are you?* Shoppingham, UK. *Where would rather be? What is your favourite city?* Still searching…

www.beat13.co.uk
info@beat13.co.uk

Was there a defining moment when you decided to become a visual artist? When I was 5 and won membership to the junior ornithologist's club for drawing a picture. *What would you say are your influences? And main sources of inspiration?* Barry (13), ouch… *What's your favourite book cover?* The Gadfly cover by Lothar Reher. *What's your favourite title sequence?* Saul Bass' Vertigo. *Can you describe the work(s) you've sent to us?* Ornamental rubbish. *In what context was it produced?* Taking what is others' waste and using it for other uses. The Rolls Royce was left over from a Vogue photo shoot, the van was crashed and dumped, the car was scrapped and worthless. *When are you most aware of design?* When I come across something amazingly designed and when I come across something amazingly badly designed.

00
Lucy McLauchlan

01
Bird
2005
Painting by Lucy

02
Camo
2004
Fabric design by Matt for Maharishi DPM book

03
Japanfabric
2005
Fabric design by Lucy & Matt for Laforet, Tokyo

04
LittleRIS
2005
By Lucy for JuJu calender, Berlin

05
Peace hand
2004
Poster design by Lucy for exhibition in US

06
Sonar CD
CD sleeve design by Matt for BPI's 'British music sampler' CD presented at Sonar, Barcelona 2005

07
Supersonic CD
CD sleeve design by Matt for Supersonic Festival presented by Capsule, Birmingham 2005

07
Dumped van
Lucy doodled over a van that had been left dumped

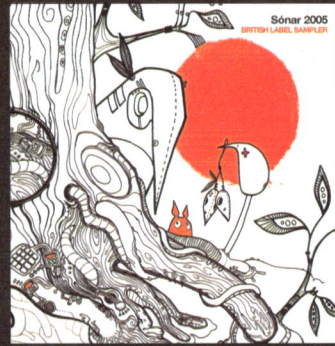

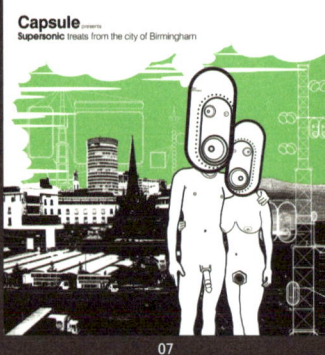

Manuel Miranda

I was born in Chicago, grew up in Seattle, and currently live in New York. My partner, Min Kyong Lew, and I collaborate on a variety of projects for various cultural organizations in New York and New Haven. I studied comparative literature as an undergraduate at The Evergreen State College in Olympia, WA, and did graduate studies in graphic design at the Yale School of Art. I am currently freelancing at Brand Integration Group at Ogilvy & Mather, New York.

manuel@minandmanuel.com
www.minandmanuel.com

What is your work about? Any central themes? I'm interested in how difference requires flexible structures. I love typography and patterning, though I like to 'freestyle' in collage from time to time. The way I like to work focuses more on the creation or selection of elements, and the structure those elements are placed into. I guess I'm sort of anti-compositional. **What medium(s) do you work with?** I like books and websites. I enjoy posters for the experimentation they allow on a flat surface, and for their size. I also program a bit, and enjoy making computationally-generated work. **What would you say are your influences? And main sources of inspiration?** It may sound clichéd, but I would say that a primary influence is New York City. It is an intensely grid-y and organized environment, yet also completely diverse and chaotic. The lowest lows and the highest highs are possible here. I suppose that sense of possibility is what keeps me aware of the world around me. **Wallpaper or paint?** Wallpaper. Walls fall within the world of signs, as they normally aren't load-bearing structures, and only serve to express social divisions and hierarchies. The opportunity for interesting narrative on wallpaper is huge.

134–137 (following pages)

Various works
Page 134
Wallpaper proposal for the lobby of the Tisch School of the Arts at New York University. Ideas of division (between inside and outside, domesticity and the street, and childhood and adulthood) inspired the work.
Page 135
A foldout brochure made for the 89th Congress of the Society for Mechanical Revelation, run by Elena Grossman. Mirroring, elements of surveillance machines, and the feeling of paranoia (all primary concerns of the Society), were used as elements within the design.
Pages 136–137
A series of posters inspired by the Calla Lily, and the themes of love, death, and rebirth that are commonly associated with the flower.

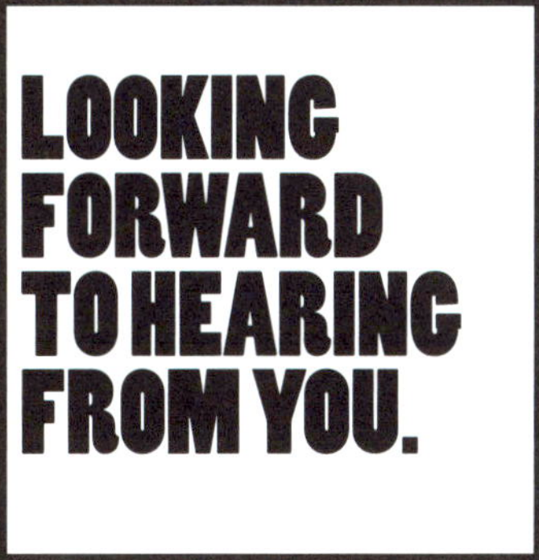

02
Pamphlet portfolio for Min and Manuel

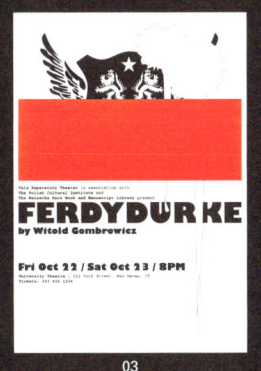

03
Theater poster for Witold Gombrowicz' play *Ferdydurke*, shown at the Yale Repertory Theater

00
Manuel Miranda

01
Poster for Jean-Luc Godard's film *2 or 3 Things I Know About Her*, shown at the Yale School of Art

04
Poster for visiting critic Micheal Beirut, at the Yale School of Art's department of Graphic Design

05
Remix of Milton Glaser's *I ♥ NY* and Herbert Matter's logo for the New Haven Railroad, used for a T-shirt design

06
Poster for the Yale Center for Cultural Sociology's conference, *Culture in the World*

07
Karel Martens Requests Your ID at Yale
Part of the visiting critic series at the Yale School of Art's department of Graphic Design. (ID is a play on the Dutch pronunciation of 'idea')

08
Impressions
A book on Seattle's 1962 World's Fair

134 *Various works*
Manuel Miranda

135

Zantedeschia

Zantedeschia is named after Professor Zantedeschi, probably Giovanni Zantedeschi, 1773-1846, an Italian physician and botanist, although there is some uncertainty about this. The name aethiopica is not directly related to Ethiopia. In classical times it meant south of the known world i.e. south of Egypt and Libya. Several southern African plants were given this specific epithet early on. Although called the arum lily, it is neither an arum (the genus Arum) nor a lily (genus Lilium). But it is associated with the lily as a symbol of purity and these elegant flowers have graced many bridal bouquets, as seen in this picture of a South African bride in 1934.

Sub-Class: Arecidae
Sub-Order: Arales
Family: Araceae
Sub-Family: Aroideae
Tribe: Zantedeschieae
Height: 1 1/2' to 4'
Rate of Growth: Fast

ranged in a complex spiral pattern on the central column (spadix). The tiny flowers are arranged in male and female zones on the spadix. The top 7 cm are male flowers and the lower 1.8 cm are female. If you look through a hand-lens you may see the stringy pollen emerging from the male flowers which consist largely of anthers. The female flowers have an ovary with a short stalk above it, which is the style (where the pollen is received).

Spathe

The spadix is surrounded by the white or coloured spathe. According to Marloth the whiteness of the spathe is not caused by pigmentation, but is an optical effect produced by numerous airspaces beneath the epidermis.

Nutritional Requirements: Balanced liquid fertilizer monthly
Light Requirements: Full sun to partial shade
Form: Clump forming herb
Leaves: 1 1/2' long, rich green. Plants become dormant in winter – leaves may shrivel but no ne...
Flowers: White, Yellow, Pink, Purple, Orange
Fruits: None.
Pests or diseases: Tolerant of most pests and di...

this attracts various crawling insects and bees which are responsible for pollinating the flowers. Cross pollination occurs as the anthers of each flower ripen before the ovaries. A white crab spider of the family Thomisidae visits the flower to eat the insects. This spider does not spin webs and uses its whiteness as camouflage against the spathe. In the western Cape, a tiny frog Hyperolius hopstocki is also attracted to the arum lily flowers. The spathe withers after flowering and covers the ripening berries. It rots away when these are ripe and the succulent yellow berries attract birds, which are responsible for seed dispersal.

North... is evergreen...duous de... on the habi... and rainfall regime. In the Western Cape it is dormant in summer and in the summer rainfall areas it is dormant in winter. It will remain evergreen in both areas if growing in marshy conditions which remain wet all year around.

Femininity

Despite the countervailing themes of mortality, masculinity, and homosexuality, the primary association remained that of the cala with femininity. The erotic import of the calla was generally comprehended by the turn of the century, especially after Sigmund Freud's identification of the flower's sexual symbolism.

Androgyny

The androgynous form of the blossom ad...to the development of the calla's symbolism... the nineteenth century. While its whiteness and dramatic co...ry bolstered associations with the female form, the prominent spadix could easily be read as a phallic symbol, making it potentially a masculine symbol as well.

...the calla was attractive for ...ation with feminine grace, ...associations with death consti-...ppeal. Although in olden times ...of the arum was considered ...e plague," some nineteenth-...cientists believed that "a ...of acridity generally pervades ...tribe, and exists in so high ...some of the..., as to render ...gerous poisons." In addition to ...ualities, the calla's color had ...l implications; as one botanist ...in 1889, "To dream of white ...s been supposed to prognosticate death." These associations ...ality made the calla an ideal mourning flower.

Arts:

...y twentieth century, the calla lily enjoyed a heightened popularly in the 1920s and 1930s, as dozens of painters and ...hers of varying reputations and approaches to image-making ...e subject of their work. Modernist painters, such as Preston ...and Charles Sheeler, best known for their Precionist ap-...ere drawn to the elegant, curvilinear, yet bold forms of the calla ...o depicted by artists whose work reveals a more specific ...cy on European Cubism, such as Alfred Maurer and Joseph ...n Stanton Macdonald-Wright, known for his highly abstracted ...ist paintings, used the calla as subject matter. And the sleek ...nt forms of the plant appealed to a variety of photographers of ..., such as Marjorie Content, Imogen Cunningham, Clara Sip-... Edward Weston.

...merican modern to make recurrent use of the motif of eroti-... calla lily was Marsden Hartley. A pastel of call lilies, which ...n 1920, is his most straightforward depiction of the subject; the ...are isolated against a dark, creased background of the type ...employed in other still-life compositions of that period. In 1917, ...fe No. 9, Hartley began to take liberties with his floral subject, ...and patterning its blossoms and foliage in stylized designs ...his Provincetown abstractions of the preceding year. The sense ...ss and contour shown in the pastel is here sacrificed for two-...cal silhouettes, to which the calla's dramatic spathe and broad, ...ped leaves were uniquely well suited. The decorative patterns ...upon calla-lilies appeared in several key still-life compositions ...y produced around 1920.

...d Berlin between 1922 and 1924, Hartley turned with new ...still-life painting, initially inspired by Georges Braque's decora-...ositions and subsequently by Paul Cezanne's more structured ...simple composition on the calla in goblet is well developed ...tral alignment is emphasized by the manner in which the artist ...hed the edges of the small canvas. This was a trait common to ...is still-lifes and caused critic Paul Rosenfeld to complain that "a ...ll be painted with relish and verve. But the rest of the canvas, ...er the brush of a Renoir or a Cezanne would have been no ...tant, will by Hartley be left half alive, treated with an irritating ...of attention." Although sketchily handled, the still-life gives ...nce of the spadix and the spathe, whose form echoes the ...ilt of the goblet that contains it. The alignment of goblet and ... with elongated spadix, and their insertion in the conjoin-...ings of blossom and bowl, create a pattern whose sexual ...ons are considerably more obvious than those of his earlier

calla lily compositions. The following year Hartley enriched his symbolic configuration in The Window, in which a calla with enormous spadix tops a complicated arrangement of fruit and floral bounty. Again, the artist aligned the vertical thrust of erect pear, spadix, and rising mountain, which peaks in an opening flanked by rich foliage. Although Hartley had earlier foresworn programmatic symbolism in his painting—"I weary of emotional excitement in art"–both he and the commentators of his day were thoroughly imbued with the pervasive interest in psychological symbols, which was a prime legacy of the turn of the twentieth century.

Doubtless the most ambivalent blossoms of modern times have been the numerous calla compositions by which Georgia O'Keefe's fame was secured in the 1920s. Her earliest efforts with the single blossoms are similar to the formal concerns that Mondrian and others explored in their still-life designs. O'Keeffe was familiar with the calla studies by her colleague, Marsden Hartley, and with the sexual allusions that Rosenfeld and others discovered in them. Her own Paintings of closely viewed and enlarged leaves and flowers, which she began about 1922, had similarly excited critics and gallery visitors. "I couldn't understand what all the talk was about, what they were seeing in my flowers," she later explained. "I had seen Hartley's calla lilies, and thought I would try one to see if I could understand what it was all about."

O'Keeffe's early exercises with Hartley's blossom, dating from 1923, generally treated single blooms placed in long-necked containers and often isolated against dark, monochromatic backgrounds, such as the Calla Lily with Red Background. The isolation of the flower and the dramatic contrast of white spathe with dark ground were remarkably similar to nineteenth-century examples by Lambdin and other late Victorian painters. The formal elegance and simplicity of the design owed more, however, to modernism's reductive vision and paralleled (probably fortuitously) Mondrian's lily. The precision with which the flower was drawn and brushed was typical of O'Keeffe's work at that juncture; her coloring was well applied to such tight, sculptural forms as the calla. The waxy blossom offered the same type of clear outline and organic form that later drew the artist to profiles of adobes, sunbleached pelvic bones, and water-smoothed rocks. In the callas O'Keeffe discovered the ideal combination of organic subject and formalist design that was to motivate her finest work.

As a child of the fin de siècle, O'Keeffe was certainly familiar with the traditional associations clustered about the calla lily. As a self-conscious modernist, she was aware of the more novel interpretations given to

the blossom. As a formalist, she was attuned to the artistic possibilities that close study of the flower afforded. Her achievement rests in the disingenuous play of these contradictory properties against each other. For some, her calla lily paintings recalled traditional sentiments. Alfred Stieglitz, reflecting such associations of whiteness and the lily purity, or perhaps with tongue in cheek–referred to his wife's callas as "the Immaculate Conception." And Miguel Covarrubias caricatured O'Keeffe as "the Lady of the Lily." Another contemporary echoed the nineteenth-century gift books' equation of the flower and "Magnificent beauty" by reproducing a calla subject to illustrate the conclusion that O'Keeffe's paintings "contain the emotional and spiritual properties inherent in pure beauty."

Marsden Hartley, Still-Life with Artichoke 1924–1925
Imogen Cunningham, Two Callas 1925
Edward Weston, Two Callas 1929
Charles Sheeler, Cactus 1931
John Dickson, Calla Lilies 1920s
Marsden Hartley, Calla Lilies 1920s
Rebecca Salsbury James, Echo of New England c.1930
Kanami Kubinyi, Calla Lily c.1936–37
George Cochran Lambdin, In the Greenhouse c.1870s
John La Farge, Calla Lily 1862
Stanton Macdonald-Wright, Still Life with Arum Lilies and Fruit 1923
Alfred Maurer, Still Life with Calla Lily c.1925–26
Alfred Maurer Floral, Still Life with Calla Lily c.1926–28
Alfred Maurer, Calla Lily Turned Away 1923
Georgia O'Keeffe, Calla Lily in Tall Glass—No. 2 1923
Georgia O'Keeffe, Calla Lily with Red Background 1923
Georgia O'Keeffe, Calla Lilies 1924
Georgia O'Keeffe, Yellow Calla 1927
Georgia O'Keeffe, Calla Lily for Alfred 1927
Georgia O'Keeffe, Calla Lilies on Red 1928
Georgia O'Keeffe, Calla Lilies on Grey 1928

...cci Patterns:

...most of us have never taken the time to examine very carefully the number or arrangement of petals on a flower. If ...do so, several things would become apparent. First, we would find that the number of petals on a flower is often ...Fibonacci numbers. One-petalled (white calla lily) are not common.

...o Pisano is better known by his nickname Fibonacci. He was the son of Guilielmo and a member of the Bonacci ...nacci himself sometimes used the name Bigollo, which may mean good-for-nothing or a traveller. Did his coun-...h to express by this epithet their disdain for a man who concerned himself with questions of no practical value, or ...word in the Tuscan dialect mean a much-travelled man, which he was?

...ci was born in Italy but was educated in North Africa where his father, Guilielmo, held a diplomatic post. His ...o was to represent the merchants of the Republic of Pisa who were trading in Bugia, later called Bougie and now ...lia. Bejaia is a Mediterranean port in northeastern Algeria. The town lies at the mouth of the Wadi Soummam near ...uraya and Cape Carbon. Fibonacci was taught mathematics in Bugia and travelled widely with his father and ...d the enormous advantages of the mathematical systems used in the countries they visited. Fibonacci writes in his ...ok Liber abaci (1202):-

...y father, who had been appointed by his country as public notary in the customs at Bugia acting for the Pisan ...going there, was in charge, he summoned me to him while I was still a child, and having an eye to useful-...uture convenience, desired me to stay there and receive instruction in the school of accounting. There, when I ...introduced to the art of the Indians' nine symbols through remarkable teaching, knowledge of the art very soon ...e above all else and I came to understand it, for whatever was studied by the art in Egypt, Syria, Greece, Sicily ...nce, in all its various forms.

...ci ended his travels around the year 1200 and at that time he returned to Pisa. There he wrote a number of im-...ts which played an important role in reviving ancient mathematical skills and he made significant contributions to ...ibonacci lived in the days before printing, so his books were hand written and the only way to have a copy of one ...ks was to have another hand-written copy made. Of his books we still have copies of Liber abaci (1202), Practica ...e (1220), Flos (1225), and Liber quadratorum. Given that relatively few hand-made copies would ever have been ...we are fortunate to have access to his writing in these works. However, we know that he wrote some other ..., unfortunately, are lost. His book on commercial arithmetic Di minor guisa is lost as is his commentary on Book ...'s Elements which contained a numerical treatment of irrational numbers which Euclid had approached from a ... point of view.

...he Renaissance, mathematicians took special interest in how many objects in nature reflected mathematical prin-...they discovered connections, they developed mathematical ideas to help us understand the relationship between ...nature.

...cept of the golden mean, also known as the golden measure, was used by many Renaissance artists and archi-...learned about it from studying the ancient Greeks. It describes what people thought was a "visually pleasing"

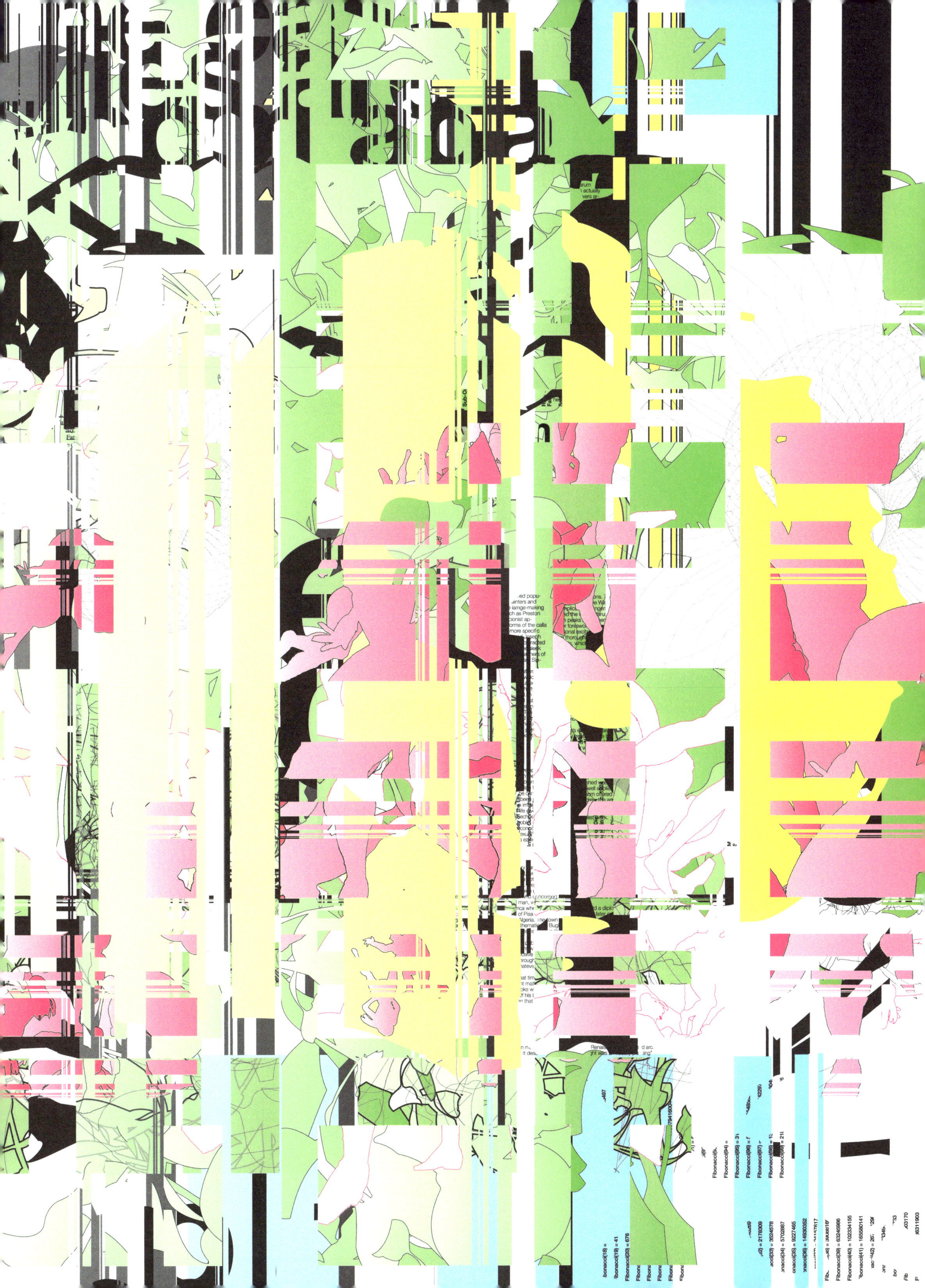

Pylon; Parachute; Pearl Harbour; Shark + Ribbon Girl
Mr&Mrs

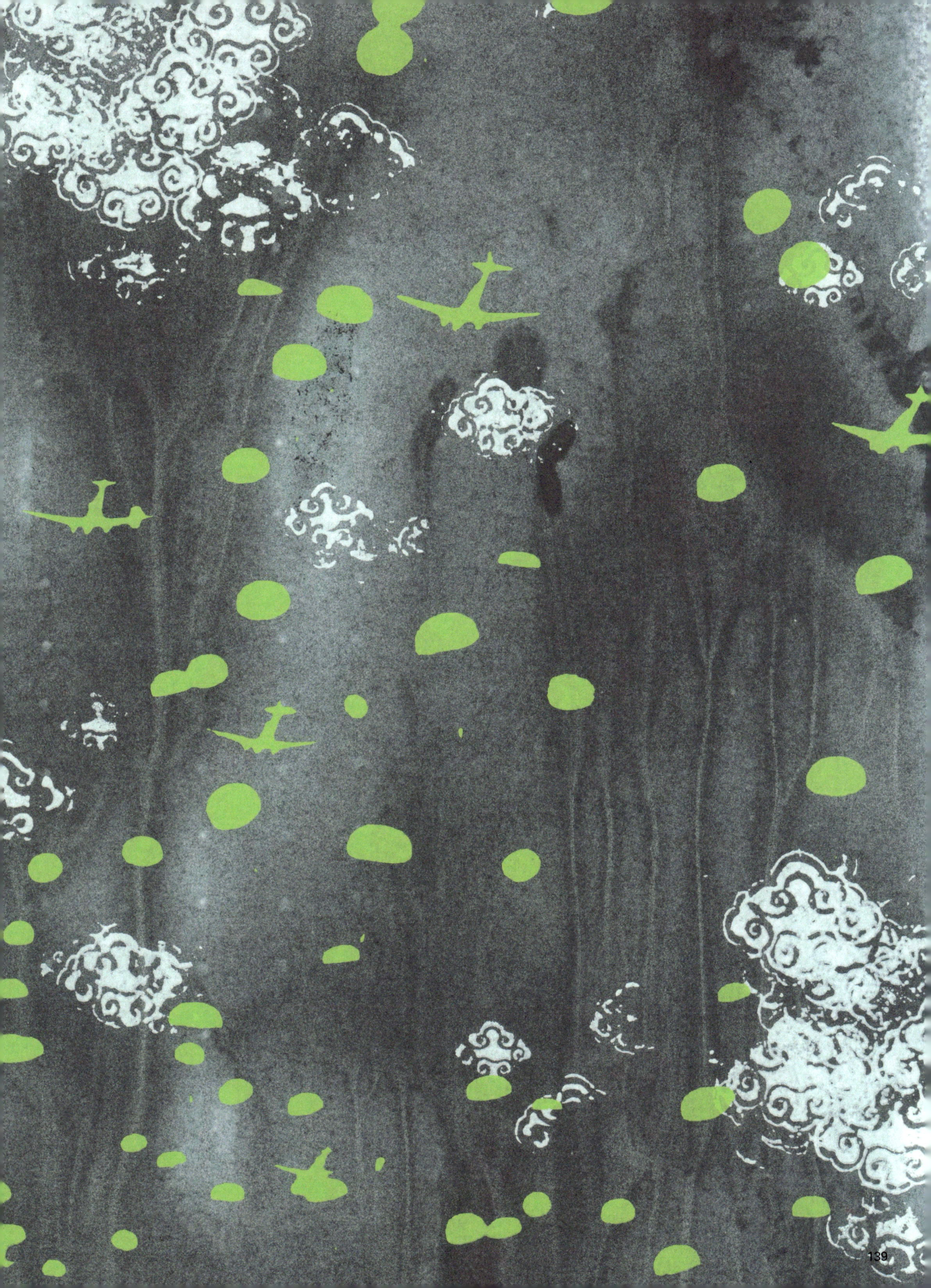

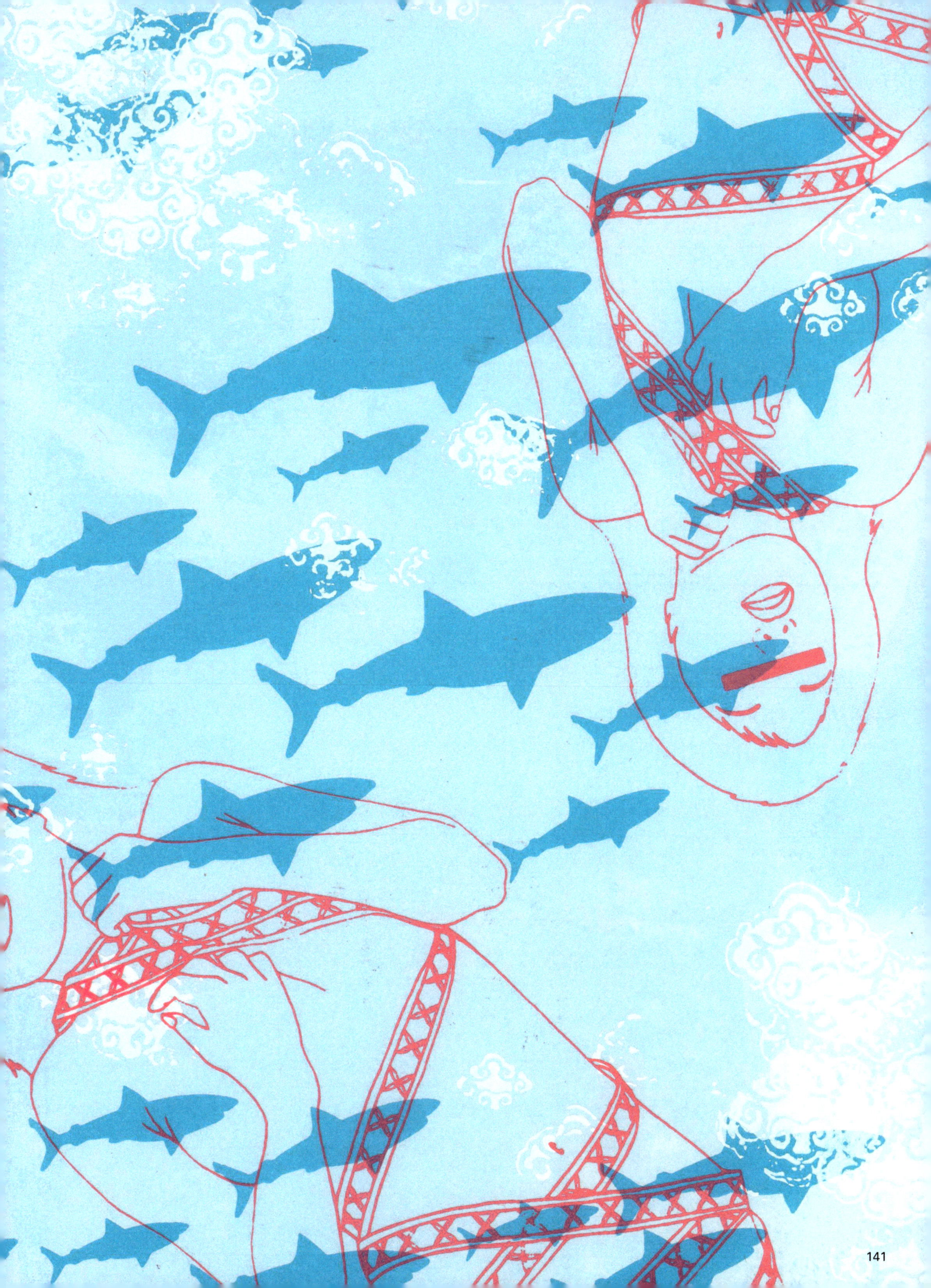

138–141
(preceding pages)

Mr&Mrs

Pylon; Parachute; Pearl Harbour; Shark + Ribbon Girl
08.2005

This series of patterns is composed from varying layers of transfer and computer print, screen-print and drawing. Initially we printed a cherry blossom design onto metallic papers to produce something deliberately beautiful. Because we often use patterns as an initial layer before adding other imagery to form final compositions, these prints felt a bit empty and lacking. We then began to use source material with more content, including maps relating to our family histories and military assault images and diagrams and combined this with sharks, clouds, pylons and other elements. We have tried to create something decorative out of elements not normally used to make patterns.

Who are you? Mr&Mrs: husband and wife team Damion and Katherine McClung-Oakes. *What are your star signs?* Mr: Aries (Tiger) Mrs: Gemini (Dragon). *Where do you come from?* We are from mixed family backgrounds. Mr: English/Welsh/Estonian/Belgian, Mrs: Chinese/ English. But we were both born at Birch Hill hospital in Rochdale, Greater Manchester. *Where in the world are you?* Bury, Greater Manchester. *Where would rather be? What is your favourite city?* Kuala Lumpur for family, food, weather, good vibes, people and being only one hours flight from a tropical island. *What is your work about? Any central themes?* Our work explores issues of acceptability and morality. Continuing themes of sex and war are merged in multiple and decorative layers amongst maps, sharks and historical references. *What is the most interesting book you've read or the most interesting film you've seen in the past year?* 2046 by Wong Kar-Wai, whose films are always beautiful. *What's your favourite title sequence?* Chunking Express (another Wong Kar-Wai film) for its fast camera work, bold and short title text but mostly the soundtrack.

When are you most aware of design? Mr: when travelling I'm really aware of information design such as maps and signs. I can't help but examine and compare the standard of transportation maps everywhere I go. And no matter how many times I fly I'm still fascinated by aeroplane travel, every available space has a designated function. Mrs: when unwrapping onagiri bought from a convenience store in Japan (usually from one of the many Lawsons in Tokyo). The clever design of the wrapper separates the rice from the seaweed, ensuring that awesome first crispy bite! *Is there such a thing as over design?* Not sure. *Does form always follow function?* Not always. *On a scale of 1 to 10 – where 1 is fanatical minimalism and 10 is gilded rococo – where would you place your work? Why?* Somewhere in the middle, we appreciate space but get absorbed in multiple layers. *What is your definition of ornament?* Decoration just for the sake of it.

00
Mr&Mrs

01
Blindfold bombers
2003
Screenprint on fabric

02
Bottoms up
2001
Gloss paint on polyboard

03
Sakura Pattern

04
Geta
2004
Mr&Mrs collaboration with electricity

05
Highway No. 206
2003
Nagasaki screenprint on fabric

06
Prisoners
2003
Screenprint on metallic paper

07
Looking down on Hiroshima
2003
Screenprint on fabric

08
Warning – harmful – misplaced – napalm
2003
Screenprint on paper

Nice Design

Based in London, design and illustration service Nice find inspiration in everything from greasy-spoon interiors to Kinder Eggs and ceramic animals found at car boot sales. With ideas taken from everyday life and some taken out of thin air, Nice aim to inject humour into their image making. Always aiming to try something new, Nice particularly like exploring new ways of applying their designs; whether it is on bespoked interiors, T-shirts, scarves, wallpaper or tiles.

sales@niceness.co.uk
www.niceness.co.uk

Who are you? Matt Duckett & Sofie Eliasson. *What is your star sign?* Badger & Snake carrier. *Where do you come from?* Wales & Sweden. *Where would you rather be?* Canoeing. *What is your favourite city?* Bangla City. *What's your background (training, education, other)?* Chemistry teacher & hairdresser. *What is your work about? Any central themes?* No themes but we try to avoid skulls, guns & deer. *What medium(s) do you work with?* We like screen-printing but our dream is to work with Paul McKenna. *What would you say are your influences? And main sources of inspiration?* Clip art. *What kind of work do you really like? What turns you on as an artist?* Everything from fashion & interiors to Arnold Schwarzenegger films. *What is the most interesting book you've read in the past year?* Clip Art Heaven Vol 2, great visuals. *When are you most aware of design?* In the spring. *What is your definition of ornament?* Gold. *Wallpaper or paint?* No comment. *Who would you never, under any circumstances, do work for?* Each other. *Computers, more or less?* Less is more. *If money and time were no object what would your ideal project be?* Design a castle.

**144–145
(following pages)**

Hybrid wallpaper collection
01.2005

The Hybrid wallpaper range is a self-initiated project which consists of four designs: Mammals, Insects, Sea Creatures and Reptiles. The collection looks to push the concept of wallpaper by making the consumer part of the design process as it allows for a number of unique patterns to be created using one or a combination of the four designs.

00a
Matt Duckett

00b
Sofie Eliasson

01
Amazing (detail)

02
Apple lungs

03
Bonsai tree

04
Line lady

05
Mechanica (detail)

06
Nice logo

07
Ribbon head (detail)

Hybrid wallpaper collection
Nice Design

145

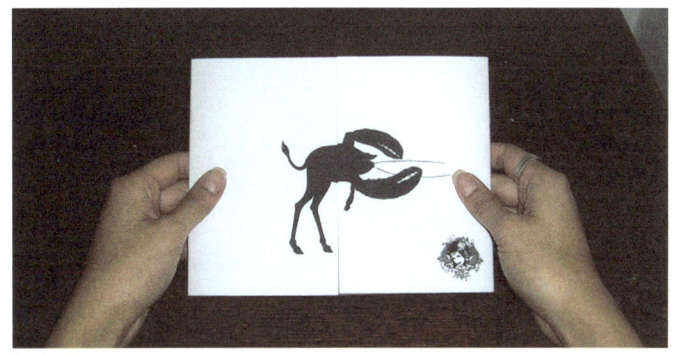

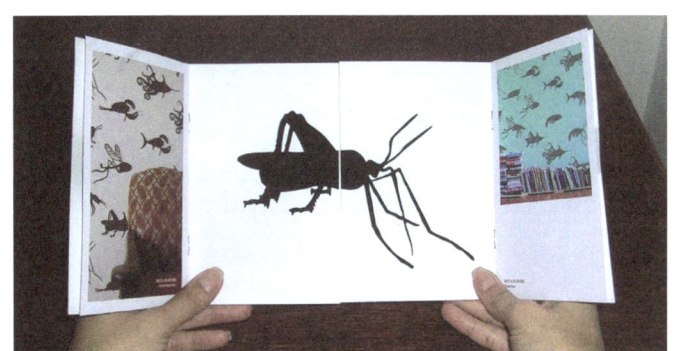

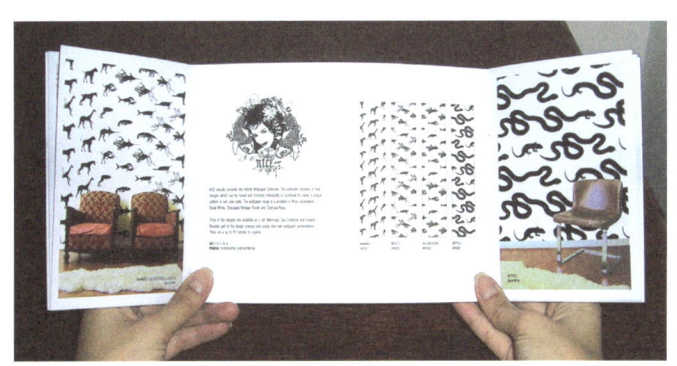

Ballerina, Marine, Gypsy, Surrealism
Linn Olofsdotter

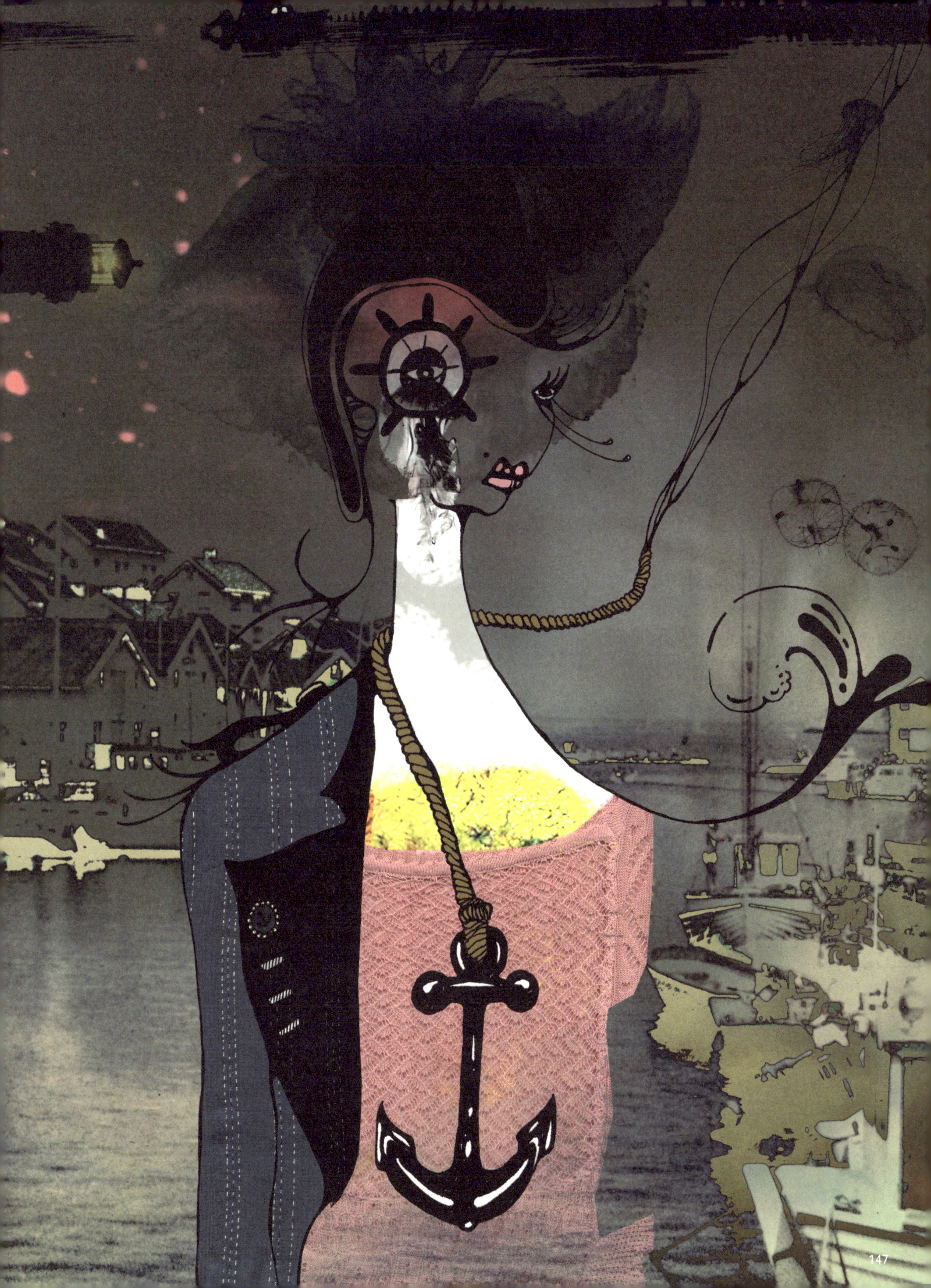

148

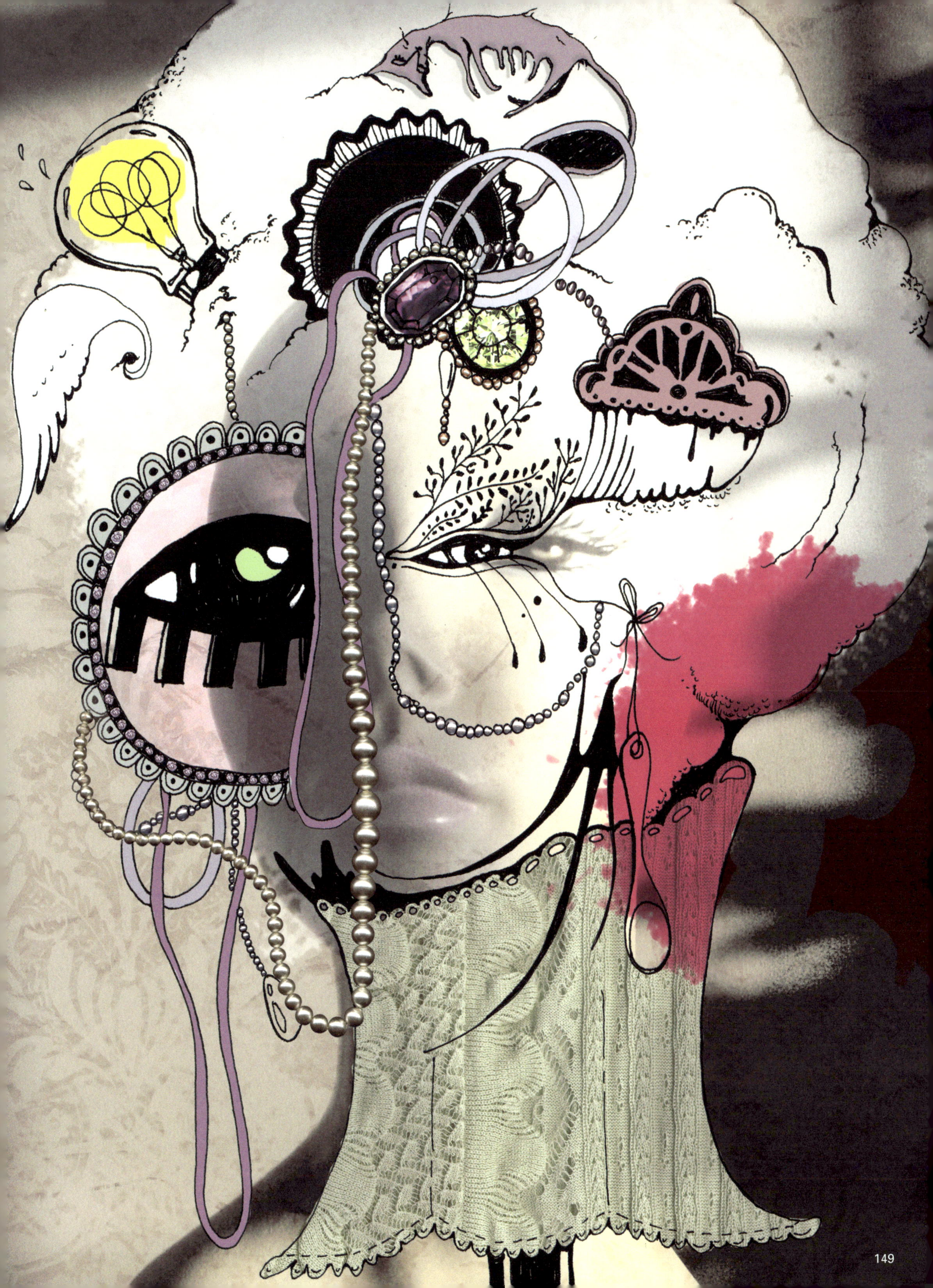

148–151
(preceding pages)

Linn Olofsdotter

Ballerina, Marine, Gypsy, Surrealism
01–05.2005
The four images I made for Bon Magazine are a product of me working with the great editor-in-chief Salka Hallström Bornold. I tried not to think so much about the fashion but about which associations I made with the different themes. Therefore the images turned out a little dreamlike, disconnected, which I like. The teeth were more about fear of going to the dentist, not for me but for others. The 44 Boards project is a project where 44 designers / artists received a blank skateboard deck to use as their canvas. They will be auctioned and the proceeds will go to the Human Rights Campaign. I burned my illustration into the board so it will be a bit more permanent if it actually gets used. It's about life and death.

Designer / illustrator Linn Olofsdotter didn't begin illustrating until fairly recently. After studying graphic design and advertising at various locations around the world she followed her heart and moved to Rio de Janeiro together with her husband Nando Costa. In Rio they launched Nakd.tv, a motion graphics company, working with clients such as MTV, Fine Living Network, The Anime Network, and Country Music Television among others. Her intriguing illustrations have been used in fashion catalogues, bottle labels, posters, record covers, music videos, tattoos and have also been showcased in various books, magazines and exhibits at various locations world wide.

Currently Linn is an art director at respected advertising agency *Modernista!* of Boston. There she is helping her husband Nando set up the agency's multimedia department as well as working on selected broadcast and print projects.

linn@olofsdotter.com
www.olofsdotter.com

Was there a defining moment when you decided to become a visual artist? When an extremely grumpy 80-year-old woman complimented me on the sign on my door. *What is your work about? Any central themes?* No central themes. I like drawing women and nature though. *What medium(s) do you work with?* Ink on paper, colour pencils, any texture that can fit onto my scanner. I colour my images digitally. *What would you say are your influences? And main sources of inspiration?* Inspiration can come from everything. Sometimes it's my nightmares and sometimes a beautiful tree I pass on my way home. *What's your favourite book cover?* I don't have a favourite but in general I think the pocket book covers in Sweden are often very nicely designed. *On a scale of 1 to 10 – where 1 is fanatical minimalism and 10 is gilded rococo – where would you place your work? Why?* 6. I like decorating. Sometimes I feel like an image is finished but then I start decorating and it's just so much fun. *What is your definition of ornament?* Sparkles and swirls. *Wallpaper or paint?* Silk. *Computers, more or less?* In moderation.

00
Linn Olofsdotter

01
Relationships
Chapter break for *Violet* magazine
via *Modernista!*

02
Predator
Self-portrait for exhibition in Singapore
by Design Taxi

[03–08]
Illustrations for *Bon* magazine on upcoming
fashion trends

03
Beatnik

04
Edwardian

05
20s

06
Ancien-couture

07
Vixen

08
Auf dem bahnhof

Tal Rosner

Tal Rosner (b. 1978, Jerusalem) is an experimental filmmaker, director, and graphic designer. He was educated at Bezalel Academy of Art and Design, Jerusalem (1999–2003), and received an MA from Central Saint Martins College of Art and Design, London (2003–2005). His most recent film, *Doppelgänger,* has been screened in various moving image festivals, including the Onedotzero festival at the ICA, London in May 2005, the Brighton Festival Fringe ('Final cut' experimental film screening), and the 2005 Design Prima Expo, London. He has worked as an independent graphic designer in Los Angeles and as a graphic designer in a post-production studio for Israeli network television. His graphic work appeared in the summer 2004 issue of *Graphic* magazine (Graphic 05). *Doppelgänger* was recently chosen from among a select group of finalists in the forthcoming Global Student Animation Awards (Stash DVD magazine) for a screening at the Hype Festival, Los Angeles.

tal.rosner@gmail.com
www.cubic-ds.co.uk

Was there a defining moment when you decided to become a visual artist? Getting a set of calligraphic pens for my 10th birthday. *What medium(s) do you work with?* Video, photomontage, computer graphics. *What would you say are your influences? And main sources of inspiration?* Sergei Eisenstein, Dziga Vertov (*The Man with a Movie Camera*), François Truffaut (*Fahrenheit 451*), Peter Saville, Stuart Bailey, Julian House. *What's your favourite book cover?* The Penguin crime series (1961-64, design Romek Marber). *What's your favourite title sequence?* *Six Feet Under* (TV), *Gattaca* (film). *When are you most aware of design?* The way people dress. *Is there such a thing as over design?* No. **On a scale of 1 to 10 – where 1 is fanatical minimalism and 10 is gilded rococo – where would you place your work? Why?** 3, but sometimes 7. *What is your definition of ornament?* Something pretty and complex simultaneously. *What would you rather have: More of... Less of...* More hard drives. Less bread. *If money and time were no object what would your ideal project be? What would you most rather do?* Run a houmous deli in Covent Garden.

152–153
(following pages)

Doppelgänger
01.2005
A daydream travel between real and imaginary, steel and concrete, clouds and smoke. The project is a sketchbook-in-motion, which explores the process of personalizing public spaces by 'de-' and 're-' constructing them using screen-based grid systems and various editing techniques.

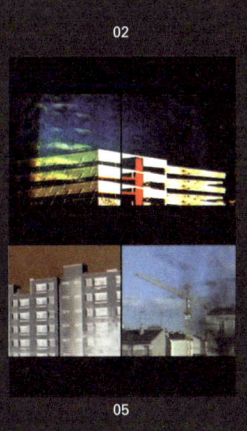

00
Tal Rosner

01
the slow drug

02
teli 2

03
someone is watching me behind the telescreen

04
Easy pieces III galop

05
Concerto for two pianos

06
Old Street

07
The Erpingham Camp

08
Brockwell Park

152 *Doppelgänger*
Tal Rosner

153

154 *Various work*
Studio Job

This spread
Viking
2004
The Central Museum invited us to design an exhibition on the Vikings (800–1200 AD). The space was about 1,300m² divided into 9 spaces. For each room we designed (huge) patterns and drawingswhich were printed out on canvas and installed in the museum like gigantic paintings. Every room had a theme, from monastery to slaughterhouse.

Following spread
Insect pattern
Our idea was to let the world get overgrown with insects. So we designed a copyright-free pattern to be used by anyone who likes it. It was launched as a fashion pattern for Viktor & Rolf (women 2004–2005), and then used for tiles, books, lamps, bags, a facade, stickers, fabrics and even as graphics on trucks. Every day people mail us to get it for private use, like homemade lamps etc. It went from 'haute couture' to 'industrial purpose' in 6 months…

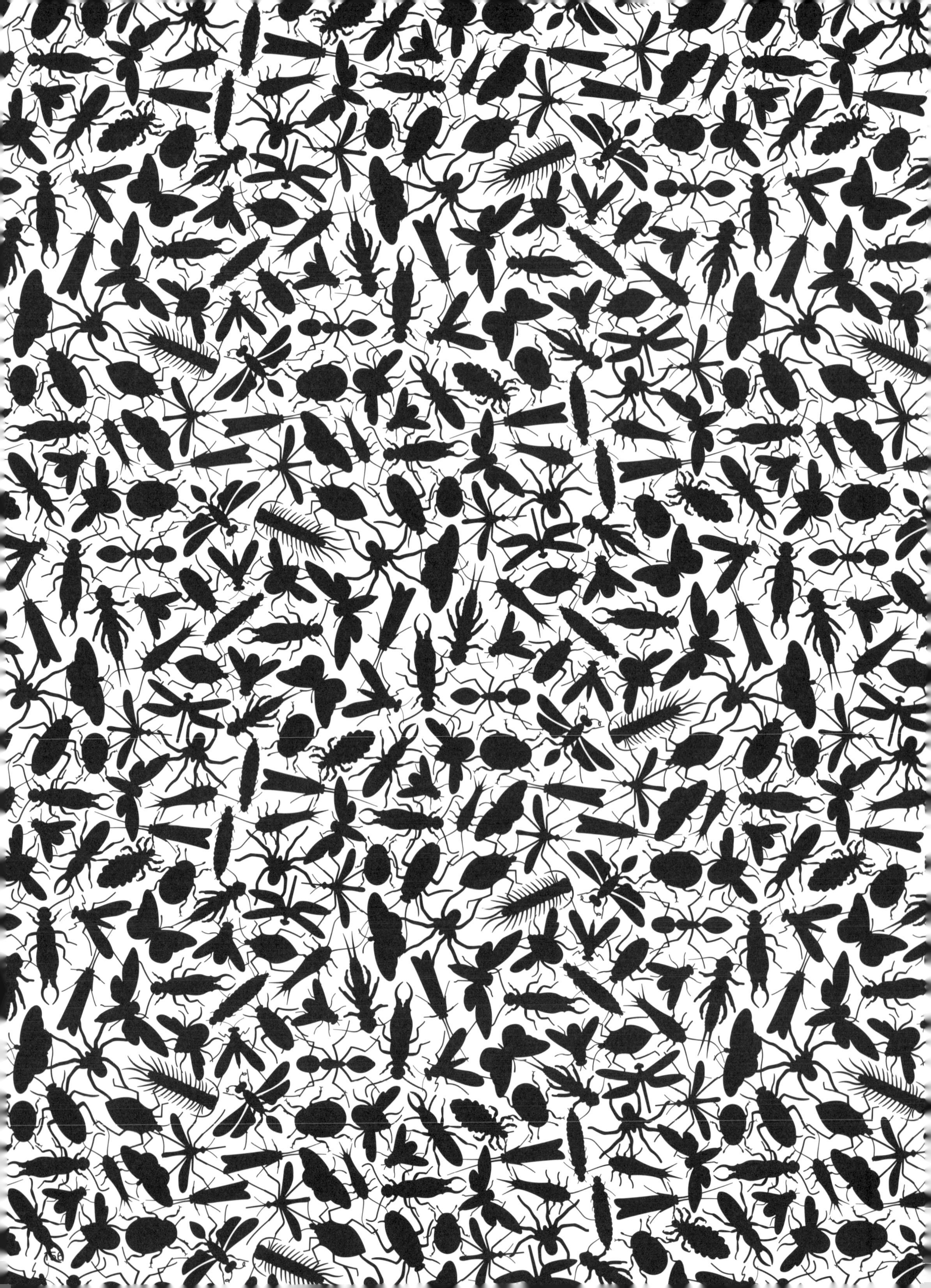

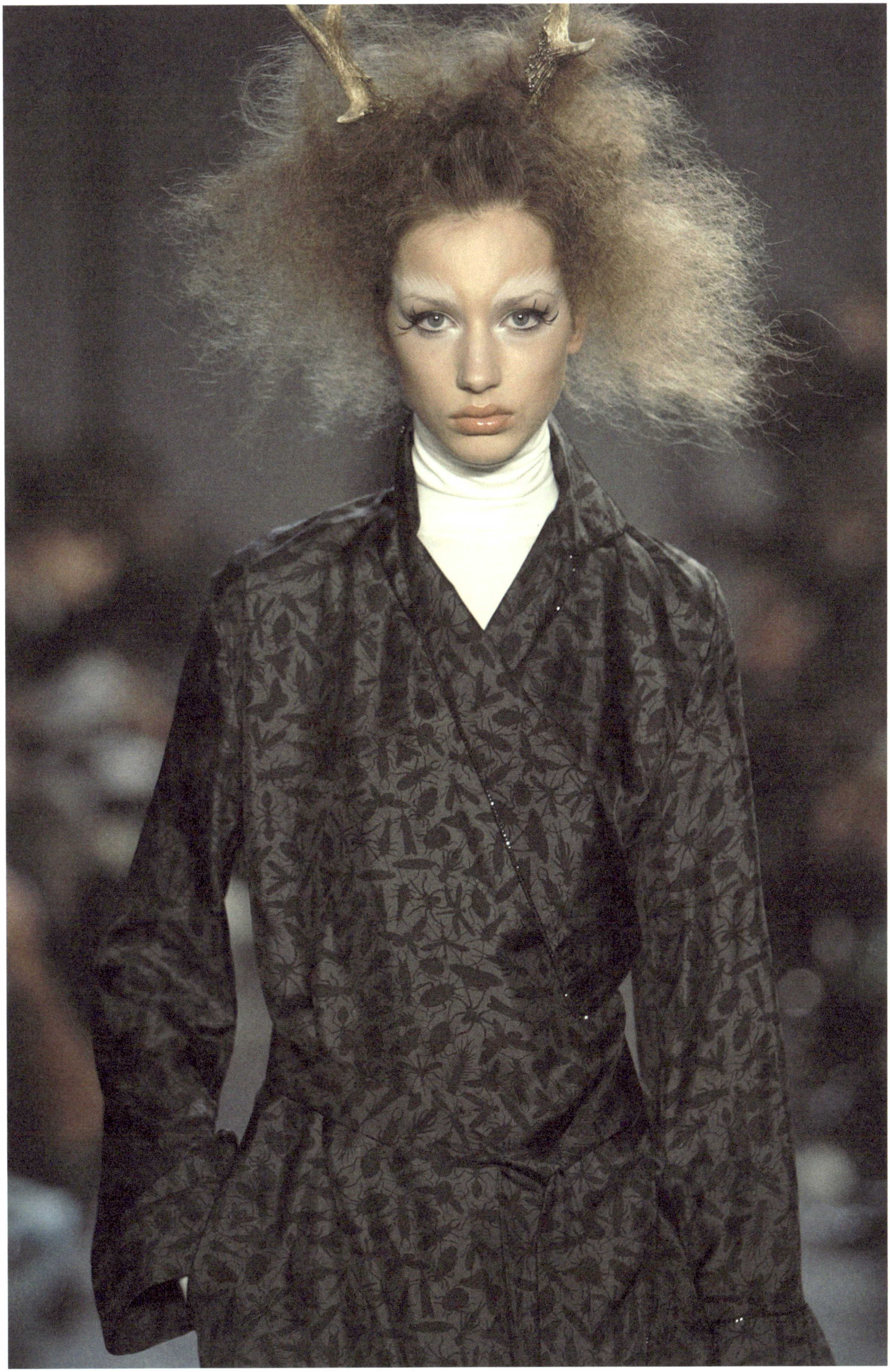

Charm Chandelier
2003
We designed a 'masterpiece' for Swarovski. The chandelier is about 3 metres high and weighs about 800kg. It was published in the New York Times as one of the most expensive design pieces (more than $450,000). It is inlaid by hand with 2,000,000 Swarovski crystals. You can see hundreds of sillouettes making a mishmash of machines and animals. It's in the collection of Swarovski London.
Now we have designed a Mini-Charm for them which will be more within reach for for people's homes. This one is only 5kg and is deliverable with or without electric lights. The different coloured beads are hotfixed on a golden frame. In the Mini-Charm we play 'good citizens'.

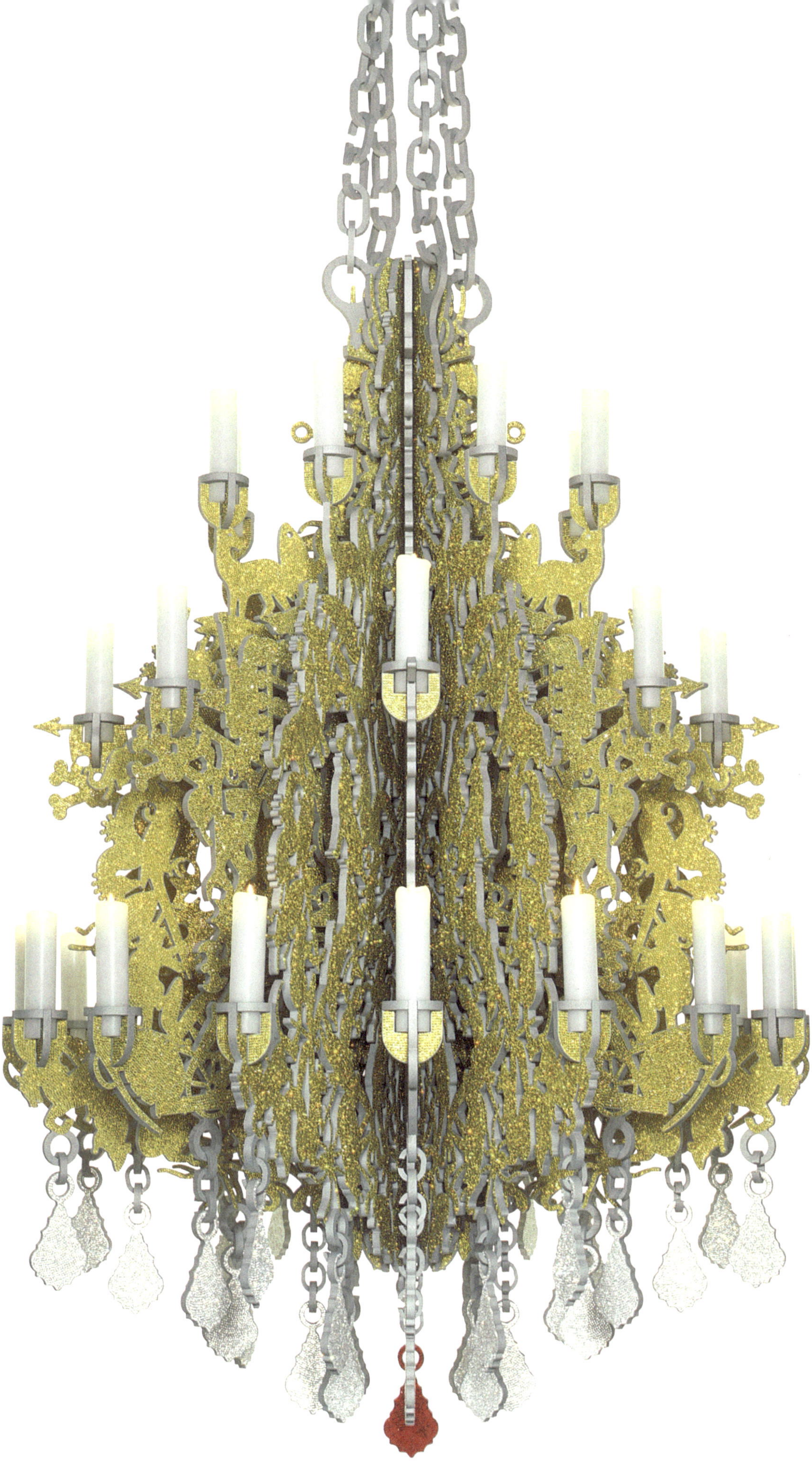

This spread
Circus pattern
2004
Fool and Princess was the invitation for an installation in a contemporary gallery in Rotterdam, the Netherlands. Part of the installation is 'circus': on a printed canvas you can see us performing as entertainers / acrobats. The structure of the design is based on a classical grid used for wallpaper.

Following spread
Machine
Patterns composed out of machine parts, flowers, and other industrial archetypical forms and parts. Project Alabama used them for their womenswear collection, bags and accessories.

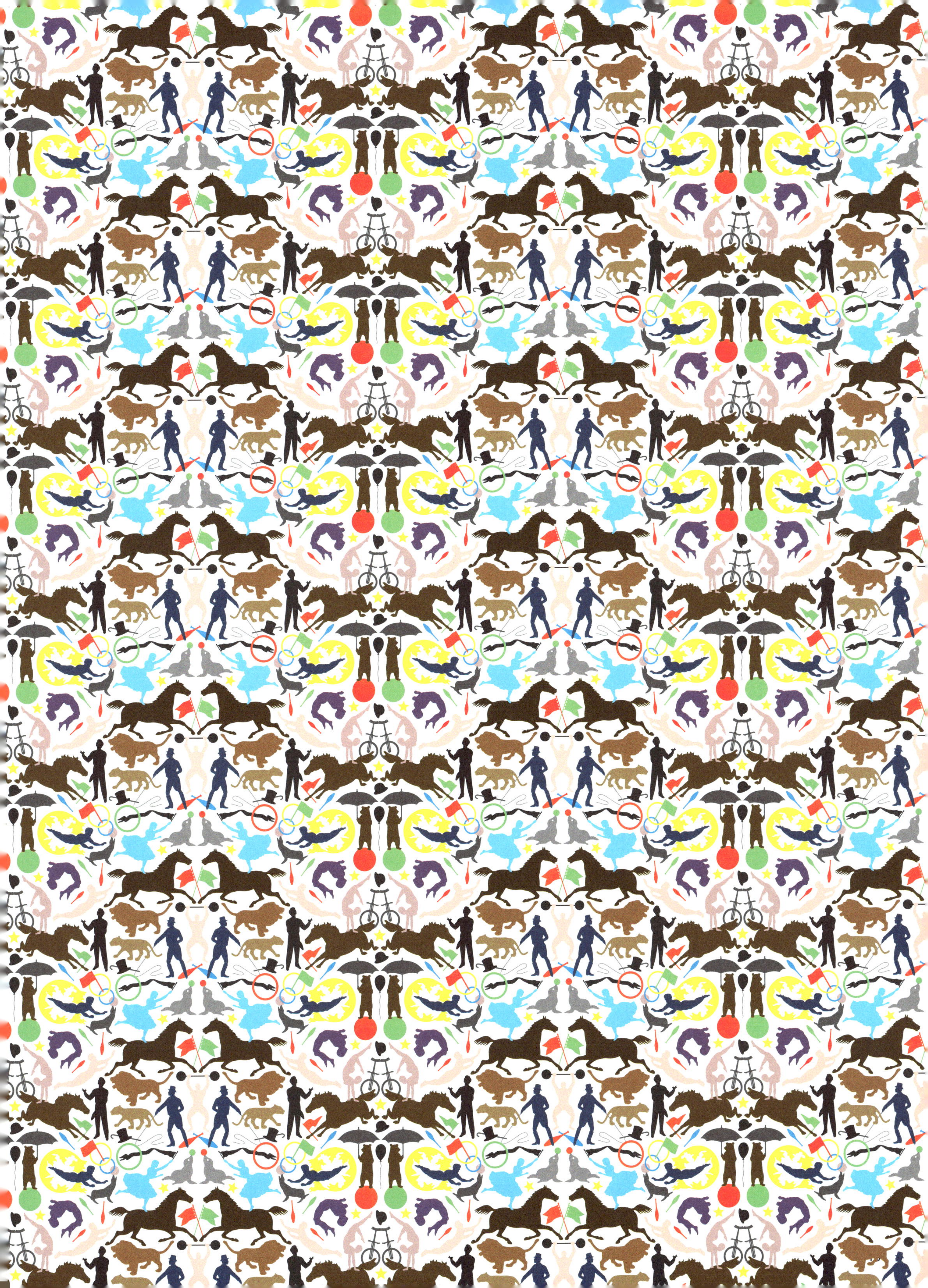

163

154–163
(preceding pages)

Studio Job

Various works
See captions for description of work

Studio Job (Job Smeets and Nynke Tynagel) is known for its rebellious, scale-less way of creating an own universe. The objects are often based on personal fascinations varying from unique pieces, editions, installations, interiors and assignments for public space. The way Studio Job is walking a tightrope between design and art gives the work an autonomous position in international design. More than once Studio Job created a fresh discussion within on the existing norms of the contemporary field.
Drs. S A van Zijpp, curator of contemporary art, Groninger Museum 2004

www.studiojob.be

Was there a defining moment when you decided to become a visual artist? Somewhere in puberty. *What is your work about? Any central themes?* Anything is a possible theme: so, you have to be your own curator and pick out the right theme at the right time. *Do you make a distinction between commercial and non-commercial work?* As little as possible, but working with a client is a collaboration. *When are you most aware of design?* It's love and hate… always around but never welcome. *Is there such a thing as over design?* Don't know, but there is 'bad taste'. *Does form always follow function?* Of course not! *On a scale of 1 to 10 – where 1 is fanatical minimalism and 10 is gilded rococo – where would you place your work? Why?* All levels. We do not want to exclude anything. *What is your definition of ornament?* A definition 'narrows'. *Computers, more or less?* As many as needed. *What would you rather have: More of… Less of…* A little bit of this and a little bit of that. *If money and time were no object what would your ideal project be? What would you most rather do?* Maybe just the same…

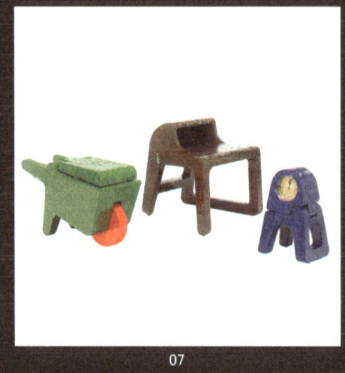

00
Studio Job

01
Rock chair mould

02
Centrepiece

03
Charm chain

04
Containers

05
Craft

06
Elements 2000

07
Elements 2001

08
Excavator

Timorous Beasties

Timorous Beasties is a design-led manufacturing company based in Glasgow, specialising in Fabrics and Wallpapers. Timorous Beasties was started by Alistair McAuley and Paul Simmons, who met at Glasgow School of Art in the mid-eighties. Paul Simmons went on to study at the Royal College of Art, whilst Alistair McAuley finished a post graduate at the GSA and started their first studio in Glasgow; the duo were finally established in 1990.

Their early work has been described as 'William Morris on acid', and could be seen as a wayward take on the often 'twee' world of textiles, with heavily illustrative insects, triffid-like plants and large-scale fish swirl in intricate patterns and repeats that adorn rich and heavy fabrics. Their more recent work is as graphic and modern as it is varied, with designs ranging from target and arrow motifs to large 3-D damasks.

Timorous Beasties studio mixes design and production under one roof, allowing them a free reign to create their unique style.

info@timorousbeasties.com
timorousbeasties.com

What is your work about? Any central themes? Beauty, surprise, irony. *What kind of work do you really like? What turns you on as an artist?* We're designers but anything that's good, different, radical, and funny. *Can you describe the work(s) you've sent to us?* The way textile design should be. *In what context was it or were they produced?* Pressured. *Do you work from a studio? Home? Other?* Studio, and from home when it's late. *Do you manage to make a living out of your artwork?* Yes, and for others. *When are you most aware of design?* In the morning. *Does form always follow function?* Depends on the function; it was the decorative architect Louis Sullivan who was supposed to have coined the phrase, and not Mies van der Rohe (although it probably dates way back to ancient history). Louis Sullivan meant it to mean: if the building is majestic, like a palace or bank, then the form can be decorative, because it still fits its function (although simplicity can be grand too). Mies van der Rohe used a cladding on his most important building, the Siegram, and technically one could say he used decoration… so in a sense everybody sort of got the meaning a bit wrong, but to answer the question – yes!

166–169 (following pages)

Glasgow Toile and other works
09.2004

Glasgow Toile is a take on the 18th century fabrics produced in France in the town of Jouey. Toiles often depict idealistic rural scenes of children playing, sheep being led by their shepherdesses, lovers on swings. We simply replaced these romanticised scenes with scenes of urban chaos, so an old man sitting on a stool with a glass of wine was replaced by a tramp drinking super lager on a park bench in Glasgow's Kelvingrove Park. The fabric is designed and printed like an old toile, so that from a distance the fabric looks like traditional fabric, but on closer inspection becomes something quite different.

00
Paul Simmons, Alistair McAuley

01
Blue on blue deft bomber fabric

02
Dovecamo wallpaper

03
Pheasant and pineapple

04
Lobster wallpaper border

05
Oriental orchid red wallpaper

06
Tank rose wallpaper

07
Velvet eel velvet fabric

08
Velvet fish velvet fabric

166 *Glasgow Toile*
Timorous Beasties

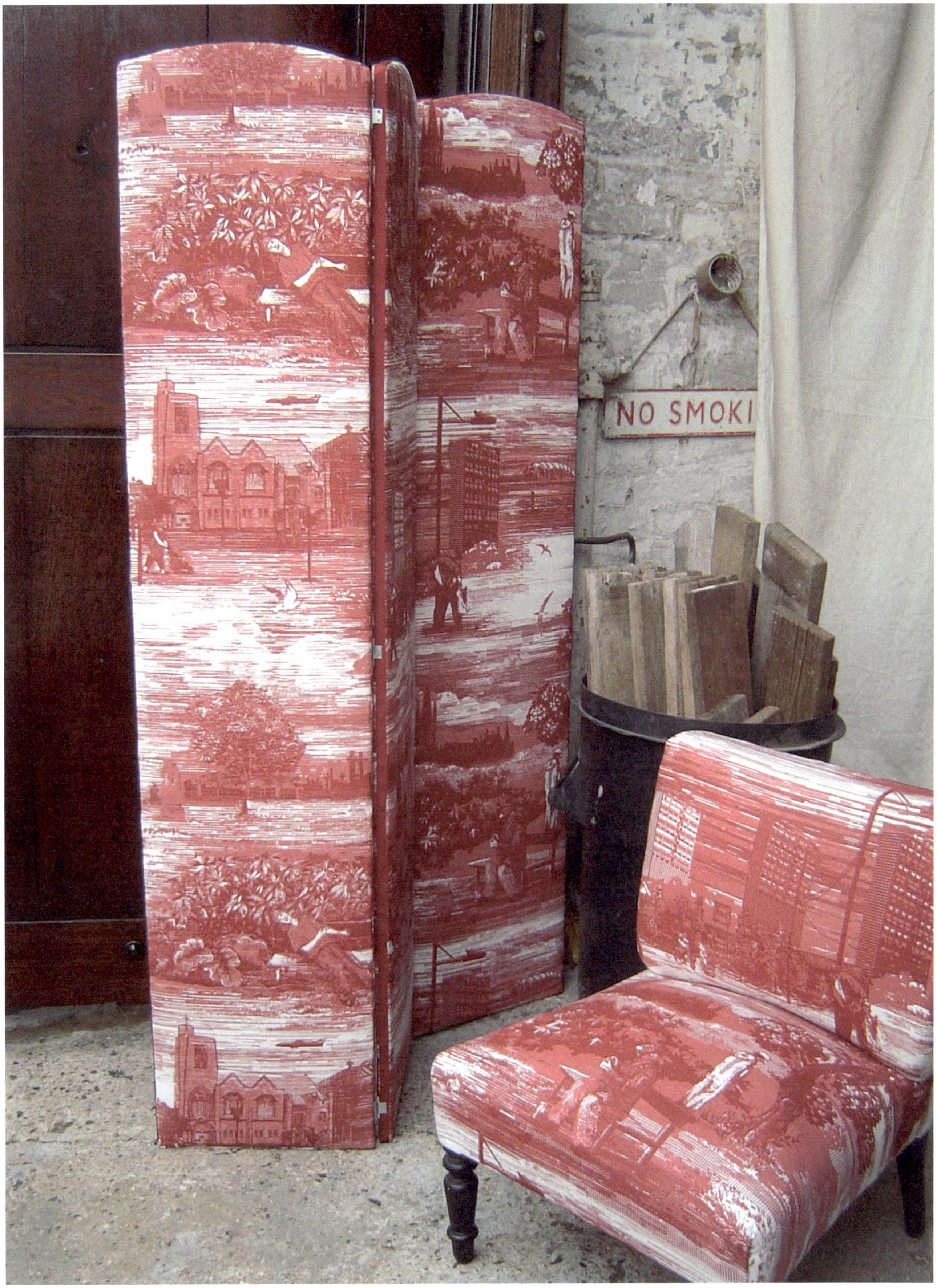
NO SMOKI

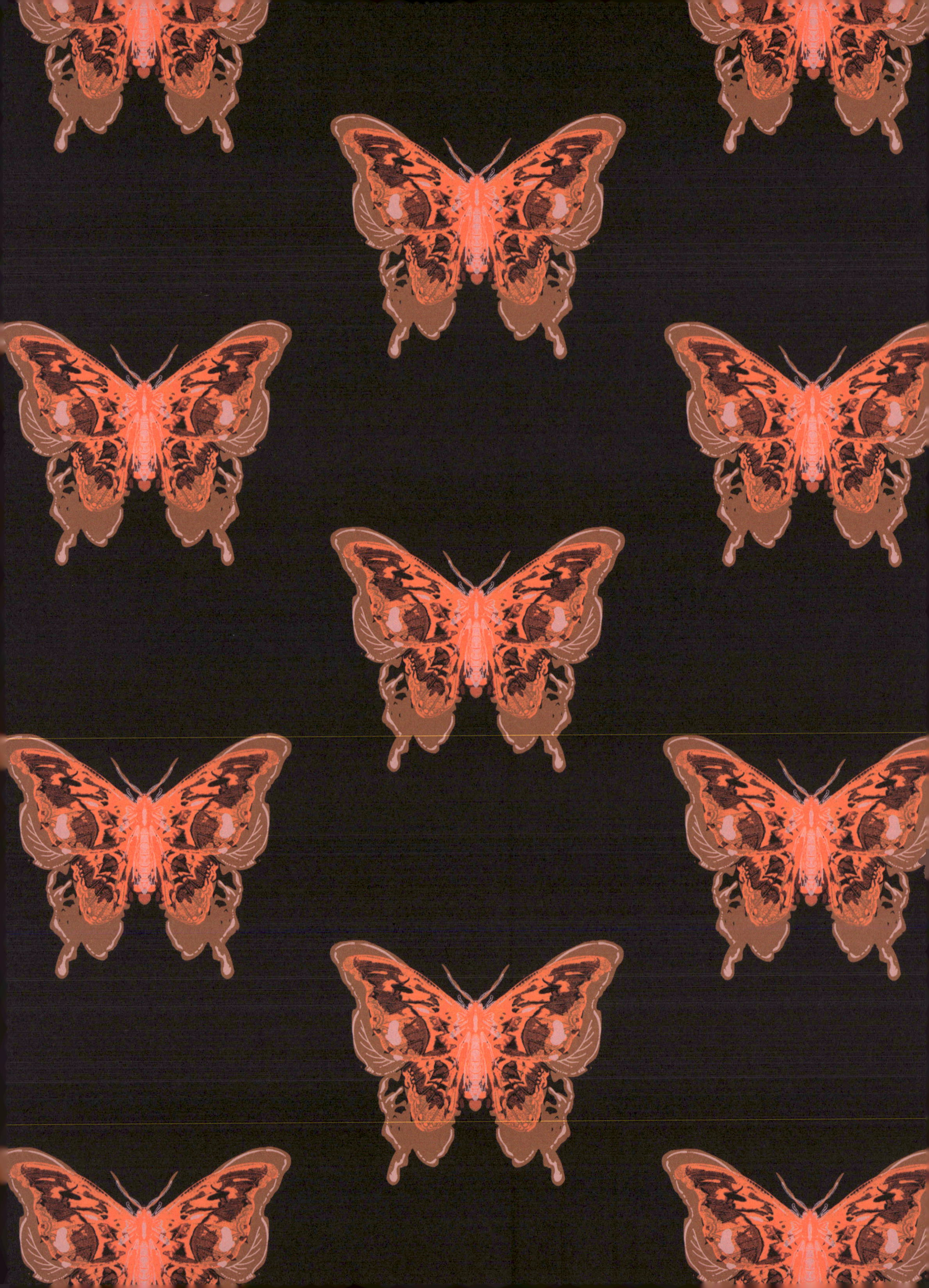

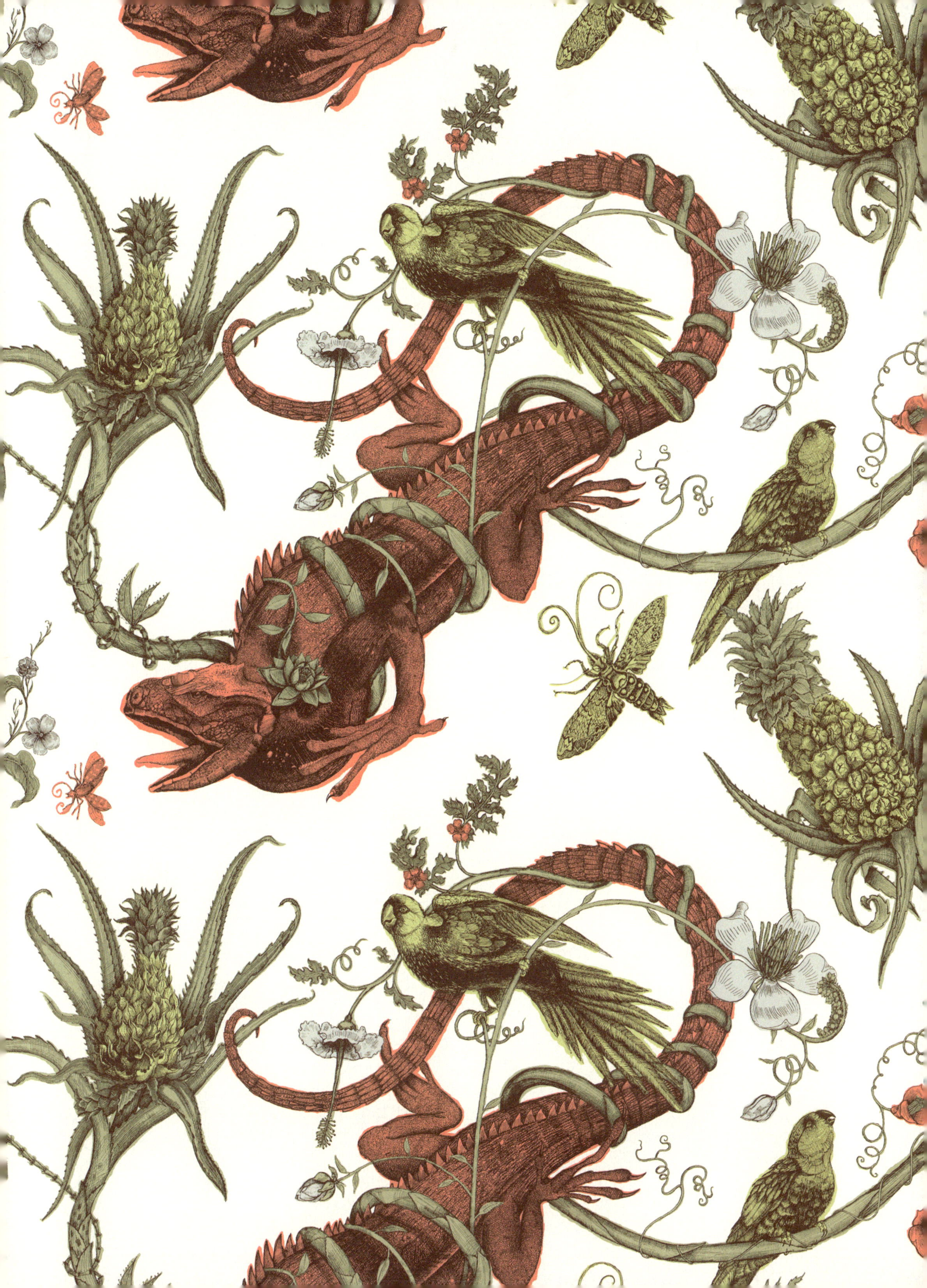

Various works
Liselotte Watkins

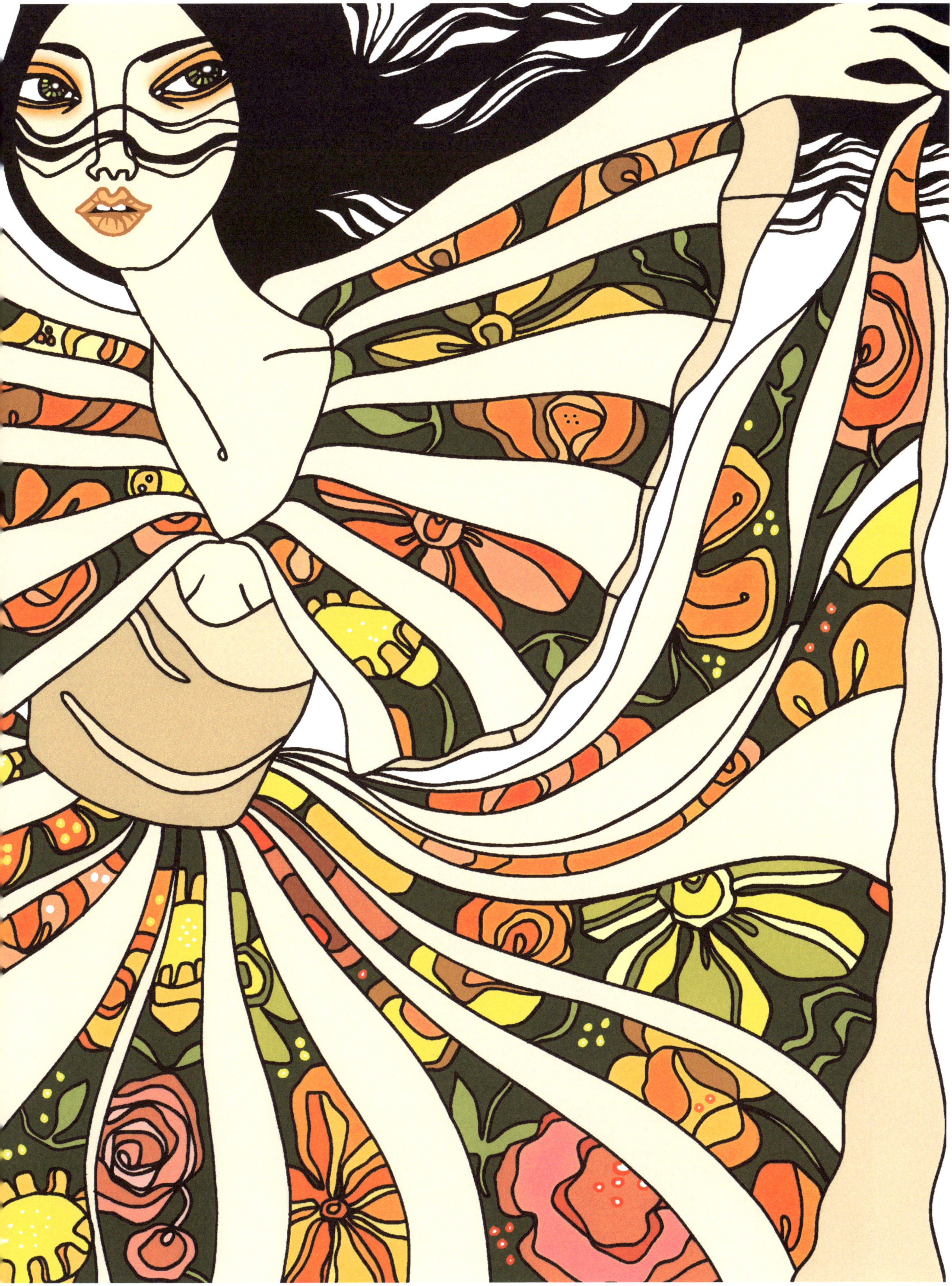

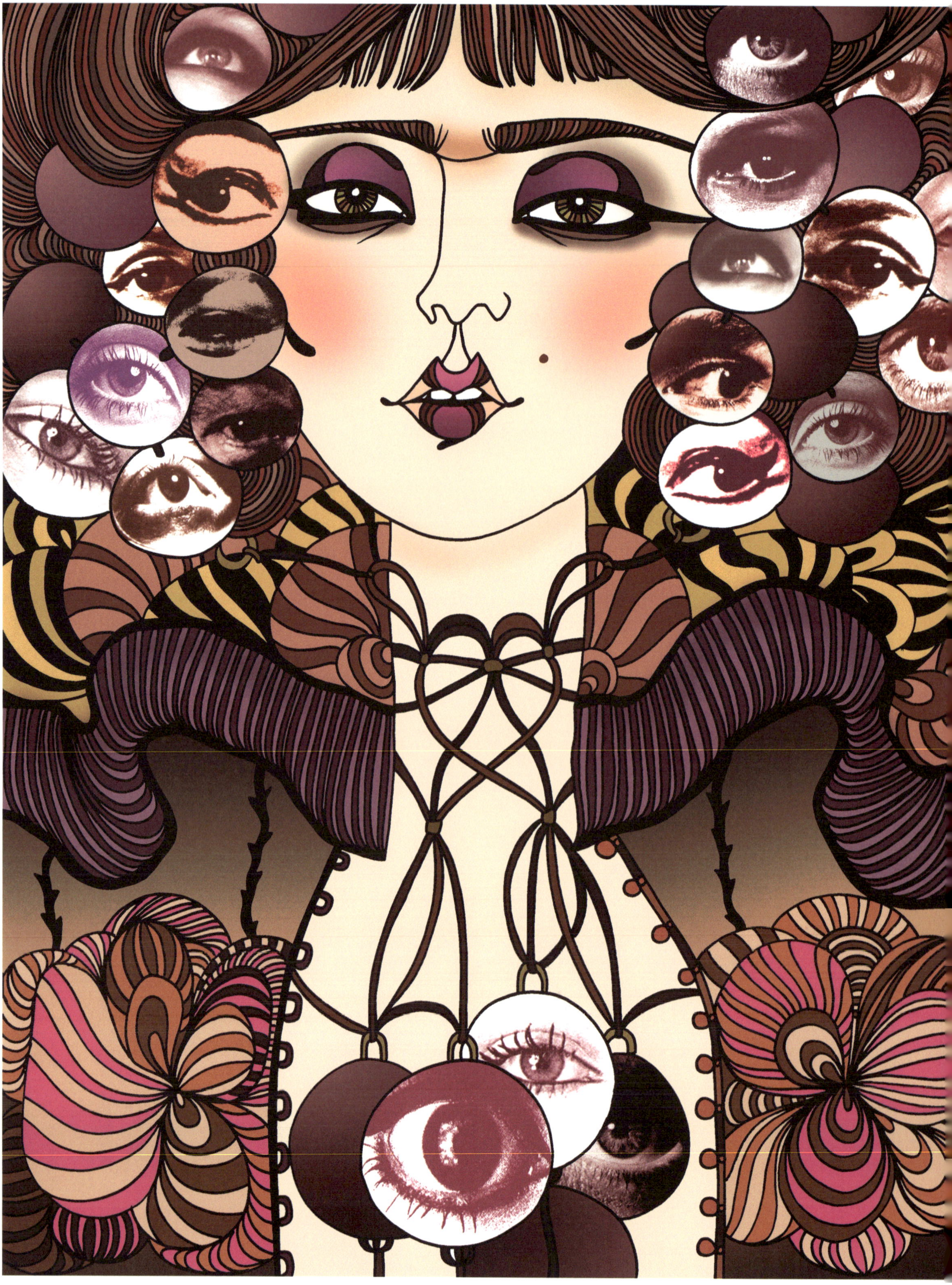

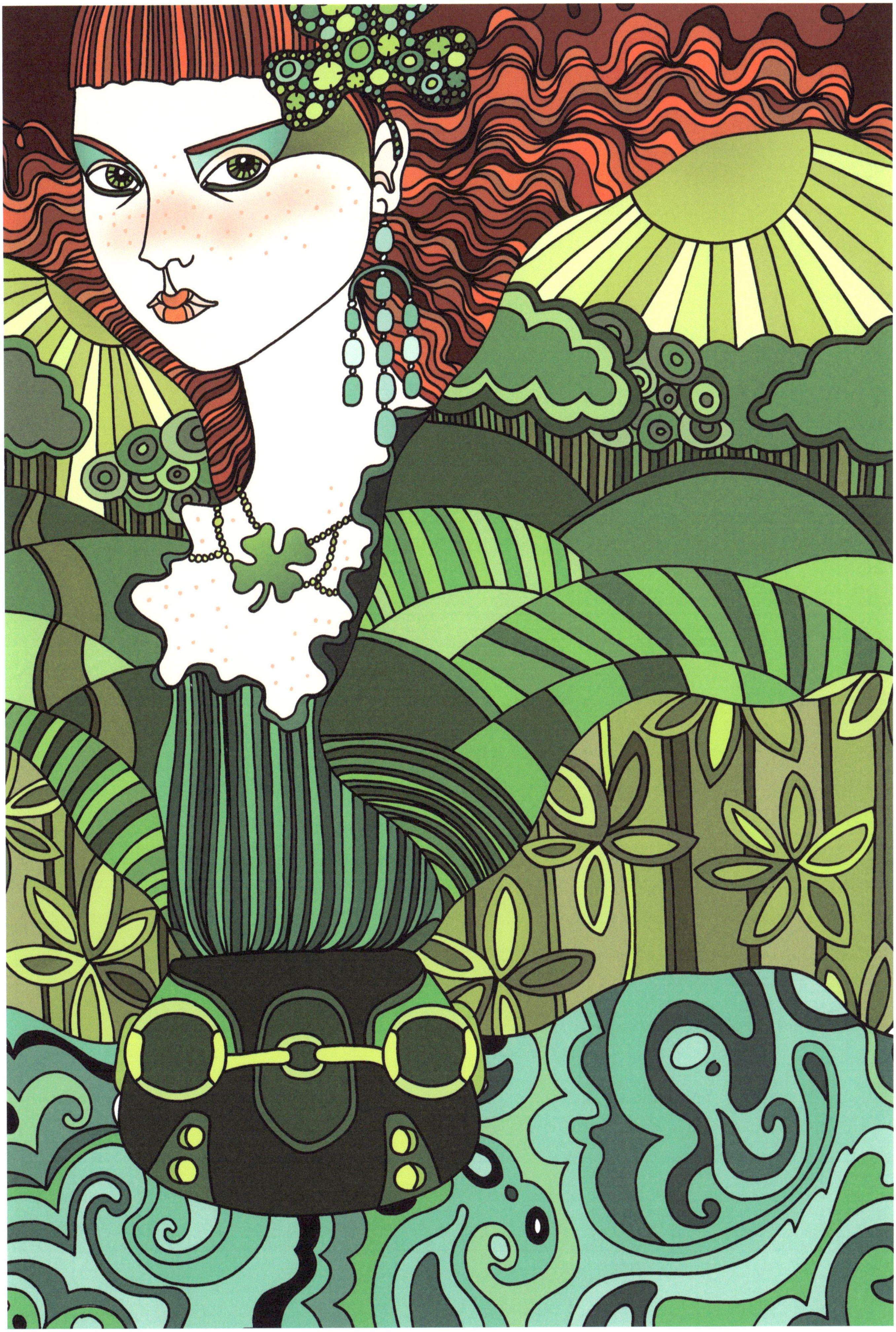

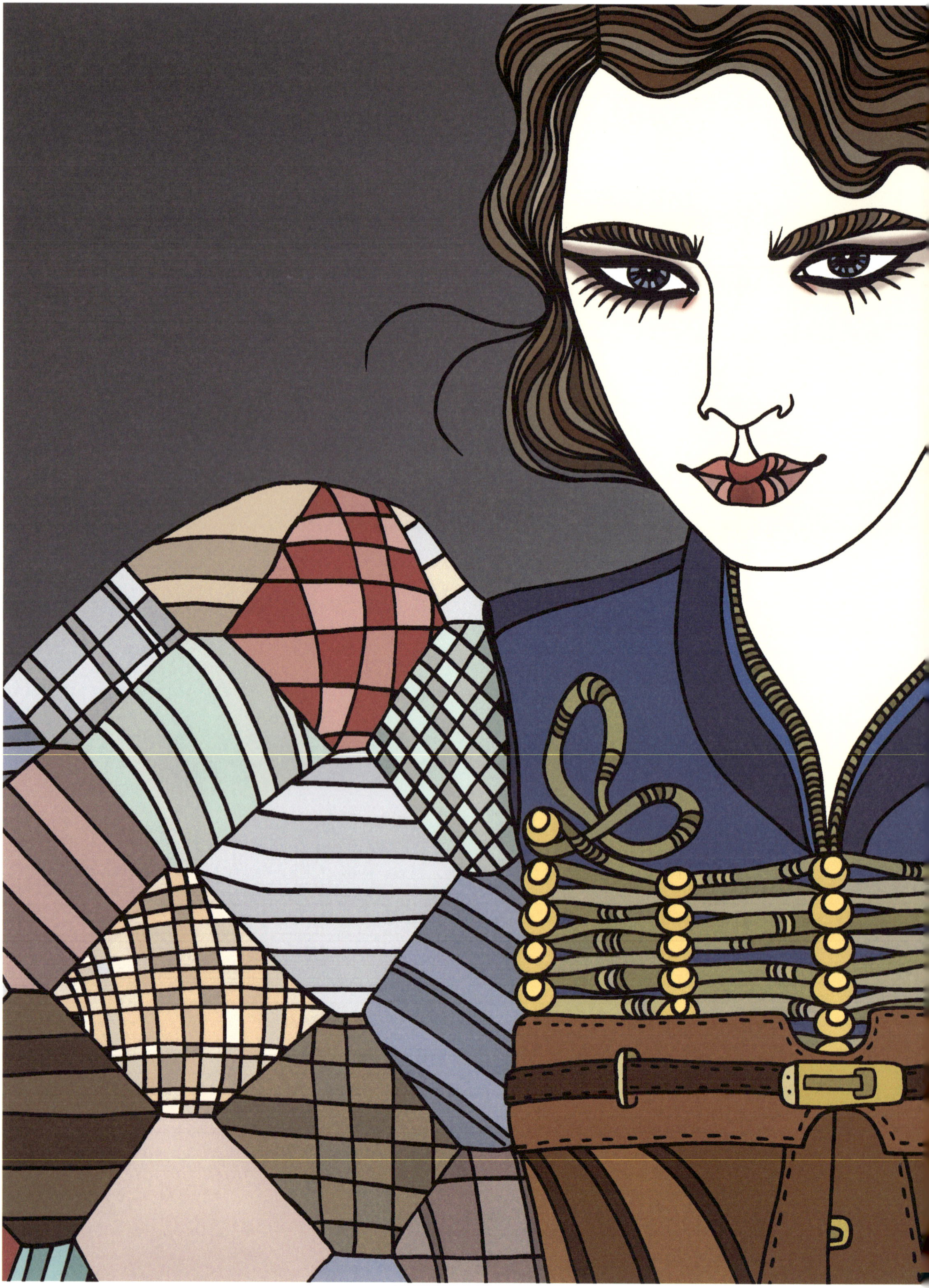

175

170–175
(preceding pages)

Liselotte Watkins

Tigergirl
Started out as a personal unpublished piece but the leopard later starred in the *Warm Night* video

Swe-Elle
Image used for trend forecast. The dress is by Viktor & Rolf

Le Book
Commissioned by Le Book but never used

Squint – Ireland, England
Work done for German magazine Squint. Free assignment on the theme 'Landscape'. I chose to do a story called 'Odyssey' together with a stylist friend. A travel around the world in couture

Born in the countryside of Sweden, 1971. Grew tired of cows and pine trees and moved to Texas at the age of 17. Went to high school for a year and after that the Art Institute of Dallas. Tried to go back to Stockholm and work but no-one was very impressed with the Southern education, so moved to the Big Apple and the YMCA in Chelsea. Got lucky and knew someone who knew someone at the in-house agency for Barneys New York. Started making cosmetic ads for them every Sunday in the Style section of the New York Times. That lasted for 4 years and in that time also managed to have 2 agents and own apartment. Fell in love with a Swede and moved back home after 5 years in NY. People in Stockholm were more impressed this time after working with clients such as Sony, Anna Sui, Vogue UK, MAC Cosmetics, Bergdorf Goodman, Amica, etc. Still spend at least four months out of the year in NY. Not liking Stockholm very much but it's quiet and good for working morale!

liselotte.watkins@chello.se

Was there a defining moment when you decided to become a visual artist? When I was a little girl in the Swedish countryside and I watched Flashdance, and then started reading Italian Vogue because she did in the movie. I also learnt how to weld but drawing girls from Vogue was more my thing. *What would you say are your influences? And main sources of inspiration?* Except for my friends, I am very inspired by the aesthetics of the 70s, biographies about people like Cecil Beaton, Diana Vreeland and Marchesa Casati, photographers like Scavullo and Ron Gaella, Movies like *Gray Gardens, Darling* and *The Cockettes*. Music like The Concretes, Amadou & Mariam, Talking Heads, Anthony and the Johnsons and CocoRosie. Going to the flea market on 13th street and AveA and Beacons Closet in Brooklyn and much, much more. *What kind of work do you really like? What turns you on as an artist?* Yves Saint Laurent, John Currin, Wes Anderson, Ines van Lamsweerde, Dave Eggers, and all the people mentioned above. *What would you rather have: More of… Less of…* More quality, less quantity.

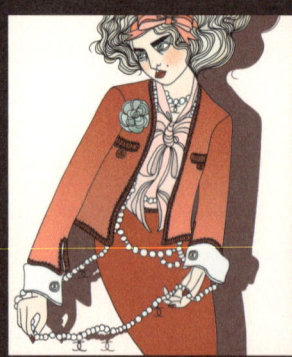

00
Liselotte Watkins

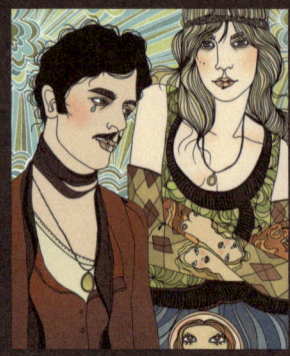

Anja & Mattias
Atomica Magazine

Army Girl
Atomica Magazine

03
Balenciaga
Avantgarde Magazine

04
Chanel
Creative Magazine

05
YSL
Creative Magazine

06
Secret Lisa

07
Jesper&Mathias
Squint magazine

08
Thomas
Squint magazine

Hanna Werning

Hanna Werning studied Graphic Design at Central St Martins College in London, where she lived and worked for six years. In 2004 she moved back to Stockholm to set up her own studio, specialising in pattern design, art and design concepts. Hanna has been most recognised for her AnimalFlowers wallpaper-posters. Vivid patterns of the unlikeliest couples of butterflies and pigs or seahorses and tigers made as graphic silhouettes mixed with beautiful floral shapes. In 2004, she won the Swedish Elle Decoration Design Award (EDIDA) for 'wall-coverings and wallpaper'. Her wallpaper is sold at Svenskt Tenn, DesignTorget and David Design and has been exhibited at Millesgården, Svensk Form and Liljevalchs in Stockholm. In London, Hanna was employed as a senior designer at Foundation 33, working on projects for Channel 4, Island Records, MTV etc. She has also been designing patterns for the bag company Eastpak and fashion labels, including Boxfresh (UK) and Stüssy (USA). This year (2005) she is getting her first interior textiles produced in collaboration with Borås Cotton.

hello@byhanna.com

What's your favourite book cover? *Gula sidorna* by Dan Wolgers. The artist, Dan Wolgers, got to do the cover of the Swedish Yellow Pages in 1992. He simply put his own name and number in big black type on the yellow cover. **Does form always follow function?** You decide yourself what you want your object to be – functional or not. I find it more interesting when an object has an idea rather than a pretty surface. Where the form is derived by a system. But then I'm also interested in the form itself. When I went to college I came to the conclusion that if the design does not have a visual surprise it will not trigger your eye and therefore not your mind. And that's one of my main interests – to make people look and think. **What is your definition of ornament?** Something that decorates or beautifies. I think of an Oscar Wilde quote: 'Beauty is a form of genius – is higher, indeed, than genius, as it needs no explanation'. Sounds a bit pretentious, but 'beauty' does not need an 'idea' for me. It is just beauty, and that is what an ornament is for me. An idea explains itself and ornaments tend to be more decorative and perhaps poetic. But of course an idea is beautiful in itself.

178–181 (following pages)

AnimalFlowers wallpaper-poster collection: Djurträdgård; Krokodillöv; Zebraskog; Ekorreblad
2005
The wallpaper-posters work as a single poster as well as wallpaper. They are available in 8 different pattern designs that repeat from top to bottom, left to right. The idea of the wallpaper-posters are that you simply buy as many poster sheets as you need to cover a certain area.

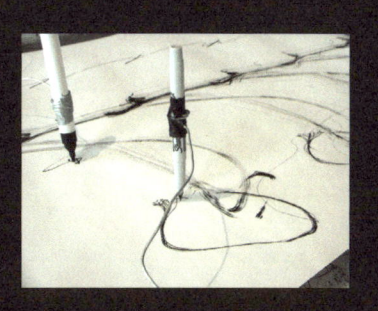

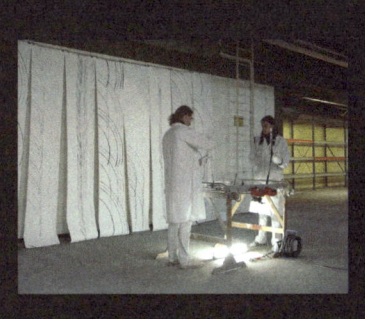

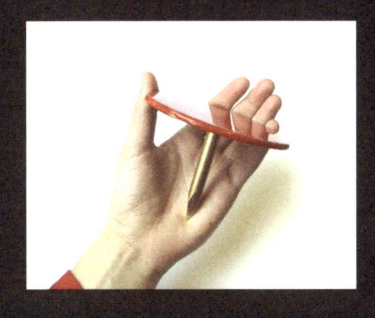

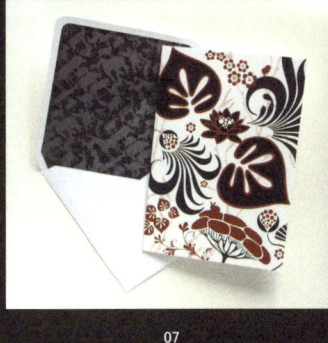

00
Hanna Werning

01–03
Apparat No. 1
'Suddenly my wall was a mess – and i like it.' by Hanna Werning and Joakim Ericsson. Wallpaper drawing machine creating patterns at random repeat. Black permanent marker on white coated wallpaper. Exhibited at Konstens Dag & Konstens Natt at the old factory of ECO-tapeter in Anneberg and at Short-Stories at Färgfabriken in Sweden

04
Eastpak bag
2005
Pattern Name: Fishpond Flush

05
Eastpak bag
2005
Pattern name: Ocean star

06
'Giant Pin' coat hanger
2005

07
Nackrossyss' greeting card
2005
Produced by Beaumonde

08
Bike streamers in rip-stop nylon

AnimalFlowers
Hanna Werning

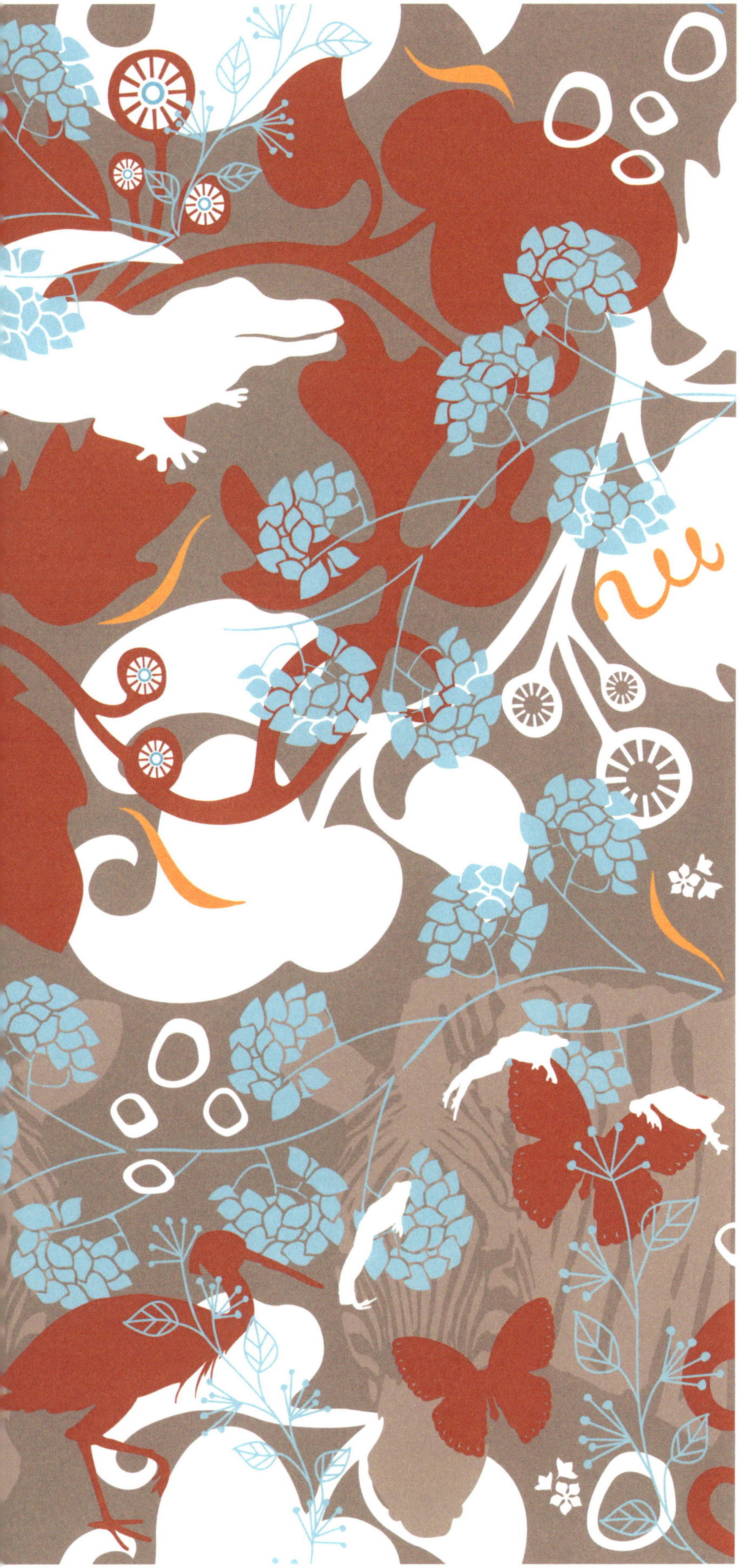

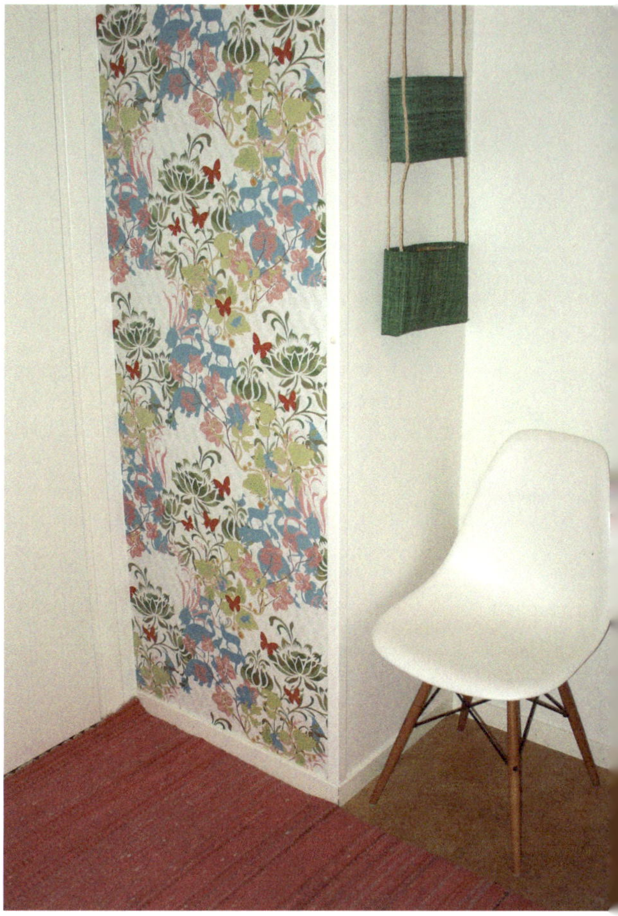

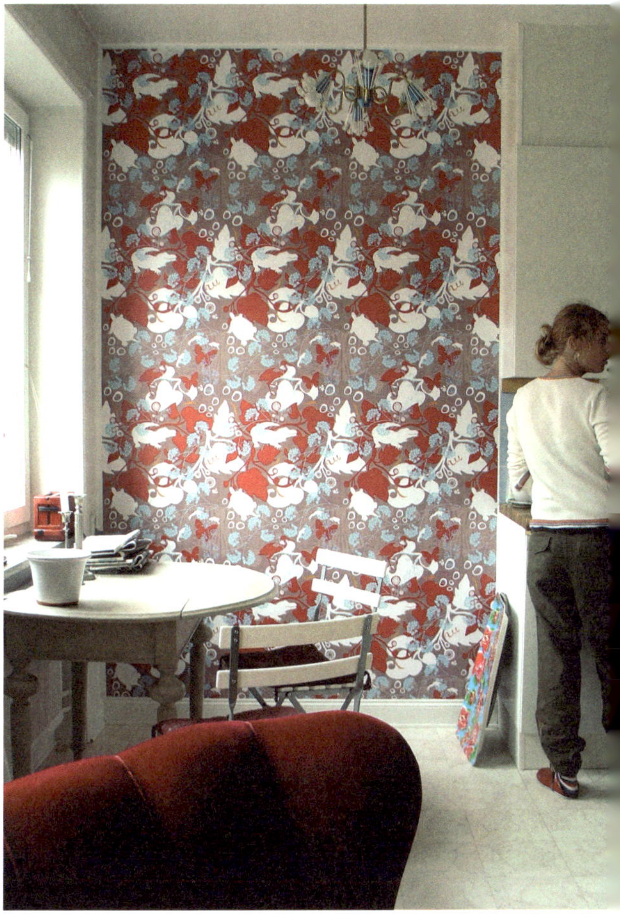

180

181

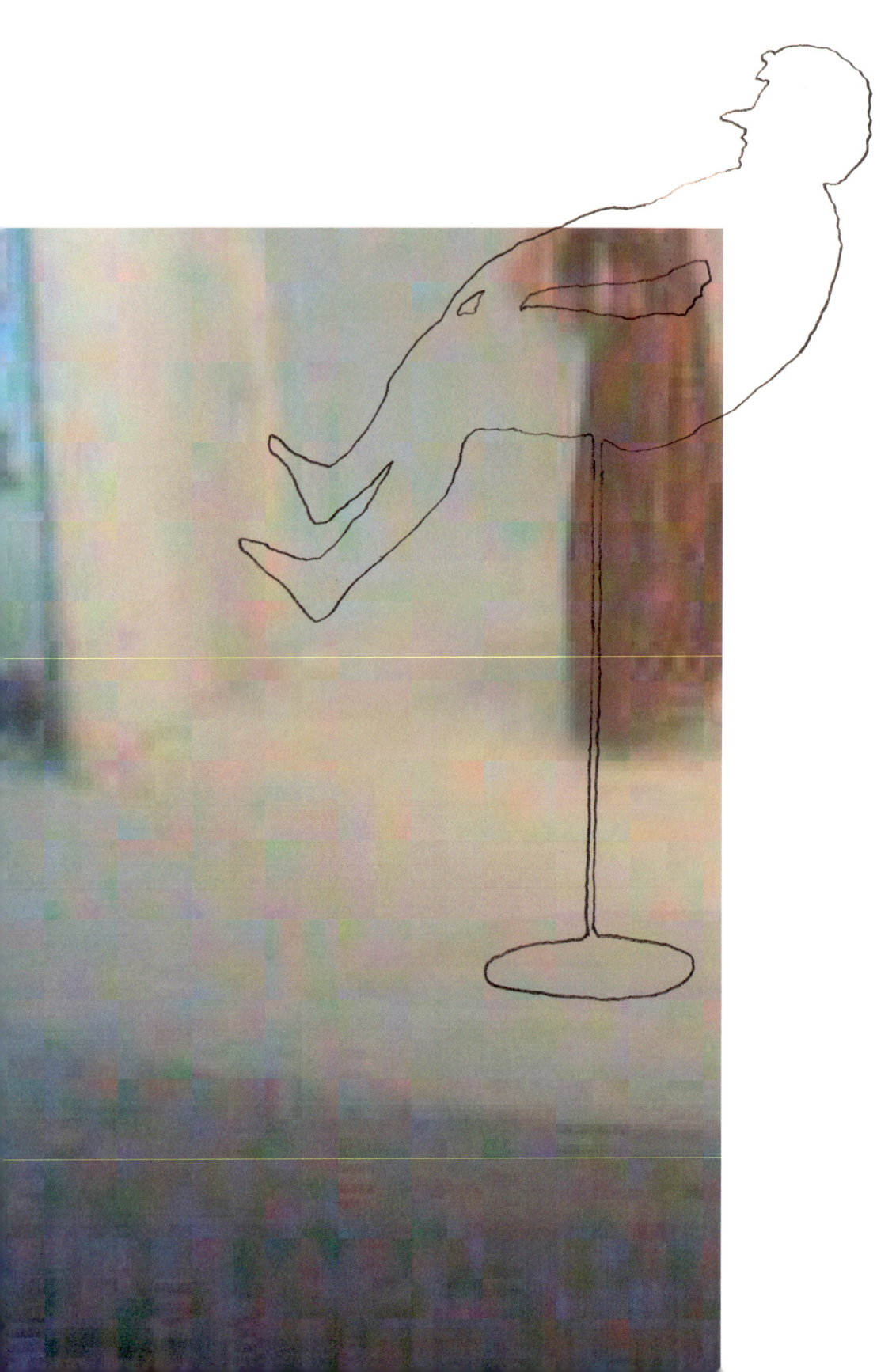

182 *Against Interpretation*
Paul Davis & Stefania Malmsten

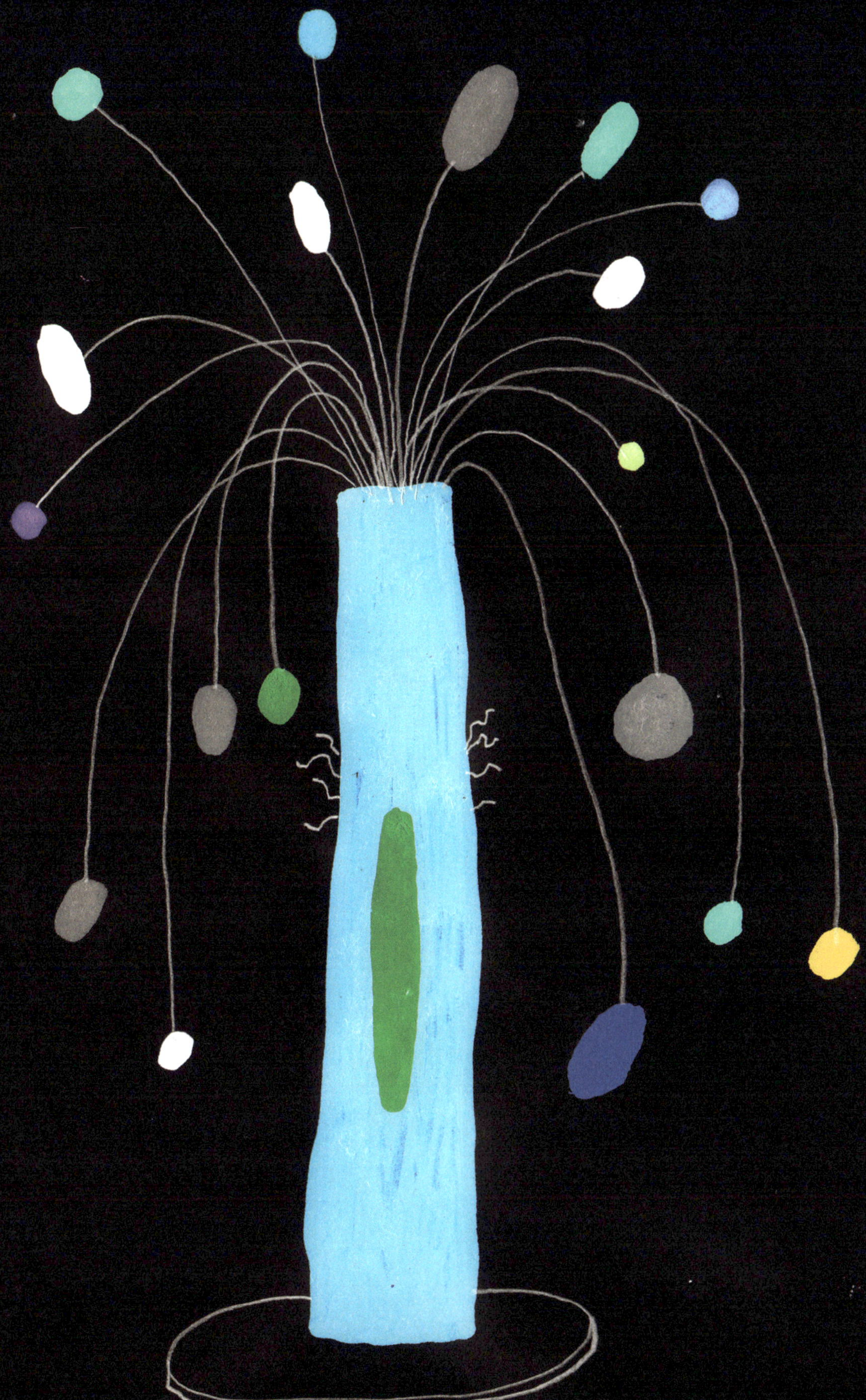

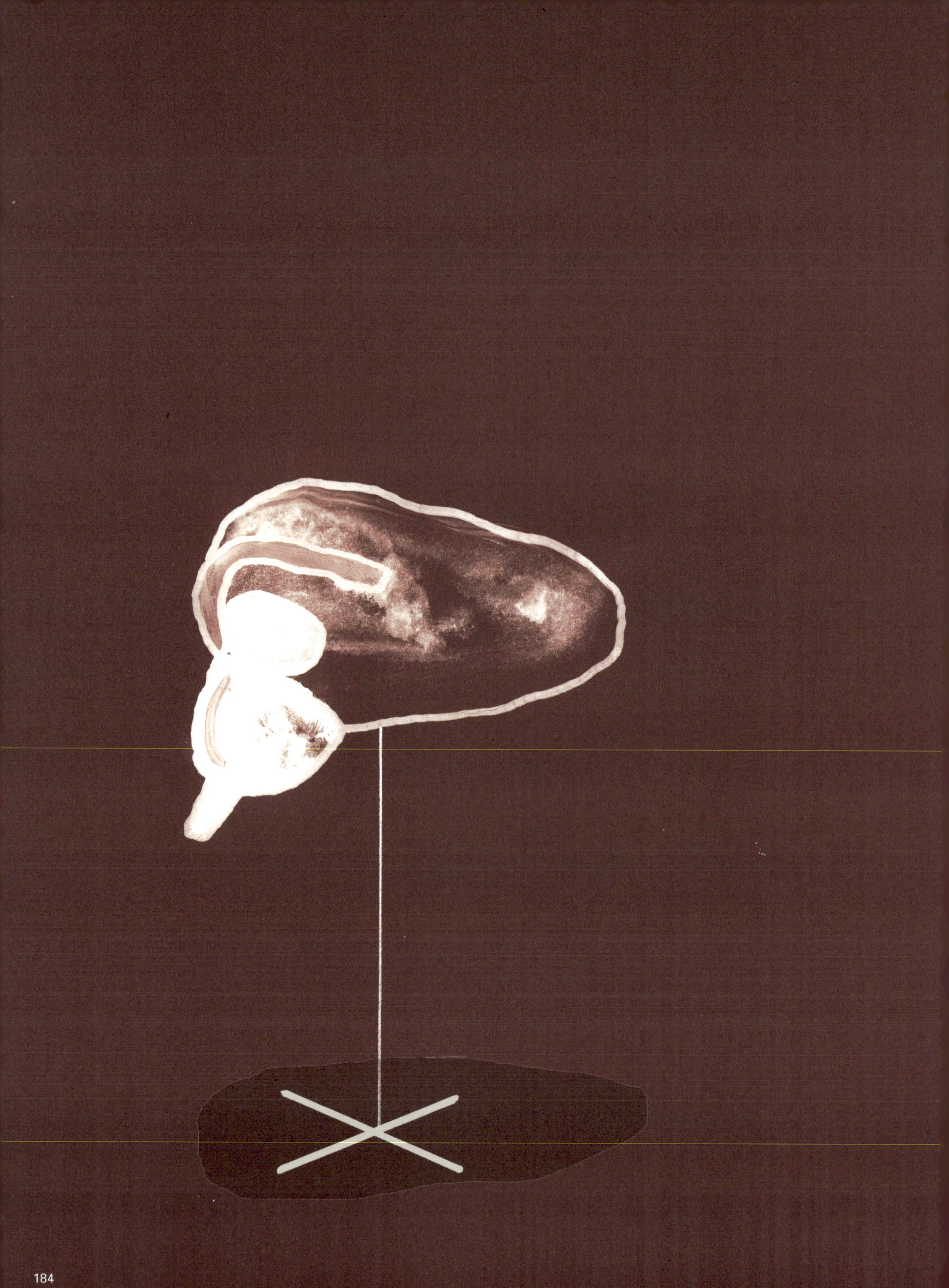

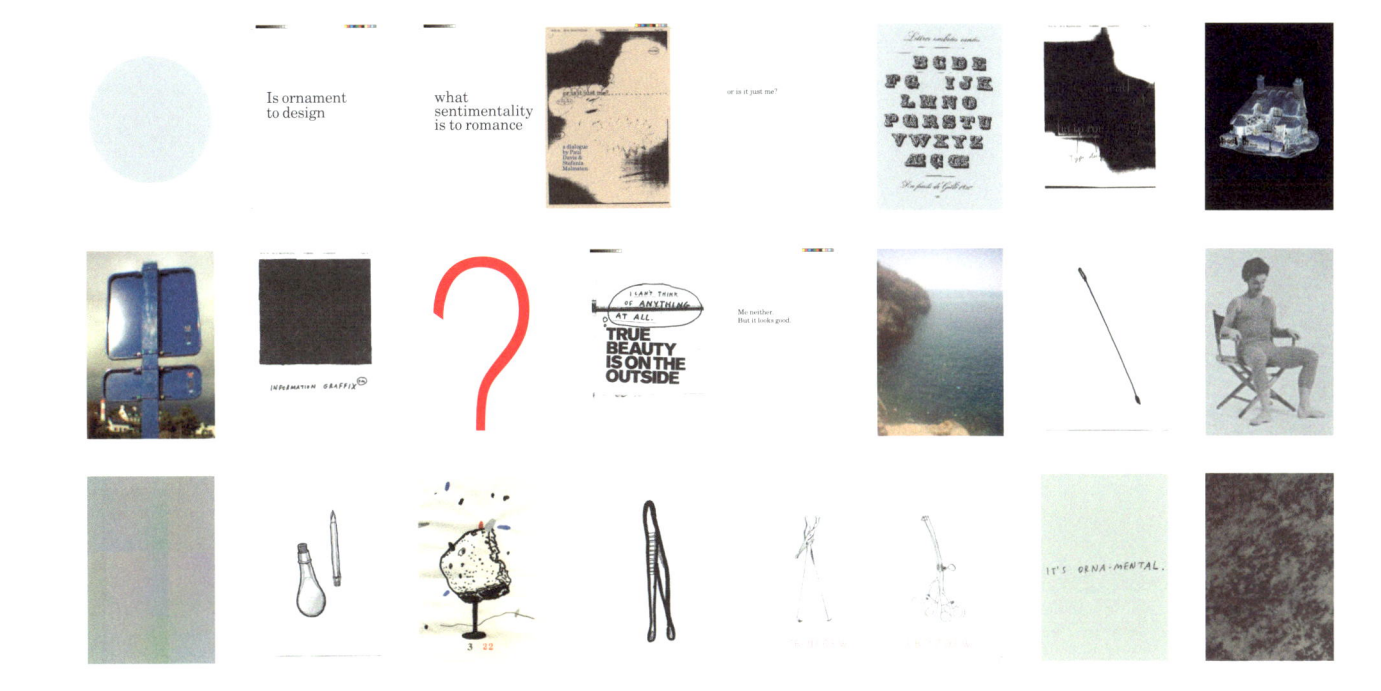

Is ornament to design

what sentimentality is to romance

or is it just me?

Me neither. But it looks good.

IT'S ORNA-MENTAL.

185

[ment]

is to rou

Type design

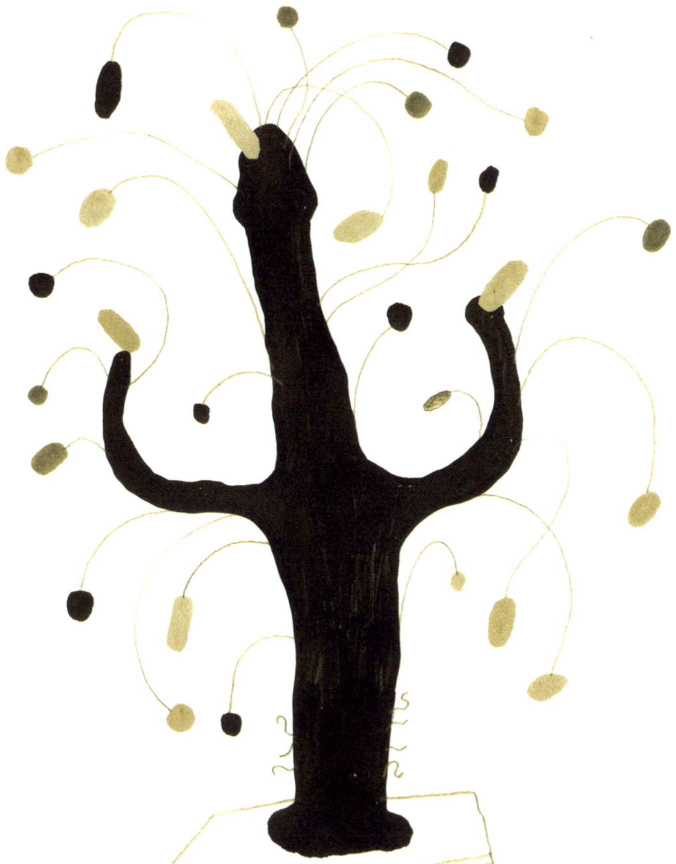

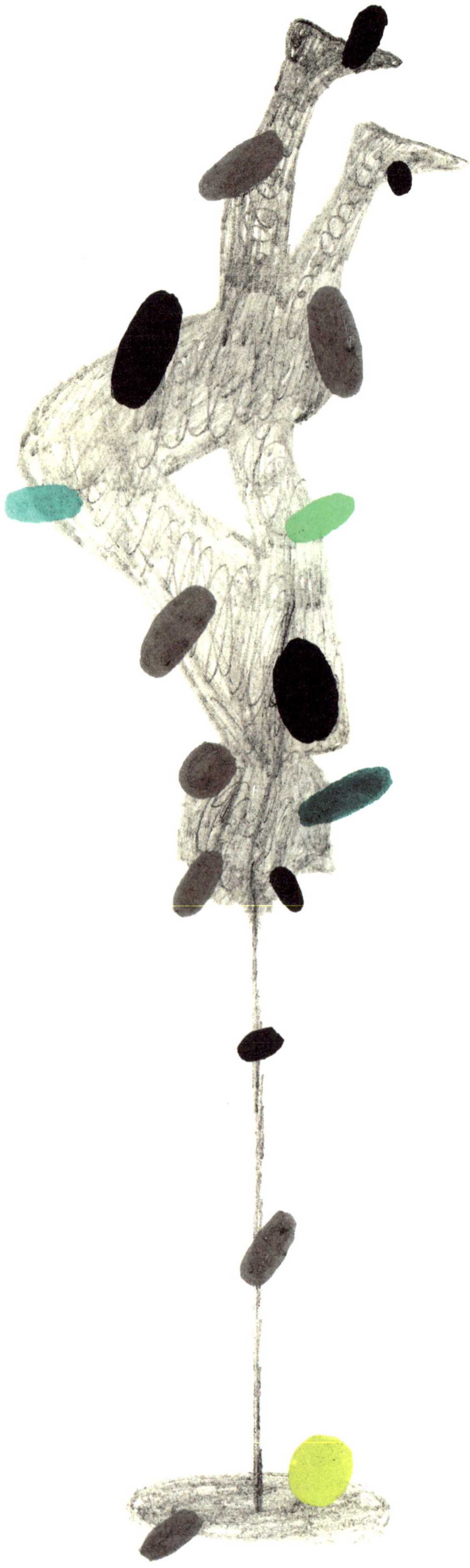

The New Graphic Ornate

Adrian Shaughnessy

It could be argued that everything in art and design is ornamental. Even the most hardcore art minimalists – Carl Andre, Donald Judd, Dan Flavin – who strip out every frill and visual nicety from their work to reduce it to pure unadorned form, cannot evade the charge that their art, no matter how reductive, is also ornamental. Every time Judd smoothes out a panel of stainless steel, or chamfers the edge of a piece of wood, it is an act of ornamentation. It may not have the 'ornateness' of Baroque churches, lace doilies or flock wallpaper, but it is ornamentation none the less.

In the book *Minimalism* (Phaidon, 2003), the writer James Mayer notes: 'Minimal art tends to consist of single or repeated geometric forms. Industrially produced or built by skilled workers following the artists instructions, it removes any trace of emotion or intuitive decision-making…' Hardly a description of ornamentation, you might say. But with its use of 'repeated geometric forms', Minimalism contains the primary element of ornamentation – pattern.

Yet when we think of ornamentation, we don't think of Dan Flavin's neon light installations. Instead, we think of the decorative, the flowery and the baroque. We think of Egyptian tomb carvings; Islamic holy architecture; Renaissance tapestries; flowery wallpaper with ceramic ducks flying across it and, well, Axminster carpets. As the Victorian architect and designer Owen Jones wrote in *The Grammar of Ornament* (Dorling Kindersley, 2001), his definitive study of the subject:

> From the universal testimony of travellers it would appear that there is scarcely a people, in however early a stage of civilisation, with whom the desire for ornament is not a strong instinct. The desire is absent in none, and it grows and increases with all in the ratio of their progress in civilisation. Man appears everywhere impressed with the beauties of nature which surround him, and seeks to imitate to the extent of his power the works of the Creator.

The ornamental instinct – the urge to make, or be surrounded by, decoration – appears universal. Nature isn't enough, it seems, we want more. Yet it is to nature that designers turn for inspiration for their decorative motifs. Owen Jones writes: '…whenever any style of ornament commands universal admiration, it will always be found to be in accordance with the laws which regulate the distribution of forms in nature.' Owen is not advocating the copying of nature (for him this is a sign of decadent decoration). Instead he advocates 'observation of the principles which regulate the arrangement of form in nature…' In other words, study the way nature arranges curves, colour, symmetry and other staples of designer language, but don't copy her.

Ornamentation is linked in the minds of many with idolatry, decadence and fetishism. Nice old ladies with their frilly blouses, and Martha Stewart fans with their flouncy 'bed skirts', might disagree. But there's something in the love of rich and elaborate decoration that suggests heightened sensuality and a love of beauty for beauty's sake. Throughout history, periods of decadence and excess are usually followed by periods of piety and visual austerity. Compare a Scottish Presbyterian church with an Italian Baroque cathedral, for example.

But a love of beauty is fundamental to human beings. It is apparently not something we learn, or a taste we acquire over time, rather it comes hardwired into our systems. Given a choice, we prefer the lovely to the gross; the elegant to the malformed; the beautiful to the downright ugly.

The writer Virgina Postrel, in her book *The Substance of Style* (Harper Collins, 2003), makes the point that a desire for aesthetic satisfaction is woven onto every aspect of modern life. Her book is subtitled 'How the rise of aesthetic value is remaking commerce, culture and consciousness', and designers, she argues, are on hand to reap the benefits.

Or are they? For many graphic designers, the notion of gratuitous beauty is hard to take. For these pragmatists, graphic design is about communication, business and the relaying of commercial messages. Why would anyone, they argue, want to interfere with design's practical and functional aims by introducing the distraction of superfluous decoration? Paul Rand, the celebrated American designer, expressed the professional designer's view when he wrote: 'A design that is complex, fussy, or obscure harbours a self-destructive mechanism.' But Rand was no philistine; although he was quick to dismiss much contemporary design as 'squiggles, pixels and doodles' and as damaging as 'drugs or pollution',